DAYTRIPS
IN
ITALY
40
One Day Adventures
by Rail, Bus or Car

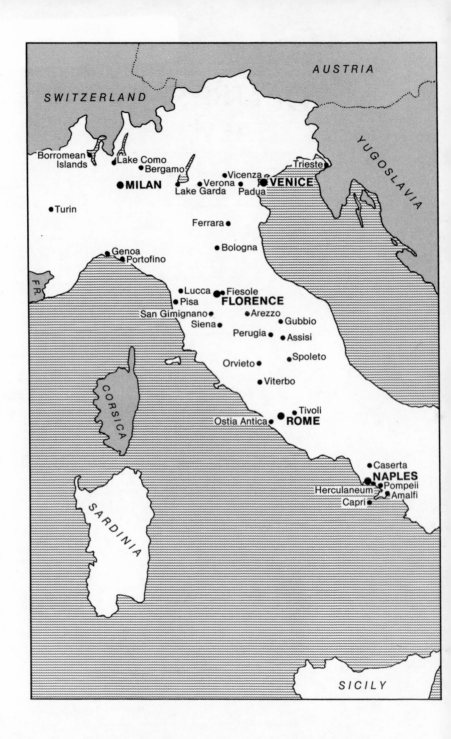

DAYTRIPS
IN
ITALY
40
One Day Adventures by Rail, Bus or Car

Revised Edition

by
Earl Steinbicker

HASTINGS HOUSE
MAMARONECK, NEW YORK

We are always grateful for comments from readers, which are extremely useful in preparing future editions of this or other books in the series. Please write directly to the author, Earl Steinbicker, % Hastings House, 141 Halstead Avenue, Mamaroneck, NY 10543; or FAX (914) 835-1037. Thank you.

All photos are by the author, except as noted.
Distributed to the trade by Publishers Group West, Emeryville, CA.

ISBN: 0-8038-9343-4

10 9 8 7 6 5 4 3 2 1

Contents

Introduction

More so than any other Western European nation, Italy presents an enormous diversity of individual towns and regions, each stubbornly clinging to its own culture and traditions. Visitors can choose from a veritable potpourri of experiences, with magnificent cities and unspoiled hill towns to explore, splendid palaces and placid lakes to visit, history to relive, and wines to taste. Few countries can match its scope of art, architecture, or regional cuisines. The possibilities for adventures are endless, but the premise of this book is that many of the very best attractions can easily be enjoyed on a daytrip basis. The pages which follow describe 40 of Italy's most intriguing destinations and tell you, in step-by-step detail, exactly how to go about probing them on your own.

Daytrips in Italy is not intended to be a comprehensive guide to the entire nation. It focuses, instead, on five broad areas of maximum tourist interest—Central Italy, the North Central provinces, the Northwest, the Northeast, and the South. Each of these has one major city which, for reasons of transportation and accommodation, makes it the most logical base for one-day adventures in its region. These are Rome, Florence, Milan, Venice, and Naples. Other towns, of course, could be substituted as bases, and these possibilities are suggested in the text whenever practical.

Daytrips have many advantages over the usual point-to-point touring, especially for short-term visitors. You can sample a far greater range in the same time by seeing only those places that really interest you instead of "doing" the region town by town. They also lead to a more varied diet of sights, such as spending one day on the Riviera, the next exploring medieval Verona, and the third cruising an Alpine lake.

The benefits of staying in one hotel for several days are obvious. Weekly rates are often more economical than overnight stays, especially in conjunction with airline package plans. You also gain a sense of place, of having established a temporary home in a large city where you can get to know the restaurants and enjoy the night life. Then, too, you won't waste time searching for a room every night. Your luggage remains in one place while you go out on a carefree daytrip. There is no need to pre-plan every moment of your vacation since you are always free to go wherever you please. Feel like seeing Florence today? Ah, but this is Monday, when many of its major sights are closed, so maybe it would be better to head for San Gimignano instead, or visit the Leaning Tower of Pisa. Is rain predicted for the entire day? You certainly don't want to be on Capri in a shower, so why not try the wonderful museums in Naples? The operative word here is flexibility—the freedom of not being tied to a schedule or route. You may run up more mileage this way, but that is easily offset by using one of the prepaid unlimited transportation plans described in Section I.

All of the daytrips in this book may be taken by public transportation or by car. Full information for doing this is given in the "Getting There" section of each trip. A suggested do-it-yourself walking tour is outlined in both the text and on the street map provided. Time and weather considerations are included, along with price-keyed restaurant recommendations, background data, and sources of additional information.

The trips have been arranged in a geographic sequence following convenient transportation routes. In several cases it is possible to combine two trips in the same day. These opportunities are noted whenever they are practical.

Destinations were chosen to appeal to a wide variety of interests. In addition to the usual cathedrals, palaces, and museums, there are Roman ruins, boat cruises, seaside resorts, major cities, great seaports and enchanting lakes, preserved hill towns, lush gardens, massive fortresses, splendid villas, magical islands, places where history was made, places of literary association, natural beauty spots, and many others. You should really read through all of them before deciding which intrigue you the most.

Many of the attractions have a nominal entrance fee—those that are free will come as a pleasant surprise. Cathedrals and churches will appreciate a small donation in the collection box, which helps pay their maintenance costs.

Finally, a gentle disclaimer. Places have a way of changing without warning, and errors do creep into print. If your heart is absolutely set on seeing a particular sight, you should always check first to make sure it isn't closed for renovations, or that the opening times are still valid. Phone numbers for the local tourist information offices are included for this purpose.

One last thought—it isn't really necessary to see everything at any given destination. Be selective. Your one-day adventures in Italy should be fun, not an endurance test. If they start becoming that, just stroll over to the nearest outdoor café, sit down, and enjoy yourself. There will always be another day.

Happy Daytripping!

Getting Around

Nearly all of the daytrips in this book can be made by rail or car, and some by bus or boat. Which of these you choose depends on purely personal factors, but you may want to consider some of the following information before deciding.

BY RAIL:

A great many Italians prefer to travel by rail for reasons of both speed and economy. In a land of high gasoline prices, expensive toll roads, congested traffic, and difficult parking, trains are usually the quickest and easiest way to travel the medium distances described in this book. The **Italian State Railways** *(Ferrovie Italiane dello Stato,* or *FS)* operates more than 1,500 passenger trains a day over nearly 10,000 miles of track, serving about 2,500 stations. Fares are exceptionally low when compared to most other European countries.

In recent years the system has been noticeably improved with new equipment, smoother tracks, and better on-time performance. Whatever problems they may have had in the past, the service is now becoming nearly comparable to that enjoyed by most northern European countries—at a fraction of the price.

There are very few places of tourist interest in Italy that cannot be reached by train, and even those without service—primarily hill towns and secluded fishing villages—almost invariably have a connecting bus to the nearest rail line. Stations are usually located right in the heart of the cities, so close to the major attractions that most of the walking tours described in this book start right at the station.

Seasoned travelers often consider riding trains to be one of the best ways of meeting the local people and making new friends. It is not at all unusual to strike up an engaging conversation that makes your trip all the more memorable. You can also get a marvelous view of the passing countryside from the large windows, and have time to catch up on your reading.

All trains operated by the State Railways belong to one of the fol-

lowing categories, as indicated on schedules and departure plat-
forms:

EC—*EuroCity.* High-speed international expresses with special
comforts. Both first- and second-class seating is offered, and there is
a supplementary fare that is covered by the various Eurailpasses internationally and by the BTLC Italian Rail Pass within Italy only. Dining
facilities are provided as indicated on the schedules. Reservations may
be required on some routes, and are suggested on others during peak
travel periods.

IC—*InterCity.* Express trains used in both domestic and some international services. Both first- and second-class seating is usually
available, but a few trains are first class only. Dining facilities are often
provided, as indicated on the schedules. Many IC trains require pay-
ment of a supplementary fare, which is waived for holders of Eurail or
BTLC Italian Rail passes. Seats may be reserved if desired, while only
a few IC trains require reservations.

IC "ETR-450"—*InterCity "Pendolino".* Ultra high-speed, high-tech,
all-first-class luxury trains linking Rome with other major cities such
as Florence, Bologna, Milan, Genoa, Turin, Naples, and Bari. Meal
service and mandatory reservations are included in the ticket price.
Railpass holders must pay a supplement to cover the meal, whether
desired or not.

EXPR—*Espresso.* These ordinary expresses, often in international
service, usually carry both first- and second-class cars—although a very
few are second-class only. There is no supplementary fare, and reservations are not necessary. Food and drink service is available on
some trains, as indicated on schedules.

DIR—*Diretto.* Semi-express trains that make many stops, often with
second-class seating only. Many of these consist of modern commuter cars, and are uncrowded during off-peak hours.

LOCALE—Sometimes called *Accelerato,* a misnomer if ever there
was one, these slow locals are usually not given any particular desig-
nation. They stop everywhere and can take you to very rural locations.
New commuter equipment is often used. First class is not usually offered, although second class is fairly empty during off-peak hours.

Schedules for train service are available at the information offices
in stations. While there, be sure to check the return schedules as well
to avoid any remote possibility of being stranded in some quaint hill
town. Tables of departure *(Partenze)* and arrival *(Arrivi)* are posted
throughout the stations and are arranged in a time sequence using
the 24-hour clock. Thus a departure at 4:52 p.m. would be marked as
16.52. Be doubly sure that you are looking at the right table, and watch
out for trains that are first-class only or that require reservations *(Pren-*

otazione Obbligatoria, or the letter "R" in a square box). Fast trains are shown in red ink.

Destinations are, of course, given in Italian; thus Venice is *Venezia,* Florence is *Firenze,* and so on. This can be very confusing in some stations, notably Milan, where even foreign cities are in Italian—did you know that *Monaco* can mean Munich, or *Nizza* Nice? You should also be very careful about places that have more than one station—sometimes your train makes stops at several, sometimes only one. These cautions are mentioned in the "Getting There" section of each trip when appropriate.

Most of the larger stations have free printed schedules for popular destinations. A few, including Rome, Florence, and Milan, feature self-operated multi-lingual computer terminals in which you enter your destination and approximate time frame and receive information, in your choice of languages, of all the possible routings within that period. The best way to check schedules, however, is to purchase a schedule book—called an *Orario*—which is available in both national and regional editions at a modest price from newsstands. The complete pages of this are posted in nearly all stations. The compact Thomas Cook European Timetable, sold in some travel book stores in North America, by mail from Forsyth Travel Library (P.O. Box 2975, Shawnee Mission, Kansas 66201; phone toll-free 1-800-FORSYTH for credit-card orders), or at Thomas Cook offices in Britain, is very useful for travel throughout Europe, although it does not list *every* local service.

Reservations are required for all IC "ETR-450" as well as a few EC and IC trains—look out for *Prenotazione Obbligatoria* or the letter "R" in a box on schedules and departure boards. They are also a good idea for other EC and IC trains during peak travel seasons. The letter "R" *without* a box, by the way, means that reservations can be made but are not mandatory. Eurailpass or "Kilometric Ticket" holders must pay a small fee for this, although reservations are free to holders of the BTLC pass. All reservations must be made at least one day prior to travel. In actual practice, however, you can make a "reservation" on board the train itself by paying a small penalty fee to the conductor—if there are any seats left.

Advance reservations can be made at the *Prenotazione* window in large stations and have the advantage of allowing you to specify a smoking or non-smoking section, and a window or aisle seat. They also guarantee you a place to sit, although this is rarely a problem in first class. Those traveling without reservations should be careful not to sit in someone else's reserved seat, which is marked by a card at the compartment entrance or above the seat.

Italy is one country where it really pays to travel first class, unless you are on a starvation budget. The second-class cars on EC, IC, and

A RAIL TRAVELER'S GLOSSARY

Agenzia di Viaggi . . . . Travel agency
Andata . . . . To go one way
Andata e Ritorno . . . . Round trip
Aria Condizionata . . . . Air conditioned
Arrivi . . . . Arrival
Autobus . . . . Bus
Automatrici . . . . Railcar
Azienda di Turismo . . . . Tourist information office
Bagagli . . . . Baggage
Biglietteria . . . . Ticket office
Biglietto . . . . Ticket
Binario . . . . Track
Cambiare Treno . . . . To change trains
Cambio . . . . Money exchange
Capolinea . . . . Bus terminal
Capotreno . . . . Conductor
Carrozza . . . . Car (of train)
Carrozza Letti . . . . Sleeping car
Carrozza Ristorante . . . . Dining car
Chiuso . . . . Closed
Coda . . . . Rear (of train)
Coincidenza . . . . Connection
Composizione Treno . . . . Train make-up diagram
Conduttore . . . . Conductor
Corridoio . . . . Aisle (seat)
Cuccetta . . . . Inexpensive sleeping car with bunks
Deposito Bagagli . . . . Checkroom, left luggage
Dintorni . . . . Nearby areas
Diretti . . . . Direct
Dogana . . . . Customs
Donne . . . . Women
Entrata . . . . Entrance
Espresso . . . . Express
Estero . . . . Foreign
Feriale . . . . Workdays
Fermata . . . . Stop, halt (train or bus)
Fermata Facoltativa . . . . Optional, on request stop
Ferrovia . . . . Railway
Finestra . . . . Window (seat)
FS . . . . Italian State Railways
Fumatori . . . . Smoking permitted
Gabinetti . . . . Toilets
Giorni Lavorativi . . . . Weekdays, Monday through Saturday
Ingresso . . . . Entrance

Ingresso Vietato	Do not enter
Interno	Domestic
Marciapiedi	Platform
Metà Prezzo	Half fare
Metropolitana	Subway, Underground, Métro
Noleggio Auto	Rental car at station
Occupato	Occupied
Oggetti Rinvenuti	Lost-and-found
Orario	Timetable
Partenze	Departure
Per	To, for
Pericolo	Danger
Piattaforma	Platform
Portobagaglio	Porter
Posto a Sedere	Seat
Prenotazione	Reservation
Prenotazione Obbligatoria	Reservation compulsory
Prezzo	Fare
Prima Classe	First class
Provenienza	Train coming from
Quotidiano	Daily
Rimborso	Refund
Ritardo	Delay
Sala di Attesa	Waiting room
Seconda Classe	Second class
Signore	Women
Signori	Men
Solo	Only
Sospeso	Suspended
Springere	Push
Stazione	Station
Supplemento	Supplement to fare
Testa	Front (of train)
Tirare	Pull
Traghetto	Ferry boat
Trasbordo	Transfer
Treno	Train
Ufficio Bagagli	Baggage check room
Ufficio Informazioni	Information office
Uomini	Men
Uscita	Exit
Vettura	Car (of train)
Viaggiatore	Passenger, traveler
Viaggio	Journey, trip
Vietato	Forbidden
Vietato Fumare	No smoking

ordinary express trains can be extremely crowded and uncomfortable during peak travel seasons.

It is always best to arrive at the station *(Stazione)* a little early to acquaint yourself with its layout. There you will usually find a sign marked *"Composizione Treni"* which shows the make-up of every express leaving from that station or platform, including the location of each car. This serves two purposes. First, you won't have to make a last-minute dash when you discover that the first-class cars stop at the opposite end of a long platform. Secondly, and more important, it shows which—if any—cars are dropped off en route to your destination.

The **routing** and final destination of each section of the train is shown just outside the door of the first car in that section. First-class cars are marked with the numeral "1" near the door, and with a yellow stripe above the windows.

Many express trains offer a **food and beverage service** of some sort, as indicated on the schedules. Riding in a regular or self-service dining car can be a delightful experience, or you can get snacks and drinks from the roving mini-bar. You may, however, prefer to stock up on refreshments from the trackside vendors or food shops in the station, as most Europeans do.

Railpasses can be a real bargain if you intend to ride a lot of trains. Ask your travel agent about them before going to Italy, as some of them are difficult to purchase once there. The Italian State Railways *(FS)* accepts the following passes:

EURAILPASS—the best-known and most popular pass, allows unlimited first-class travel throughout 17 European countries, excluding Great Britain. It is available for periods of 15 or 21 days, or 1, 2, or 3 months. The Eurailpass includes a wide variety of fringe benefits, nearly all of which are in countries other than Italy. Because Italian fares are so low to begin with, the Eurailpass is a good buy *only* if you are also traveling in countries north of Italy.

EURAIL SAVERPASS—an economical version of the Eurailpass which offers the same first-class travel benefits as outlined above, but for groups of 3 or more people traveling together. Between October 1st and March 31st the group size can be as small as 2 persons. This pass is available for a period of 15 days only, and the travel must always be done as a group. Again, it is worthwhile only if you are also traveling north of Italy.

EURAIL FLEXIPASS—the lastest innovation in railpasses allows unlimited first-class travel on any 5, 9, or 14 days within a 15-, 21-, or 30-day period. It is valid in the same 17 countries and has the same benefits as the regular Eurailpass. This is an attractive deal only if you intend to spend much time exploring the base cities between making daytrips, and are also traveling in countries north of Italy.

EURAIL YOUTHPASS—This low-cost version of the Eurailpass is available to anyone under the age of 26 and allows unlimited second-class travel in the same 17 European countries for periods of 1 or 2 months. A 15-days-of-travel-in-2-months flexi version is also sold.

BTLC ITALIAN RAILPASS—By far the best pass to use for train travel within Italy only. It is considerably cheaper than the comparable Eurailpass and is available in either first- or second-class versions for periods of 8, 15, 21, or 30 consecutive days.

BTLC ITALY FLEXI RAILCARD—A flexible version of the above, available for unlimited travel on any 4 days in a 9-day period, 8 days in a 21-day period, or 12 days in a 30-day period.

ITALIAN KILOMETRIC TICKET—mentioned here only because it is available and tends to confuse many tourists. This is not really a pass at all since you must still line up to get tickets for each train ride. The Kilometric Ticket, valid for 2 months, buys up to 20 trips anywhere in Italy, totaling not more than 3,000 kilometers (1,875 miles). It may be used by as many as 5 persons even if not related, but does not cover express surcharges or reservations. The Kilometric Ticket is available in both first- and second-class versions. Under some circumstances it may indeed be a real bargain, but the inconvenience of using it makes it a questionable value.

First-class passes, by the way, may also be used in second-class cars if desired, or when no first class is offered. All railpasses must be **validated** at the train station on the first day of actual use. The first and last days of validity will be entered on the pass at that time. Be certain that you agree with the dates *before* allowing the agent to write them in.

If you intend to take several of the daytrips in this book and to make at least one or two long journeys such as Venice to Naples, a railpass (especially the BTLC) will probably wind up saving you a considerable amount of money. Even if the savings are less than that a pass should still be considered for the convenience it offers in not having to line up for tickets, and the freedom of just hopping aboard trains at whim. Possession of a railpass will also encourage you to become more adventurous, to seek out distant and offbeat destinations.

The passes described above are available through most travel agents, who also have current information and prices, and by mail from the Forsyth Travel Library mentioned earlier. Alternatively, you could contact the nearest Italian State Railways office, sometimes known as CIT Tours. In North America these are located in New York, Los Angeles, Montreal, and Toronto. The address of the New York office is:

ITALIAN STATE RAILWAYS
FS
594 Broadway
New York, NY 10012
Phone (212) 274-0593

Any of their locations will happily supply you with a free brochure of sample Italian and European rail travel timetables and fares, useful in determining whether to buy a railpass. They also have offices in London and elsewhere.

Italy still has a few small private railroads, which might not accept railpasses. The only ones that might pertain to the daytrips in this book are the Milano-Nord (to Como but duplicated by an FS route) and the Circumvesuviana (Naples to Sorrento—a short ride).

If any of the information above makes train travel in Italy seem complicated, rest assured that you will quickly become familiar with the system as you join the thousands of other tourists riding the Italian rails.

BY BUS:

A few of the daytrips in this book are to destinations not served by the railroad. To reach them by public transportation, you should first take a train to the nearest town on a rail line, and then continue on by connecting bus *(Autobus)*, or in some cases by boat. Instructions for doing this are given in every case. Italy has a vast network of private bus companies linking just about every community but, in general, the service is slower and less comfortable than by train—and the savings very small. Specific information is included only for those trips where bus travel is the preferred way to go, such as Florence to Siena, or the only way other than driving, including Florence to Fiesole.

Buses usually depart from a bus stop *(Fermata)* or terminal *(Capolinea)* either in front of or very close to the train station. Tickets must be purchased before boarding, sometimes from a ticket window *(Biglietteria)* or sometimes from a nearby café, and canceled aboard the bus by sticking them into a small canceling machine. Schedules are almost invariably posted at the bus stop. Railpasses are not valid on buses.

BY CAR:

Many tourists prefer to explore Italy by car, which may be the best means of transport when several people are traveling together. Although usually slower than trains, cars offer a complete freedom from schedules. Nearly all of the daytrips in this book can be made this way, with distances and specific road directions provided for each. In addition to a car you will need a valid driver's license with an Italian translation and a good regional road map.

Driving in Italy is essentially the same as in the U.S.A. or Canada, but you will have to remain especially alert at all times. Italian drivers are often very aggressive, paying little attention to such details as speed limits, traffic lights, or one-way streets. Traffic coming from the right technically has the right-of-way, but it is usually the driver with the strongest nerves who prevails. Seat belts must be worn at all times. Parking in cities can be a nightmare, and is best done at attended lots or in garages. Leaving a car parked overnight on the street is a sure invitation to thieves.

Roads in Italy are excellent and well marked. The world-famous *Autostrade*, designated by the letter "A" preceding their number, are limited-access superhighways linking all major towns in the country. Speed limits range up to 140 kph (87 mph), depending on your engine displacement. Nearly all of them are toll roads where the price you pay—always quite high—is again determined by how large an engine your car has, as well as the distance covered.

The Automobile Club of Italy *(ACI)* offers many valuable services to motorists. Similar to the American AAA, they have offices in virtually every town as well as a national Phone Assistance Center in Rome—reached by dialing (06) 4212—which can answer your driving questions in English. For breakdown service on any Italian road just dial 116 from the nearest telephone.

A brief glossary for drivers is provided in this section. For more comprehensive automotive terms, you may want to use a pocket-sized phrase book, such as *Italian for Travellers* by Berlitz.

Car rentals *(Autonoleggio)* can be arranged in advance through your travel agent or one of the major chains such as Hertz, Avis, National, or Budget. Some of the popular European companies are Europcar, InterRent, and Maggiore. An International Driver's Permit, issued in America by the AAA or in Italy by the ACI, is theoretically required, although like most rules in Italy, this one is often overlooked. You must usually be between the ages of 21 and 70 to rent a car.

Be sure to ask your travel agent about the various fly/drive plans offered by most transatlantic airlines in conjunction with their flights, as these can save you quite a bit of money if booked far enough in advance. Another way to economize is to lease rather than rent, an option available for periods of 22 or more days. Finally, in estimating

A DRIVER'S GLOSSARY

Accendere i Fari (le Luci) . . . . Turn on headlights
Accostare a Destra . . . . Keep right
Accostare a Sinistra . . . . Keep left
ACI . . . . Automobile Club of Italy
Acqua . . . . Water
Alt . . . . Stop
Area di Servizio . . . . Service area
Attenzione . . . . Caution
Autonoleggio . . . . Car rental
Autorimessa . . . . Parking garage
Autostrada . . . . Limited-access highway, usually toll
Avanti . . . . Forward
Batteria . . . . Battery
Benzina . . . . Gasoline, Petrol
Caduta Massi . . . . Rock slides
Cambio Automatico . . . . Automatic transmission
Carabinieri . . . . National police
Carta Stradale . . . . Road map
Carta Verde . . . . Green card (car insurance)
Casello . . . . Toll booth
Centro Storico . . . . Historical part of town
Chilometro . . . . Kilometer
Circonvallazione . . . . Belt road around town
Curva Pericolosa . . . . Dangerous curve
Dare la Precedenza . . . . Yield
Deviazione . . . . Detour
Discesa Pericolosa . . . . Steep hill
Disco di Sosta . . . . Parking time-indicator disc
Divieto di Accesso . . . . No entry
Divieto di Parcheggio . . . . No Parking
Divieto di Sorpasso . . . . No passing
Divieto di Sosta . . . . No stopping
Dogana . . . . Customs
Faro . . . . Headlight
Freni . . . . Brakes
Galleria . . . . Tunnel
Gomma . . . . Tire
Incidente . . . . Accident
Ingresso . . . . Entrance
Lavori in Corso . . . . Road works ahead
Libretto di Circolazione . . . . Car registration papers
Macchina . . . . Car
Olio . . . . Oil
Parcheggiare . . . . To park

Parcheggio Autorizzato	Parking allowed
Passaggio a Livello	Grade crossing
Patente di Guida	Driver's License
Pedaggio	Toll road
Pedone	Pedestrian
Pericolo	Danger
Pianta	Map
Pneumatici	Tires
Polizia Stradale	Highway police
Posteggio	Attended parking lot
Raccordo Anulare	Ring road
Rallentare	Reduce speed
Sbarrato	Road closed
Semaforo	Traffic light
Senso Proibito	No entry
Senso Unico	One way
Stazione di Servizio	Service station
Strada	Road
Svolta Pericolosa	Dangerous bend
Tangenziale	Bypass
Tenere la Destra	Keep to the right
Tenersi in Corsia	Keep in lane
Velocità non Superiore	Speed limit
Uscita	Exit
Uscita Autocarri	Truck exit
Vicolo Cieco	Dead end
Vietato l' Accesso	No entry
Vigili Urbani	Town police
Zona Pedonale	Pedestrian zone

DAYS OF THE WEEK: SEASONS:

Lunedi	Monday	**Stagione**	Season
Martedi	Tuesday	**La primavera**	Spring
Mercoledi	Wednesday	**L'estate**	Summer
Giovedi	Thursday	**L'autunno**	Fall
Venerdi	Friday	**L'inverno**	Winter
Sabato	Saturday		
Domenica	Sunday		
Oggi	Today		
Domani	Tomorrow		

APPROXIMATE CONVERSIONS

1 Mile = 1.6 km   **1 U.S. Gallon** = 3.78 liters
1 KM = 0.6 miles   **1 Liter** = 0.26 U.S. gallons

your expenses, remember that gasoline *(Benzina)* costs roughly three times as much in Italy as in North America. Before returning a rental car, be sure to fill up the tank to avoid a high refilling charge.

WHEN TO GO:

Italy may be enjoyed at any time of the year, but bear in mind that July and August can sometimes be quite hot, especially in the south. The best seasons for a visit are undoubtedly the late spring and early fall, when the weather is milder and the sights less overrun with tourists. You will get more personal attention then, as well as better value for your money. Remember, also, that the hours of sunlight are longer in the late spring and early summer, which gives you more time to enjoy your daytrips. Some attractions, mostly in the north, may be closed or have sharply curtailed schedules during the winter. These variations are noted in the "When to Go" section for each trip when appropriate.

FOOD AND DRINK:

To savor Italian cuisine in its native land is one of the most compelling reasons for a trip to Europe. In order to help you do that, several choice restaurants are listed for each destination in this book. Most of these are long-time favorites of experienced travelers, with a few new discoveries added. Their relative price range, based on the least expensive full meal, is indicated by these symbols:

$ — Inexpensive, but may have fancier dishes available.

$$ — Reasonable. These establishments may also feature daily specials.

$$$ — Luxurious and expensive.

X: — Days closed and vacation months.

Those who take dining *very* seriously should consult an up-to-date restaurant and hotel guide such as the classic red-cover *Michelin Italia,* issued annually around the beginning of each year.

Restaurants, of course, are forever changing. What is good one year may not be the next. Far more important than any list of suggestions is to develop the ability to spot good establishments. It is always wise to check the prices posted outside the restaurant before entering, and to take a peek at who's dining there. A large proportion of locals, especially businessmen, almost guarantees an excellent meal—while a place full of foreign tourists may not. Those prominently displaying menus in English festooned with little British or American flags are at least suspect. You won't need the security blanket of an English menu anyway, since language is never really a serious problem in any Italian restaurant. The use of a pocket-sized translator book such as the *Marling Menu-Master for Italy* will help you enjoy even the most unfamiliar dishes without anxiety. Try to order local specialties, which vary considerably from town to town, whenever possible.

Many restaurants in Italy offer a fixed-price *(Prezzo Fisso)* "Tourist Menu," a complete multi-course meal almost invariably consisting of decent but rather unadventurous dishes. Unless you are counting every *lira*, it is much more satisfying to order à la carte. The *Carta* offers quite a few courses, but no one expects you to choose from all of them. Most commonly, these are: *Antipasti* (appetizers), *Primi Piatti* (soups, pasta, and other starches), *Secondi Piatti* (main courses), *Contorni* (vegetables and salads), *Formaggi* (cheeses), *Frutta* (fruit), and *Dolci* (desserts). Again, it is not necessary to follow a strict meal order. If you feel like having only soup, pasta, and salad, by all means go ahead and do so.

Lighter, faster, and less expensive meals can be had at the ubiquitous *Pizzerie,* which often double as simple restaurants and offer a large variety of pizzas along with other typical Italian dishes. Another money-and-time-saving possibility is to eat at a *Tavola Calda, Rosticceria,* or self-service cafeteria. Then, too, there is always the option of making a picnic lunch from ingredients purchased at a local market or grocery store. You can also buy delicious ready-made sandwiches to take out or eat on the spot at just about any *Caffè* or *Bar.* Fast-food outlets are slowly gaining a tentative acceptance in the larger cities, particularly among the young.

Lunch *(Pranzo)* is usually served between 12:30 and 2:30 p.m., and is often considered the main meal of the day. If the practice of spending two hours in the middle of the day to eat a meal seems like a waste of valuable tourist time to you, remember that most of the attractions—and all of the shops, banks, and so on—are closed then anyway. Dinner *(Cena)* begins no earlier than 7:30 p.m. and is commonly available until about 10 p.m. or so. Virtually all eating establishments are closed one day a week. A strange law—often ignored—requires you, the patron, to demand a receipt *(Ricevuta Fiscale)* for all meals and to retain this until you are at least 60 meters from the restaurant in order to discourage them from pocketing the money and avoiding taxes. Although a service charge is usually included in the menu price, and a small cover charge *(Coperto)* added, an additional modest tip is expected in all but the humblest establishments.

Italian wines are both delicious and usually quite inexpensive, particularly the house wine *(Vino della Casa),* which is most often local and chosen to complement the cuisine. Vintages are of little importance as the weather hardly varies from year to year. Red is called

Rosso, white *Bianco,* and rosé *Rosato.* A bottle of chilled mineral water *(Acqua Minerale),* with or without gas, is frequently ordered along with a meal in place of wine—or to mix with it. Another alternative is beer *(Birra),* which may have a German brand name but is usually brewed in Italy. Beer is fairly expensive throughout the country, sometimes costing more than wine. From the tap it is called *Birra alla Spina.* Soft drinks *(Bibita Analcolica)* and fruit juices *(Succo di Frutta)* are universally available.

Meals are commonly ended with a tiny cup of *Espresso,* that marvelously strong coffee that jolts you back to reality.

Italian ice cream *(Gelato),* probably the best in the world, comes in a bewildering variety of unusual flavors which may be mixed to suit your fancy. Take a short break from your walking tours and stop in at a local *Gelateria* for a cone or dish, but be sure to look first for the sign *Produzione Propria,* which means that it is homemade and not mass-produced.

SUGGESTED TOURS:

The do-it-yourself walking tours in this book are relatively short and easy to follow. On the assumption that most readers will be traveling by public transportation, they always begin at the local train station or bus stop. Those going by car can make a simple adjustment. Suggested routes are shown by heavy broken lines on the maps, while the circled numbers refer to attractions along the way, with corresponding numbers in the text.

It is important to cover as much of each tour as possible before stopping for lunch as many of the sights are closed in the afternoons. This was taken into consideration when the routes were devised, and the opening hours for each major attraction are indicated in the text.

Trying to see everything in any given town could easily become an exhausting marathon. You will certainly enjoy yourself more by being selective and passing up anything that doesn't catch your fancy in favor of a friendly *Caffè* or *Gelateria.* God will forgive you if you don't visit *every* church.

Speaking of churches, you should be aware that many—especially the great cathedrals—have strictly enforced dress codes and will not admit people wearing shorts or having bare shoulders. In general, the works of art in churches are dim and badly lit. Coin-operated light switches are very frequently provided, so be sure to carry plenty of small change.

Practical information, such as the opening times of various attractions, is as accurate as was possible at the time of writing. Everything is, of course, subject to change. You should always check with the local tourist office if seeing a particular sight is crucially important to you.

As a way of estimating the time any segment of a walking tour will take, you can look at the scale on the maps and figure that the average person covers about 100 yards in one minute. The maps, by the way, were drawn to best fit the page size. North does not necessarily point to the top, but is always indicated by an arrow.

HOLIDAYS:

Legal holidays *(Giorni Festivi)* in Italy are:

January 1	*Capodanno*
Easter Monday	*Lunedi dell' Angelo*
April 25	Liberation Day *(Liberazione)*
May 1	Labor Day *(Festa del Lavoro)*
August 15	Assumption *(Assunzione S. Vergine)*
November 1	All Saints' Day *(Ognissanti)*
December 8	Immaculate Conception *(Immacolata Concezione)*
December 25	*Natale*
December 26	*Santo Stefano*

Trains operate on holiday schedules on these days, and some attractions may be closed, as are banks. In addition, some cities celebrate their local patron saint's day, which are mentioned in the text where appropriate.

TOURIST INFORMATION:

Virtually every Italian town of any tourist interest has at least one information office, which almost invariably has at least one person on staff who speaks English. All of them can help you with specific questions and furnish maps and brochures, while most will also book local accommodations. Sometimes these offices are closed on Sundays, holidays, or over the noon meal period.

The location of the tourist offices is shown on the town maps in this book by the word "**Info.**," and repeated along with the phone number under the "Tourist Information" section for each trip. To phone ahead from another town in Italy you must first dial the area code *(Prefisso Telefonico)*, which always begins with 0 and is shown in parentheses, followed by the local number. If the number you are calling from has the same area code you would, of course, omit it and dial only the local number.

Calling ahead is useful if the whole reason for your daytrip hinges on seeing a particular sight that might be closed (a common occurrence in Italy), or perhaps to check the weather. Pay phones usually require the use of special tokens called *Gettoni*, which are sold by vending machines or at newsstands, tobacco shops, cafés, and similar establishments. Instructions for use are on the phones themselves, many of which now also accept coins. For inter-city calls *(Interurbano),* be sure to have at least six or eight *gettoni* or coins ready, but don't release them into the slot until the party answers. Unused tokens or coins will be returned after you hang up.

ADVANCE PLANNING INFORMATION:
   The **Italian Government Travel Office** *(ENIT)* has branches throughout the world that will provide help in planning your trip. In North America these are located at:

630 Fifth Ave.,
New York, NY 10111
Phone (212) 245-4822

500 North Michigan Ave.,
Chicago, IL 60611
Phone (312) 644-0990

360 Post St.,
San Francisco, CA 94108
Phone (415) 392-6206

1 Place Ville Marie, No. 1914
Montreal, P.Q., H3B-3M9
Canada
Phone (514) 866-7667

In England, they are at 1 Princes Street, **London** W1R-8AY, phone (071) 408-1254.

Section II

Daytrips from Rome

Central Italy

Chances are that your Italian adventures will begin and end in Rome—the heart of the ancient empire, the capital of a diversely fascinating nation, and the center of Christianity throughout the world. While the Eternal City is among the most fabulous tourist attractions anywhere, its surrounding regions of Latium (*Lazio* in Italian) and Umbria are all too often overlooked in favor of Rome's undeniable charms. The fact is that most of these outlying sights can be enjoyed on easy daytrips from the city, freeing you from the bother of frequent hotel changes and the nuisance of traveling with luggage. Just settle down in a Rome hotel, become a temporary Roman and—between explorations of the city—make delightful one-day forays into the countryside.

But first you will probably want to probe the main attractions of Rome itself. The following chapters describe three "get acquainted" walking tours in the heart of the city, beginning with a focus on classical civilization, then moving on primarily to the glories of the Renaissance and later periods, and finally exploring what lies across the Tiber, including the Vatican. Each of these tours can be done at a leisurely pace in the better part of a day if you don't spend too much time in museums.

After that, there are two short excursions to the outskirts of Rome, both of which can be done by subway, and both of which could be combined in the same day.

Now the real adventures begin. Of all the major destinations within daytrip range of Rome, the seven described in this book were chosen for their relative ease of access as well as the wide range of intriguing experiences they offer. Tivoli and Assisi are, of course, well known and popular with tourists, but how many travelers ever get to admire the beauties of Gubbio, Perugia, or Viterbo? Some of these are really off the beaten path, while the others—Orvieto and Spoleto—lie right on main transportation routes. All, however, can be reached without trouble by train and bus, or by private car.

Most of the daytrips described in Section VI (Southern Italy) can also be made from Rome if you don't mind the extra travel time involved.

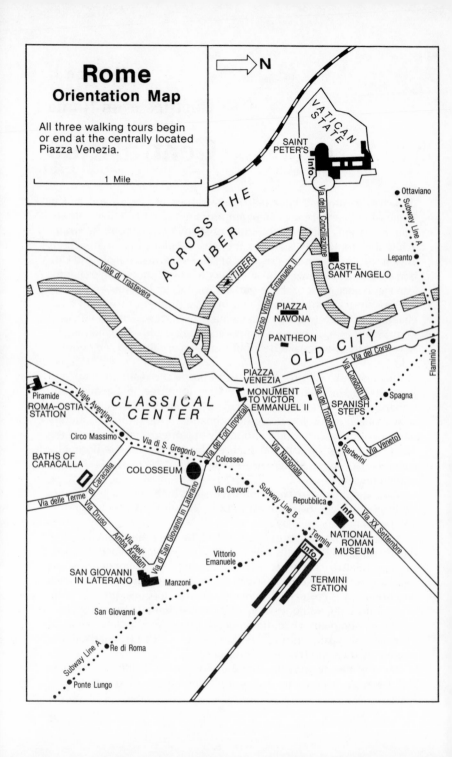

Rome

(Roma)

The Classical Center

Dig a hole anywhere in Rome and you're bound to run into ancient ruins. This is both the curse and the fascination of this magnificent city, where remnants of over two and a half thousand years of continuous civilization are heaped on top of each other, layer by layer. Throughout its long history it has always been a vital, living place, more concerned with the present than with its glorious past. One thing Rome is most emphatically not is a museum. Although some of its old structures are preserved for posterity, the majority of those unearthed are put to some kind of contemporary use, if only to serve as a bench at a bus stop or to support a laundry line.

According to legend, Rome was founded on April 21st, 753 B.C. by Romulus, who had been abandoned as an infant on the banks of the Tiber along with his twin brother Remus. There they were rescued by a she-wolf and raised by shepherds. Romulus later killed Remus in a territorial dispute and then founded a village on the nearby Palatine hill, populating it with a variety of wandering outlaws. However intriguing the story may sound, the actual evidence is that there were settlements on that spot long before then, and that the date probably refers to the time when all were first united under a common government. The Etruscans, who occupied the right bank of the river, came to dominate the small kingdom until they were overthrown by the Latins and Sabines of the left bank around 500 B.C. A republic was soon formed, which grew to become the most powerful force in the Mediterranean. This eventually evolved into the mighty Roman Empire, whose first emperor, Augustus, is reputed to have found Rome a city of brick and to have left it one of marble.

Many of the greatest monuments of that era are along the route of this one-day walking tour. It requires more than a little bit of imagination to re-create, in your mind's eye, what they might have looked like during the height of the Empire, but this can be helped considerably by purchasing one of the several excellent illustrated guidebooks available locally. On the other hand, you may find it equally enjoyable—and certainly easier—just to appreciate them as romantic ruins.

The suggested walking route can be cut short without losing too much of interest by going directly from the Colosseum (23) to the Baths of Caracalla (28) or the Circus Maximus (29). Other aspects of Rome will be covered in the next several chapters.

GETTING THERE:

Trains from all over Italy and Europe call at Rome's modern Termini station. Some typical running times are: Florence—3 hours; Milan—6 hours; Venice—6 hours; and Naples—2 hours. Schedules to northern cities are being speeded up considerably as sections of the new *Direttissima* line become operational. A very few through trains stop at Rome's Tiburtina station instead, in which case you will have to change trains or take a taxi into town.

By car, it is 172 miles to Florence, 355 miles to Milan, 328 miles to Venice, and 136 miles to Naples—all by Autostrada. Park as close to your hotel as possible and avoid driving in the city.

By air, Rome is served with direct flights from every corner of the world. Nearly all of these land at Leonardo da Vinci Airport, commonly known as Fiumicino. Located some 20 miles southwest of the central city, it has both international and domestic terminals, and is connected by frequent trains to the air terminal at Ostiense station. Cabs are also available but tend to be quite expensive. A few flights—mostly charters—land at Ciampino Airport instead, from which you can take either a taxi or a bus/subway combination, changing at Cinecittà.

GETTING AROUND:

The suggested walking tour through the classical center begins and ends at centrally located Piazza Venezia, easily reached by bus or taxi. If you use the bus, be sure to buy your ticket or pass before boarding through the rear door, and to cancel it in the machine provided. Always leave the bus by the center door. Tickets and passes, along with maps, are available from the ATAC booth near the front of the Termini train station, and tickets are also sold at many newsstands, bars, and tobacco shops.

The subway (*Metropolitana,* indicated by a large letter "M" at the entrances) is of limited use for this walking tour, but if you get tired you may want to return from one of the three stops along the route. These are at the Colosseum (23) (*Colosseo,* line B), the Basilica of St. John Lateran (26) (*San Giovanni,* line A), and the Circus Maximus (29) (*Circo Massimo,* line B). The two lines intersect at the Termini train station. Tickets are sold by vending machines in the stations.

WHEN TO GO:

Avoid taking this walk on a Tuesday or major holiday, when the most important sights are closed. They also close early, at 1 p.m., on Sundays. The Baths of Caracalla are closed on major holidays, and on Sunday and Monday afternoons.

Good weather is essential as nearly the entire day will be spent out of doors. Comfortable and sturdy walking shoes are a necessity, since many of the paths are stony or unpaved. An early start, arriving at the Roman Forum at 9 a.m., will help you beat both the mobs and the mid-day heat in the unsheltered Forum area.

In general, Rome is best visited in the spring or early fall. Summers are often hot and always crowded, while winters—though mild—can sometimes be dismally wet.

FOOD AND DRINK:

The hearty cuisine of Rome originated with the ancient Etruscans, and has borrowed heavily from other regions of Italy during the thousands of years since. Some local favorites to look for are, among the pasta dishes, *Spaghetti alla Carbonara* (with bacon, eggs, cheese, and black pepper); *Fettuccine al Burro* (and its cousin, *Fettuccine Alfredo*); and *Gnocchi alla Romana*. Meats include the ever-popular *Porchetta* (roast suckling pig), *Saltimbocca* (thin slices of veal and ham cooked in butter with wine), *Abbacchio* (milk-fed lamb), and *Pollo alla Diavola* (spicy chicken). Although none of the local table wines are truly great, there are some quite decent dry whites from the *Castelli Romani* such as *Frascati* and *Albano*. The curiously named *Est! Est!! Est!!!* is a slightly sweet white from Montefiascone, north of Rome. You might want to finish with a glass of *Sambuca,* an anisette liqueur usually served with floating coffee beans.

The part of town covered by this first walking tour does not offer a particularly great selection of restaurants, however those listed below—in the sequence that you will pass or come close to them—are well recommended. An inexpensive and delightful alternative idea for lunch is to buy sandwiches and drinks at a bar near the Basilica of St. John Lateran (26) to eat in the lovely gardens of the Baths of Caracalla (28).

> **Forum** (Via Tor de Conti 25, 2 blocks north of the Forum entrance) Rooftop dining at an elegant hotel that was once a palace, overlooking the Forum. X: Sun. $$$
>
> **Mario's Hostaria** (Piazza del Grillo 9, 1 block north of Via dei Fori Imperiali) Very popular with visitors to the Roman Forum. For reservations phone 679-37-25. X: Sun. $$
>
> **Da Domenico** (Via di San Giovanni in Laterano 134, near the Church of San Clemente) A traditional local trattoria. X: Mon., Aug. $$

Charly's Saucière (Via di San Giovanni in Laterano 270, near the Basilica of St. John Lateran) French and Swiss cuisine. Reservations 73-666 X: Sun., Aug. $$

Cannavota (Piazza San Giovanni in Laterano 20, opposite the basilica) Traditional Roman cooking. X: Wed., Aug. $$

Apuleius (Via Tempio di Diana 15, on the Aventine hill 2 blocks southeast of the Church of Santa Sabina) An old-fashioned tavern in an elegant neighborhood. X: Sun., late Aug. $$

TOURIST INFORMATION:

The local tourist office for Rome, phone (06) 488-37-48, is at Via Parigi 5, just off Piazza della Repubblica, 4 blocks west of Termini train station. There is also a busy branch office in the station.

SUGGESTED TOUR:

Begin your tour at **Piazza Venezia** (1), a busy intersection easily reached by bus, taxi, or on foot from your hotel. Directly facing you is one of Rome's major landmarks, the enormous **Monument to Victor Emmanuel II**, the first king of a united Italy. Erected between 1885 and 1911 and commonly known as *Vittoriano,* it gives new meaning to the word "monumental" and in fact is so sublimely hideous that all you can do is love it.

Crossing the large open square poses problems for the uninitiated, as the traffic is virtually non-stop. The best way is just to march out on the marked pedestrian crossings, secure in the knowledge that the cars will avoid hitting you. If you lack the courage for this you can always wait until you see a group of small children led by a nun, and join them.

Behind the monument rises the Capitoline hill, a small mound that was one of the original seven hills on which Rome was founded. There are several things of interest at its top, including a wonderful view of the Roman Forum, but these are best saved until the end of the walk.

Continue around the corner to the **Via dei Fori Imperiali**, a broad boulevard linking the Piazza Venezia with the Colosseum. Built in 1932 by Mussolini as a suitable locale for his military parades, it is one of the few modern streets in Rome. Actually, its future is in doubt as there are many significant Roman ruins buried beneath it that the archaeologists would love to dig up.

To your left, across the Via dei Fori Imperiali, are several of the **Imperial Forums**, begun by Julius Caesar and continued by later emperors after the old Roman Forum had become too small for the expanding empire. The most interesting of these is **Trajan's Forum** *(Foro di Traiano)* (2), built during the reign of Trajan (A.D. 98-117) at the foot of the Quirinal hill. Although not open to the public, it can easily be

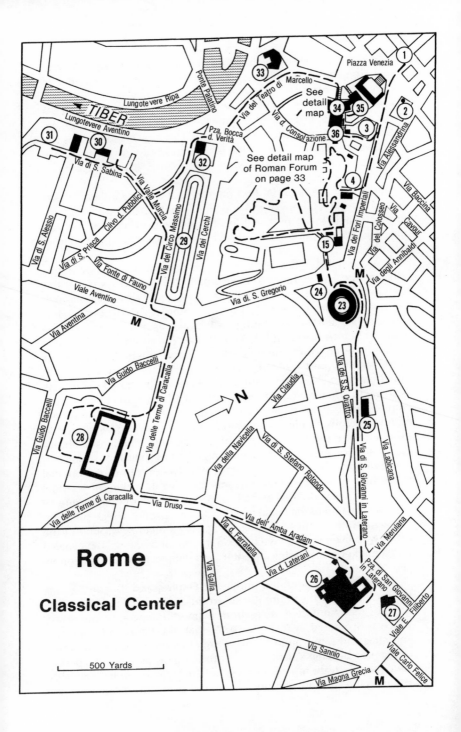

seen from the street. Beyond it, on the hill, is **Trajan's Market**, a three-storied complex of about 150 shops that was an early forerunner of modern shopping malls. It may be visited on any day except Mondays and some holidays, but is best saved for later. The entrance is on Via 4 Novembre. **Trajan's Column**, at the west end of his forum, is a magnificently carved structure, some 125 feet high, that celebrates his victories over the Dacians during the early 2nd century A.D. The bronze statue of the emperor at its top was replaced in 1588 with one of Saint Peter.

The first of the **Imperial Forums** was that built by **Julius Caesar** (Foro di Cesare) (3) between 54 and 46 B.C. with profits from his conquest of Gaul. Much of it still lies buried beneath the Via dei Fori Imperiali, but the portions that have been excavated can be seen from the sidewalk.

From here it is only a few steps to the first major attraction of this walking tour. The entrance to the **Roman Forum** (Foro Romano) (4) is open between 9 a.m. and 6 p.m. on Mondays and Wednesdays through Saturdays, and from 9 a.m. to 1 p.m. on Sundays and Tuesdays. It is closed on some holidays. During the winter season it closes on weekdays just before sunset. It is best to arrive here around 9 a.m. so that the unsheltered forum can be explored before the mid-day heat sets in. The admission charge also includes the Palatine hill, which follows the same hours. You may want to purchase an illustrated guidebook as an aid in visualizing what the forum looked like at the height of the empire, because it is mostly in a ruined state now. The walking route outlined below is only a suggestion, and may have to be altered as excavations continue. In any case this is one of the greatest archaeological sites on earth and certainly a highlight of any trip to Rome.

The Roman Forum began as a valley between four of the original seven hills of Rome, whose streams fed into it, making it a virtual swamp. This was drained as early as 510 B.C. under Etruscan rule by the construction of the Great Sewer (Cloaca Maxima), which still empties water into the nearby Tiber. Originally a meeting ground of the tribes who lived in primitive huts on the surrounding hills, it evolved into a market place, political center, and temple area during Republican times.

Development continued under the Empire, and it soon became the focal point of the entire Roman world—a dense complex of structures of many different styles from many different eras, the last of which was erected in A.D. 608. After that, the Forum fell into ruin, churches and other buildings were set amid the remains, and much of the area became a handy quarry for building stones and a pasture for cows. Excavations—the earliest of which caused much damage—began in the late 18th century and are still going on.

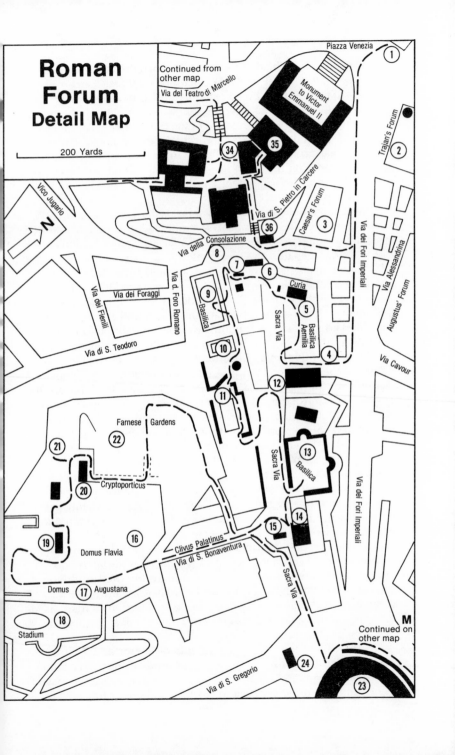

Roman Forum
Detail Map

200 Yards

Piazza Venezia

Continued from other map

Via del Teatro di Marcello

Monument to Victor Emmanuel II

Trajan's Forum

Vico Jugario

N

Via della Consolazione

Via d. Foro Romano

Via dei Foraggi

Via dei Fienili

Basilica

Via di S. Teodoro

Caesar's Forum

Via di S. Pietro in Carcere

Curia

Basilica Aemilia

Sacra Via

Via dei Fori Imperiali

Via Alessandrina

Augustus' Forum

Via Cavour

Farnese Gardens

Cryptoporticus

Basilica

Via dei Fori Imperiali

Domus Flavia

Clivus Palatinus

Via di S. Bonaventura

Domus Augustana

Stadium

M
Continued on other map

Via di S. Gregorio

The main thoroughfare through the Forum is the **Sacra Via** (Sacred Way), the oldest street in Rome. Victorious generals once rode in chariots drawn by four horses in triumphal processions here, preceded by captives and followed by soldiers. Turn right on its ancient paving stones to the scanty remains of the **Basilica Aemilia**, a meeting place first erected in 179 B.C. and rebuilt several times. The world "basilica" has no religious significance in classical architecture. Near its western end, on the Sacra Via, are the foundations of the circular Shrine of Venus Cloacina, dedicated to the goddess who protected the Great Sewer.

One ancient building that is still intact is the **Curia** (5), dating originally from the earliest times but often rebuilt. The present unadorned structure was erected by Diocletian in A.D. 303. Long a meeting place of the Roman Senate, it was converted into a church in A.D. 638—which assured its preservation—and restored to its 3rd-century appearance in 1937. The interior is now open and used for exhibitions.

In front of the Curia, under a modern roof, is the **Lapis Niger**, a pavement of black stones. Beneath this was found a stone slab with the oldest known Latin inscription, probably from the 6th century B.C. According to legend, this is the tomb of Romulus, the founder of Rome.

The **Arch of Septimius Severus** (6), one of the most grandiose of Roman arches, was erected in A.D. 203 to celebrate the emperor's victory over the Parthians and the Arabs. To the left of this are the remains of the **Rostra** (7), a raised speakers' platform moved to this site in 44 B.C. by Julius Caesar. Once decorated with the iron prows of captured enemy ships, its oratorical function declined as the absolute power of the emperors increased.

Next to this, to the left, are the eight remaining columns of the **Temple of Saturn** (8), built in 497 B.C. and heavily restored in the 4th century A.D. In its basement was located the State treasury, presumably protected by the gods above—although Caesar certainly got his hands into it. In front of the columns is the Golden Milestone, from which all distances in the empire were measured.

Continue on past the **Column of Phocas**, erected in honor of the Byzantine emperor. Dating from A.D. 608, this was the last monumental addition to the Forum. Just south of it are the ruins of the once-extensive **Basilica Julia** (9), begun by Julius Caesar in 54 B.C. and completed by Augustus. A meeting place for the civil courts, it is interesting for the scratched designs on some of is paving stones, used by idlers for little games of chance.

To the east of this stands the **Temple of Castor and Pollux** (10), also known as the *Dioscuri*. Three very beautiful Corinthian columns, each 40 feet high, are just above all that survives of this once-magnificent structure, originally built in 484 B.C. and reconstructed several

The Arch of Titus

times since. Next to it is the **Temple of Caesar**, erected in 42 B.C. by Augustus on the site of Julius Caesar's cremation. It marks the first time that a mortal was elevated to the rank of a god.

The **Temple of Vesta** and the **House of the Vestal Virgins** (11) were concerned with the cult of the sacred fire, which was kept burning in the temple and which symbolized the continuity of the State. Ironically, the temple burned down several times but was always rebuilt, the last time in the 2nd century A.D. The flames were tended by the six Vestal Virgins, who lived in the strictest morality in the luxurious house next door. They served a term of 30 years, usually beginning around the age of ten. Any of them who broke their vow of chastity were buried alive.

You have now come full circle through the western part of the Forum. Next to the entrance road is the **Temple of Antonius and Faustina** (12), which was converted into a Christian church during the 11th century and given a baroque façade in 1602—resulting in a very strange structure indeed. The original temple, still mostly intact, dates from the 2nd century A.D.

Now follow the Sacra Via east past traces of an Iron Age necropolis to the enormous **Basilica of Maxentius and Constantine** (13). Built in the 4th century A.D., it was the last such structure erected in Rome, and is still a very impressive sight. Nearby is the **Antiquarium of the**

Forum (14), a museum housed in a former convent, which displays treasures discovered during the excavations. It is usually open from 9:30 a.m. to 12:30 p.m.

The eastern part of the Forum ends at the **Arch of Titus** (15), set atop the highest point of the Sacra Via. This lovely structure was erected in A.D. 81 to commemorate the victories of Titus and Vespasian in the Judean War, which ended in the sack of Jerusalem.

The route now leaves the Roman Forum and climbs the **Palatine** hill, where the history of Rome began. Throughout the Republic this remained a quiet residential area, but when Augustus become the first emperor in 27 B.C. great palaces (the word derives from Palatine) began to be built. During the Middle Ages churches and convents were constructed over the pagan remains, and later sumptuous villas for the wealthy appeared. Today almost everything is in ruin, but the many trees and the parklike ambiance makes it a very enchanting place to visit—and the perfect spot for a picnic. It also offers magnificent panoramic views across the Forum and the city.

At the top of the hill is the **Domus Flavia** (16), the official palace built for the emperor Domitian at the end of the 1st century A.D. Although in ruin, it is possible to reconstruct in your mind's eye the splendor that it once possessed. Adjoining this to the east is the **Domus Augustana** (17), the actual residence of the emperor and his family. Despite its misleading name, it was also built by Domitian, not the earlier emperor Augustus. Domitian also ordered the construction of the adjacent **Stadium** (18), usually considered to be a sports arena for the amusement of the emperor, although some authorities maintain that it was his private garden. Art treasures unearthed during the excavations can be seen in the **Antiquarium of the Palatine** (19), a small museum located between the two palaces. It is open from 9:30 a.m. to noon, with tours every half-hour.

The best-preserved ancient structure on the Palatine is the so-called **House of Livia** (20), named for the wife of Augustus. It is now believed that this was actually the residence of the first emperor himself. Famous for its wall paintings, its fascinating interior may be seen by asking the custodian in the shelter by the entrance. Below this, reached by the Steps of Cacus, are traces of an **Iron Age Hut Village** (21) associated, at least in legend, with Romulus himself.

The lovely 16th-century **Farnese Gardens** (22) cover most of the remains of the Domus Tiberiana, a palace built for the emperor Tiberius in the early 1st century A.D. You can explore parts of the Cryptoporticus, a network of underground passages that linked various imperial palaces together. According to tradition, this is where the emperor Caligula was murdered in A.D. 41. Continue on to the northwest corner of the gardens, where you will have a fabulous **view** of

The Colosseum

the Roman Forum. From here follow the map downhill back to the Arch of Titus (15) and exit the enclosed area onto Piazza del Colosseo.

You are now standing in front of Rome's most famous landmark, the **Colosseum** *(Colosseo)* (23), known in ancient times as the *Flavian Amphitheater* after the imperial dynasty that built it. The Venerable Bede, that great 8th-century English historian, prophesied that "While the Colosseum stands, Rome shall stand; when the Colosseum falls, Rome shall fall; and when Rome falls, the world shall fall." Obviously, preservation of this glorious monument—the greatest to have come down from ancient Rome—is of the utmost importance.

Begun by the emperor Vespasian around A.D. 72 and inaugurated by Titus in 80, the Colosseum is an amazing feat of engineering. Some 50,000 unruly spectators were able to enter through the 80 arches and find seats within minutes. Shade from the hot sun was provided by a huge awning supported by exterior poles.

The amphitheater was built as a place of public entertainment during an era of what the contemporary satirist Juvenal called "bread and circuses." Many of the shows were extremely cruel to both man and beast, although it is doubtful whether Christians were actually fed to the lions there. What caused the populace to become so depraved as to enjoy watching pain and death is a mystery that probably has its roots in a system of government that robbed them of all sense of responsibility.

Remaining in use until the 6th century, it was made into a fortress during the Middle Ages and later used as a quarry for building stones during the Renaissance. In the 18th century it was consecrated by Pope Benedict XIV, after which some partial repairs were carried out.

Like the ancient Romans, you can enter the Colosseum free, although there is a charge to visit the upper levels. It is open daily from 9 a.m. to 7 p.m., closing before sunset in winter.

The incredibly well-preserved **Arch of Constantine** (24) stands next to the Colosseum. Erected in A.D. 315 to commemorate the emperor's victory over his rival Maxentius at Milvian Bridge, it was among the last great monuments of ancient Rome. Most of the sculptures adorning it were taken from earlier monuments as the quality of art had declined dramatically by the 4th century. Although Constantine was the first Christian emperor, the scenes depicted are pagan—his baptism was yet to come at the time.

At this point you could cut the walking tour short by going directly to the Baths of Caracalla (28) or the Circus Maximus (29) by way of Via di San Gregorio. Either way you will be spared climbing the Coelian hill.

If you choose to make the complete tour, stroll around the Colosseum and follow Via di San Giovanni in Laterano to the **Church of San Clemente** (25). Easily among the most interesting churches in Rome, St. Clement's is a 12th-century church on top of a 4th-century church on top of a 3rd-century Mithraic temple next to a 1st-century home—all of which can be visited. Be sure to see, in the upper (street level) church, the 12th-century **inlaid marble floor**, the superb **mosaic** in the apse depicting the *Triumph of the Cross,* and the lovely **frescoes** in the chapel of St. Catherine. Steps beyond the north aisle lead down to the 4th-century lower church with its interesting frescoes. Another set of steps, in the southwest corner, takes you from here down to the ancient temple and the house. The Church of San Clemente is closed between noon and 3:30 p.m., and a small charge is made for the lower sections.

Many people are under the impression that St. Peter's in the Vatican is a cathedral. It is not. The Cathedral of Rome is the **Basilica of St. John Lateran** *(San Giovanni in Laterano)* (26), reached by continuing straight ahead to the top of the hill. A cathedral church has been on this site since the 4th century, although it has been totally reconstructed many times. The present structure dates from the 17th and 18th centuries and is largely the work of the architect Borromini, with a façade by Alessandro Galilei. Some consider the restrained baroque interior to be cold, but it is in fact a masterpiece of understatement. The **doors** of the main entrance were taken from the ancient Curia in the Roman Forum, and the **statue** of the emperor Constantine on the front porch from the imperial baths on the Quirinal hill.

Step inside and take a look at the marvelous 16th-century **wooden ceiling**, the statues of the apostles in the nave, and the **papal altar**—used by the Pope to celebrate Mass—above which is a reliquary containing the heads of Saints Peter and Paul. The **cloisters**, reached through the left transept, are remarkable.

Leave via the right transept and visit the **Baptistry**, entered from Piazza di San Giovanni in Laterano. Built in the 5th century, it is the only building in the area to have survived intact from antiquity. Close to this, and adjacent to the church, is the **Lateran Palace**, which was rebuilt in the 16th century and houses Church offices. The original structure dated from the reign of Constantine and was the home of the Popes until their 14th-century exile in Avignon, France—after which they were installed in the Vatican. Curiously, the entire Lateran complex is not actually in Italy at all, as it belongs to the Vatican State.

While at the top of the hill you may want to visit the **Church of the Scala Santa** (27), diagonally across the street from the front of St. John Lateran. Inside are the famous marble stairs believed to be from the palace of Pontius Pilate in Jerusalem, which Christ ascended during His trial. The 28 steps, now clad in wood, are traditionally climbed by the faithful on their knees. At the top is the *Sancta Sanctorum*, a chapel containing precious relics including the *Acheiropoeton*, an icon bearing the likeness of Christ, supposedly painted by angels. The chapel is not open, but you can take a peek through the grate. If you would rather go up on foot there are other stairs on either side. The church is closed between 12:30 and 3:30 p.m.

The walk now leads downhill by way of Via dell' Amba Aradam and Via Druso to the **Baths of Caracalla** *(Terme di Caracalla)* (28). Although in a ruined state, enough of the enormous walls have survived to enable you to imagine the luxurious splendor they once contained. Built to accommodate 1,600 bathers, the complex was begun in A.D. 212 by the emperor Caracalla and remained in use until the 6th century, when the supply aqueducts were damaged by invading barbarians. The rear of the baths open onto a lovely park, an ideal venue for a picnic lunch. It was here that the poet Shelley wrote most of his masterpiece, *Prometheus Unbound,* in 1820. Outdoor operas are performed among the ruins during the summer season. Visits may be made Tuesdays through Saturdays, from 9 a.m. to sunset, and on Sundays and Mondays from 9 a.m. to 1 p.m.

Now follow the map to the **Circus Maximus** *(Circo Massimo)* (29). Little remains of this great racetrack set in a valley between the Palatine and Aventine hills, but you can easily imagine what it was like, as it is still an open area with the same ground contours. Horse races were held here at least as far back as the 4th century B.C. and as late as the 6th century A.D. Many different successive stadiums were built during its thousand-year history, some accommodating over 300,000 spectators. Besides chariot races, it was used for a variety of sports and triumphal parades. Naturally, there were plenty of wine taverns along its sides, and gambling flourished.

If your legs are up to it, an interesting little side trip can be made up the **Aventine** hill. The route leads past the Savello Park, worth stopping at as it offers a magnificent view of Rome, and then continues on to the ancient **Church of Santa Sabina** (30). Built in the 5th century, this has of course been altered many times, but a great deal of the original structure and its embellishments remain intact to delight you. The west door contains 5th-century carved **cypress panels**, while the nave is divided by fluted **Corinthian columns** taken from a nearby pagan temple. The **mosaic** above the entrance dates from the earliest church. Be sure to see the lovely cloisters if they are open. The church is closed between noon and 3:30 p.m.

Continue along the same street to its end, the **Piazza dei Cavalieri di Malta** (31), an utterly gorgeous square with a most unusual sight. Take a peek through the keyhold at number 3, the Priory of the Knights of Malta, and you will be rewarded with an extraordinary view of the dome of St. Peter's in the Vatican framed by trees. Skillful photographers should be able to capture this on film.

Now follow the map to Piazza Bocca della Verità and the beautiful **Church of Santa Maria in Cosmedin** (32). At the left side of its front porch is the famous **Mouth of Truth** (*Bocca della Verità*), a great stone face that was once a Roman drain cover. You can safely stick your hand into it only if your conscience is clear—otherwise, according to legend, it will be bitten off. During the Middle Ages this was used as a test for perjury. The church itself, dating from the 6th through the 12th centuries, is easily one of the most beautiful in Rome. The pleasing interior has been restored to its early appearance.

Busy Via Teatro di Marcello leads to the massive **Theater of Marcellus** (33), begun by Julius Caesar and completed by the emperor Augustus, who dedicated it to his nephew. Once seating over 10,000 spectators, it was among the largest in the Roman world. Later used as a fortress during the Middle Ages, it was converted into a palace in the 16th century. Only 12 of the original 41 rows of arches still stand, and these now form part of a large apartment complex.

Continue up the street almost to the Victor Emmanuel II Monument, where this walking tour began. As the sun is probably low by now, this would be a good time to explore the **Capitoline hill** (*Campidoglio*), the lowest and most sacred of the original seven hills of Rome. In ancient times this was both the political and the religious center of the city, and the site of its principal temple, dedicated to

Jupiter. Virtually nothing of the distant past remains today, however, as the entire area was rebuilt during the Middle Ages and the Renaissance, turned 180 degrees to face the Vatican instead of the Roman Forum.

There are two stairways leading up the hill. Take the lower of these, to the right, and climb up to **Piazza del Campidoglio** (34). Both the open square and the staircase were designed by Michelangelo in the 16th century, although some changes were made since then. The bronze **equestrian statue** of Marcus Aurelius (presently removed for restoration) that graces its center dates from the 2nd century A.D. and was long thought to represent the Christian emperor Constantine, hence its salvation from the melting pot.

The 16th-century building straight ahead is the Senatorial Palace, the official seat of the Governor of Rome, and is not open to the public. To the right is the **Conservators' Palace** which, together with the **New Palace** to the left, houses the **Capitoline Museums**—the oldest such institutions in the world. Both are devoted primarily to classical sculpture, although there is also a distinquished collection of paintings. You may want to return here on another day. The museums, sharing a joint ticket, are open on Wednesdays and Fridays from 9 a.m. to 2 p.m.; on Tuesdays and Thursdays from 9 a.m. to 2 p.m. and 5–8 p.m.; on Saturdays from 9 a.m. to 2 p.m. and 8–11 p.m.; and on Sundays from 9 a.m. to 1 p.m.

Steps between the Senatorial Palace and the Conservators' Palace lead up to a garden with a fine view of the Roman Forum. Return to the piazza and stroll out into the gardens overlooking the Imperial Forums. From here it is also possible to enter the side door of the noted **Church of Santa Maria d'Aracoeli** (35), whose main entrance is via the very steep steps from the bottom of the hill, next to the ones you climbed. The church was built in the 13th century on the foundations of the Temple of Juno Moneta, which dated from the 6th century B.C. It is filled with art treasures, including the revered *Santo Bambino,* a wooden image of the Christ Child said to be carved from the wood of an olive tree from the Garden of Gethsemane.

Now follow the narrow road that leads steeply downhill on the north side of the Senatorial Palace. At the bend continue straight ahead down steps to the **Mamertine Prison** (36), also known as San Pietro in Carcere. The lower chamber of this gloomy chapel is probably a cistern from the 4th century B.C., and was used as a prison for enemies of the State. Legend has it that Saint Peter was imprisoned here by the emperor Nero, and that while incarcerated he baptized his jailors with water from a spring that appeared miraculously. From here it is only a short stroll back to Piazza Venezia (1), the start of this walk.

Rome

(Roma)

The Old City

Although Rome is a city built on hills (considerably more than seven if you actually count), it was the flat land in the bend of the Tiber to the northwest of the Forum that saw the greatest development after the Middle Ages. Known in ancient times as the *Campus Martius,* this area was well built up during the late Empire, but little of that era remains as the stones were mostly reused in later construction. During what are conveniently called the Dark Ages the population had fallen dramatically, only to rebound towards the end of the 14th century following the papacy's return from its French exile. After that, a tremendous amount of new construction took place, first in the Renaissance and later in the baroque styles. These treasures, beautifully maintained and still in use, are there to delight you today.

Actually, you could take weeks to explore the heart of Old Rome, especially if you spend time visiting its many museums and churches. This one-day walking tour, however, covers nearly all of the highlights and provides a sound basis for further probes.

GETTING AROUND:

Like the previous tour of the classical center, this one begins at centrally located Piazza Venezia—easily reached by bus, taxi, or on foot from your hotel. The area covered is served by three subway stations, all located towards the latter part of the walk. You may want to return from one of these. They are near Piazza del Popolo (10) *(Flaminio)*, the Spanish Steps (9) *(Spagna)*, and Via del Tritone *(Barberini)*—all on line A.

WHEN TO GO:

This walk may be taken at any time, although you should avoid Sundays if you plan to visit the churches, and Mondays if seeing the inside of the Pantheon or any of the museums is important to you. It is easily possible to include the Castel Sant' Angelo, described in the next chapter, in this tour—in which case you should also avoid Mondays. Good weather is important as nearly all of the day will be spent out of doors.

FOOD AND DRINK:

The Old City is richly endowed with a vast selection of good restaurants in all price ranges, so you won't go hungry. Some of the better choices—in the sequence that you will pass or come close to them on the walking route—are listed below. For information about local specialties see the "Food and Drink" section of the previous chapter.

La Sacrestia (Via del Seminario 89, just east of the Pantheon) A large, old-fashioned restaurant and a long-time favorite. Both full meals and pizzas are available. X: Wed. $$ and $

Eau Vive (Via Monterone 85, 2 blocks southwest of the Pantheon) Run by missionaries, this popular place features various French Colonial cuisines. X: Sun., Aug. $$

L'Orso 80 (Via dell' Orso 33, 3 blocks north of Pza. Navona) A popular Roman trattoria with great antipasti. X: Mon., mid-Aug.) $$

Da Pancrazio (Piazza del Biscione 92, off the east side of Pza. Campo dei Fiori) Built into ancient Roman ruins, with lots of atmosphere. X: Wed. $$

Hostaria Farnese (Via dei Baullari 109, between Pza. Campo dei Fiori and the Palazzo Farnese) A small family-run trattoria. X: Thurs. $

Polese (Piazza Sforza Cesarini 40, in front of the palazzo of the same name) A traditional trattoria, with outdoor tables. X: Tues. $

Passetto (Via Zanardelli 14, just north of Pza. Navona) Considered to be among the best in Rome. X: Sun., Mon. Lunch $$$

La Maiella (Piazza Sant' Apollinare 45, 1 block north of Pza. Navona) Another great place, specializing in dishes from the Abruzzi region. X: Sun. $$$

Il Falchetto (Via Montecatini 12, 2 blocks south of Pza. Colonna) A rustic tavern. X: Fri., Aug. $$

Da Mario (Via della Vite 55, 3 blocks south of Via Condotti) Tuscan cuisine at reasonable prices. X: Sun., Aug. $$

McDonald's (Piazza di Spagna 47, near the Spanish Steps) For the homesick, with a salad bar. $

Margutta Vegetariano (Via Margutta 119, between the Spanish Steps and Pza. del Popolo) For the vegetarian crowd, X: Sun., Aug. $

La Buca di Ripetta (Via di Ripetta 36, 2 blocks south of Pza. del Popolo) Excellent food, always crowded. X: Sun. eve., Mon., Aug. $$

Birreria Tempera (Via San Marcello 19, 3 blocks southwest of the Trevi Fountain) German food in a noisy beer hall. X: Sun., Aug. $

TOURIST INFORMATION:
See this entry in the previous chapter.

SUGGESTED TOUR:
Begin your walk at **Piazza Venezia** (1) opposite the pompous Monument to Victor Emmanuel II. The 15th-century **Palazzo Venezia**, on the northwest corner, was built as a palace for the popes and later became the Venetian embassy, the Austrian embassy and, finally, the office of Benito Mussolini. It was from the balcony here that *Il Duce* harangued his assembled followers. Today it houses a museum of tapestries, paintings, sculpture, and other art objects. Set into it is the fine Church of San Marco, begun in the 4th century and rebuilt many times since.

A short stroll down Via del Plebiscito leads to the magnificent 16th-century **Gesù Church** (2), the main church of the Jesuit order and an important center of the Counter-Reformation. Its interesting façade combines elements of both the Renaissance and the baroque styles. Step inside to witness the incredibly rich decorations, executed at a time when the Church had discovered the use of impressive art as a means of spreading the Word. Take a look at the **ceiling fresco** of the *Triumph of the Name of Jesus* high above the nave if you want to understand what is really meant by baroque. Another not-to-be-missed sight is the **Chapel of St. Ignatius Loyola** in the left transept, an unbelievably opulent tomb for the saint. The church is closed between 12:30 and 4 p.m.

Just down the street, here called Corso Vittorio Emanuele II, is the **Largo Argentina** (3), named after a nearby 16th-century house and not the country. The Argentina Theater, on the west side, was the scene in 1816 of an operatic disaster when Rossini's *Barber of Seville* was met with boos at its première. The square itself was excavated in the late 1920s, revealing four **Roman temples** from the Republican period. Among the earliest such structures in Rome, they have not yet been fully identified, but the oldest probably dates from the 5th century B.C. You can get a good view of them from the street level.

Now follow Via dei Cestari to Piazza della Minerva, embellished with an Egyptian obelisk from the 6th century B.C., here supported on a marble elephant's back—an idea of Bernini's. Next to it is the austere **Church of Santa Maria sopra Minerva**, the only Gothic church in Rome. Founded in the 8th century and altered many times since, it is famous for its superb works of art, including pieces by Michelangelo, Mino da Fiesole, and Filippino Lippi.

Continue on to Piazza della Rotonda and one of Rome's greatest

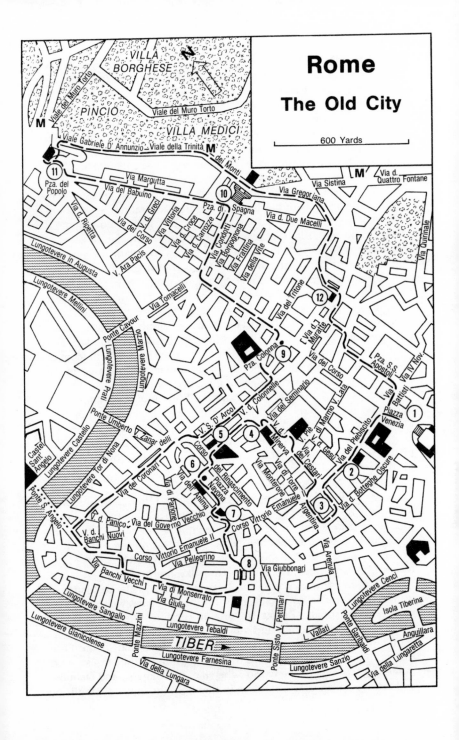

Rome

The Old City

600 Yards

VILLA BORGHESE

PINCIO

VILLA MEDICI

Viale del Muro Torto

Viale del Muro Torto

Viale Gabriele D' Annunzio

Viale della Trinità dei Monti

M

M

Via Sistina

Via d. Quattro Fontane

M

Via Gregoriana

Via d. Due Macelli

Pza. del Popolo

11

Via Margutta

Via del Babuino

Via d Ripetta

Via del Corso

V. d. Greci

Via Vittoria

Via Croce

Via d. Carrozze

V Ara Pacis

Pza. di Spagna

10

Via Condotti

Via Borgognona

Via Frattina

Via della Vite

Lungotevere in Augusta

Lungotevere Mellini

Ponte Cavour

Lungotevere Marzio

Via Tomacelli

Lungotevere Prati

Via del Tritone

12

Via d. Murate

Pza. Colonna

9

Via del Corso

V. d. Colonnelle

Via del Seminario

Pza. S.S. Apostoli

Pza. IV Nov.

Via Battisti

1

Ponte Umberto I

Lungotevere Castello

Lungotevere Tor di Nona

Via Zanardelli

V. S. D' Arco

6

5

4

V.d. Arco

Via di Marmo V. Lata

Via del Plebiscito

Minerva

V. d. Gesú

V. d. Cestari

V. d. Torre Argentina

Piazza Venezia

2

Via d. Botteghe Oscure

Castel Sant'Angelo

Lungotevere Castello

Ponte S. Angelo

Via dei Coronari

V. d. Anima

Piazza Navona

Via d. Panico

V. d. Banchi Nuovi

Via del Governo Vecchio

Corso del Rinascimento

Corso Vittorio Emanuele

7

Via Monterone

3

Via Arenula

Lungotevere Cenci

Ponte Garibaldi

Isola Tiberina

Corso Vittorio Emanuele II

Via Pellegrino

8

Via Giubbonari

Via Banchi Vecchi

Via di Monserrato

Via Giulia

Lungotevere Sangallo

Ponte Mazzini

Lungotevere Tebaldi

V Pettinari

Vallati

Ponte Sisto

Lungotevere Gianicolense

TIBER

Lungotevere Farnesina

Lungotevere della Lungara

Lungotevere Sanzio

Via della Lungaretta

L Anguillara

Lungotevere Cenci

attractions, the **Pantheon** (4). Looking as though it was only a few centuries old at most, this miraculously well-preserved structure was really first erected by Marcus Agrippa in 27 B.C. and rebuilt by the emperor Hadrian between A.D. 119 and 128. For well over a thousand years its great dome remained an unparalleled feat of engineering—actually, its diameter was not equaled until this century. Cast in solid concrete poured over a wooden mold, its only opening is at the top. Originally, the Pantheon was, as its name suggests, a temple to all the gods, but the establishment of Christianity almost brought about its ruin. What saved it was its being converted into a church in the 7th century. Despite this, it has been desecrated several times, most notably by Pope Urban VIII Barberini who, in the 17th century, melted down the bronze from the beams of the portico to make the famous baldachin in St. Peter's Basilica. This act was met with the popular quip "What the barbarians didn't do, the Barberini did."

Enter through the great **bronze doors**, the best to have come down from antiquity, to see an interior that has changed little since it was built. Two of Italy's kings are buried here—Victor Emmanuele II and Umberto I—along with the artist Raphael. The Pantheon is open Tuesdays through Saturdays, from 9 a.m. to 2 p.m., and on Sundays and holidays from 9 a.m. to 1 p.m. Entrance is free. The piazza in front of it, decorated with a lovely 16th-century fountain surmounted by an Egyptian obelisk, is a favorite gathering place for tourists.

Via Giustiniani leads to the **Church of San Luigi dei Francesi** (5), dedicated to St. Louis and serving as the French national church in Rome. Built in the 16th century with donations from various French kings, it is famous for its three fabulous **paintings by Caravaggio** depicting events in the life of St. Matthew. These nearly cover the walls of the last chapel on the left, and are the first major religious works done by the young artist, who was stylistically far ahead of his time. Caravaggio's life in Rome was short and violent. Often in trouble with the police, he fled the city after killing a man in a street fight and died four years later. Other treasures in the church's richly decorated interior include the **frescoes** by Domenichino telling the *Story of St. Cecilia*, in the second chapel on the right. The church is closed between 12:30 and 3:30 p.m., and on Thursday afternoons.

Now follow the map past the heavily guarded Palazzo Madama, which houses the Italian senate, and stroll into what may well be Rome's most popular square. **Piazza Navona** (6) occupies the site of Domitian's 1st-century stadium and still preserves its exact outline. In its center stands Bernini's glorious 17th-century **Fountain of the Four Rivers**, representing what were then thought to be the largest rivers in the four corners of the world—the Nile, the Ganges, and Danube, and the Rio della Plata. According to tradition, the figure symbolizing

The Pantheon

the Nile has his head covered to avoid looking at the adjacent Church of Sant' Agnese, designed by Bernini's arch rival, Borromini. This story does not hold water as well as the fountain, as the church was built a few years later.

Today, the piazza is a vast pedestrian area populated with tourists sitting at outdoor cafés, questionable artists peddling their works, and children playing in the square. While there, you may want to visit the lavishly decorated **Church of Sant' Agnese in Agone**, opposite the fountain. This was built in the 17th century, allegedly on the site of an ancient Roman bordello where the young saint, stripped of her clothes, suddenly and miraculously grew enough hair to cover her nakedness.

Leave the square from the south and wander through the tiny Piazza di Pasquino, named for the ancient **broken statue** in its southeast corner. Ever since the 16th century this has been used as a sort of bulletin board from which anonymous satirical comments were hung, usually to the embarrassment of the ruling powers. Pasquino has always been the most "talkative" of Rome's statues.

The ponderous **Palazzo Barschi** (7), around the corner, houses the interesting **Rome Museum**. In addition to the splendid collection of local art, there are some quite fascinating objects, including three cars from the personal railroad train built for Pope Pius IX in 1858. You can't miss seeing the fantastic staircase, which often leads to special exhibitions. The museum is open Tuesdays through Sundays, from 9 a.m. to 1 p.m., and is also open from 5–8 p.m. on Tuesdays and Thursdays, but may be temporarily closed for repairs.

Cross Corso Vittorio Emanuele II, a modern road following the old processional route between St. Peter's in the Vatican and St. John Lateran. The impressive 16th-century Palazzo della Cancelleria, to your right, is occupied by the papal chancery and so is actually part of the independent Vatican State. Continue on past it to **Piazza Campo dei Fiori** (8), an ancient square steeped in medieval history where a bustling open-air food market is held every day except Sundays, from 6 a.m. to 1 p.m. The statue of the monk Giordano Bruno, burned at the stake here in 1600 for heresy, is a reminder that this was once a common place of execution.

Just a few steps to the southwest is the 16th-century **Palazzo Farnese**, easily one of the most elegant of Renaissance palaces. Unfortunately, you cannot see its splendid interior as it is occupied by the French embassy and now closed to the public for security reasons. Continue up Via di Monserrato and turn right at the Palazzo Sforza Cesarini to the Corso Vittorio Emanuele II.

At this point you may want to make a little side trip. The **Castel Sant' Angelo**, described in the next chapter, is only a few steps out of the way, just across the footbridge over the Tiber. Seeing it today will make your tour of the Vatican more relaxed. It is open Tuesdays through Saturdays, from 9 a.m. to 2 p.m., and on Sundays from 9 a.m. to 1 p.m.

Now follow the map through an attractive and colorful old part of town to **Piazza Colonna** (9), dominated by the 2nd-century Column of Marcus Aurelius. His statue, once at the top, was replaced in the 16th century by one of Saint Paul. The Palazzo Chigi, on the north side of the square, is the residence of Italy's prime minister. On the west side is the Chamber of Deputies.

Turn left on busy Via del Corso and then right on **Via Condotti**, surely the most elegant shopping street in Italy. You'll find all of the famous fashion names here an in the adjoining streets. Chances are, however, that you'll walk right by one of the strangest oddities in town. Everyone knows that the world's smallest nation is in Rome, and most people think that this is the Vatican State. That depends on how you define a nation. The **Sovereign Military Order of Malta** (S.M.O.M.), located in a small palazzo at number 68 Via Condotti, has been accorded extraterritorial rights by the Italian government and issues its own passports, license plates, stamps, and even money. Founded around the time of the Crusades, it has a population of about 80 and carries on humanitarian work around the world. Take a look into the courtyard and see for yourself.

The **Caffè Greco**, near the top of the street, was opened in 1760

The Spanish Steps

and became a meeting place for visiting luminaries including Goethe, Wagner, Berlioz, Liszt, Byron, and many, many others. Virtually unchanged today, it is still a wonderful place to stop for a drink.

You are now standing in front of that great tourist magnet, the **Spanish Steps** *(Scalla della Trinità dei Monti)* (10). Despite the name— never used by Italians—they were built by the French in the 18th century as a way of reaching their church at the top of the hill. The square at the bottom was once in Spanish territory, being part of their embassy grounds. Today the entire area is overrun with English-speaking visitors, as you will quickly discover. The curious 17th-century boat-shaped **fountain** at the foot of the steps was an ingenious solution to the problem of lower water pressure from the supply aqueduct. To the right of it, at number 26, is the **Keats-Shelley Memorial**, a tiny museum in the house where the poet John Keats died in 1821. It is filled with memorabilia and books, and can be visited Mondays through Fridays, from 9 a.m. to 1 p.m. and 3–6 p.m.

Via del Babuino leads to the harmoniously balanced **Piazza del Popolo** (11), once the northern entrance to the city. In its center is an Egyptian obelisk brought to Rome by Augustus and originally placed in the Circus Maximus. At the northeast end of the square is the **Church**

The Trevi Fountain

of **Santa Maria del Popolo**, whose interior contains a fabulous collection of art treasures. Don't miss the magnificent **paintings** by Caravaggio in the Cerasi Chapel to the left of the chancel. Another feature is the **Chigi Chapel**, the second on the left side of the nave, which was designed by Raphael. The church is closed between 12:30 and 4 p.m.

Now take the steps opposite the church to Viale Gabriele d'Annunzio, which offers lovely views from the Pincio hill. Follow this route back to the **Trinità dei Monti Church** at the top of the Spanish Steps. Built in the 15th century by Charles VIII of France, it is still French property and is usually closed.

From here follow the map to the (finally!) last stop on this tour. You can buy an ice cream or a drink at one of the surrounding bars, then sit down for a well-deserved rest in front of the **Trevi Fountain** (12). One of the last great monuments of the baroque era, it was built in the 18th century and is the largest and by far the most spectacular fountain in Rome. Its setting, hidden away in narrow back streets, helps with the illusion of suddenly discovering something totally unexpected. The roar of the water combined with the sheer exuberance of the sculpture makes this a special place at which to end your walk. Be certain to toss a coin over your left shoulder into the water to insure your return to Rome.

Rome
(Roma)
Across the Tiber

Just about everyone who goes to Rome sooner or later winds up exploring the Vatican, and quite a few also visit the Castel Sant' Angelo. The atmospheric Trastevere district is popular for its restaurants but otherwise far too often overlooked. This one-day walking tour links all three together with an invigorating stroll across the lovely Janiculum hill, enlivened with panoramic views of Rome.

The Vatican State is either the smallest or the second-smallest independent country within Rome and in the world, depending on your definition of sovereignty. It was created in 1929 by the Lateran Treaty between the Holy See and the Mussolini government. Covering a total combined area of 110 acres and with a population of about a thousand, it consists of the Vatican City—visited on this tour—and several churches, schools, and offices elsewhere in Rome as well as a villa in the country. It operates its own postal service, mints its own money, publishes newspapers and journals, and runs its own radio station.

Prior to the mid-19th-century unification of Italy, the Papal States—covering a large section of central Italy—were ruled by the pope. This came to an end in 1870 when the troops of King Victor Emmanuel II took Rome and made it the capital of their new nation. Despite attempts at reconciliation, Pope Pius IX considered himself a prisoner in the Vatican and refused to leave, as did his successors. The dispute was finally settled in 1929 when the pope was made sovereign of the vastly smaller Vatican State.

Except for a few small installations, the right bank of the Tiber was only a minor part of ancient Rome. Originally settled by the Etruscans, a highly civilized people who predated the Romans by many centuries and controlled territory extending from here north as far as the Po valley, it was mostly inhabited by immigrants until the Middle Ages, after which some Romans began to move in. The district known as Trastevere—literally meaning "across the Tiber" (Tevere in Italian)—still retains much of its offbeat flavor, making it an exceptionally interesting place to explore.

51

GETTING AROUND:

Depending on the location of your hotel, the best way to reach the starting point of this tour is probably to take the subway *(Metropolitana* or *M)* to the northern end of line A, Ottaviano. Although you'll most likely be doing this during the height of the morning rush hour, you'll be going against the flow of traffic so empty seats should be available. Line A intersects with line B at the Termini train station. Tickets are sold by vending machines in the subway stations. You can also get there via buses marked *"San Pietro"* or by taking a taxi to *"Musei Vaticani."* Ask at your hotel for specific details.

WHEN TO GO:

The Vatican Museums are closed on Sundays and some holidays, except for the last Sunday in each month. The Castel Sant' Angelo is closed on Mondays (and closes at noon or 1 p.m. on other days), but this sight could easily be combined with the walking tour described in the previous chapter. Good weather is important for the walk across the Janiculum hill. There is so much to see at the Vatican that an early start is vital. Plan to be there around 9 a.m.

FOOD AND DRINK:

Restaurants near the Vatican are mostly geared to the tourist trade and usually overpriced. Some notable exceptions to this are listed below. There is also a self-service cafeteria with a limited selection of simple dishes at low prices in the Vatican Museums. The Janiculum hill has no restaurants, but you will pass a few outdoor snack bars offering sandwiches with a view. The Trastevere district, near the end of the walk, is famous for its wide choice of excellent restaurants.

For information about local specialties see the "Food and Drink" section in the chapter "Rome—the Classical Center."

Near the Vatican:

Les Etoiles, Atlante Star (Via Vitelleschi 34, 2 blocks northwest of Castel Sant' Angelo) This rooftop restaurant has a view of St. Peter's. $$$

Lo Squalo Bianco (Via F. Cesi 36, 5 blocks northeast of Castel Sant' Angelo) Excellent seafood, reservations (06) 321-47-00. X: Sun., Aug. $$

Il Matriciano (Via dei Gracchi 55, 5 blocks east of the museum entrance) A local favorite with simple dishes. X: Aug. $$

Hostaria dei Bastioni (Via Leone IV 29, near Vatican Museums entrance) Specializes in seafood. X: Sun. $$

Hostaria da Cesare (Via Crescenzio 13, just north of Castel Sant' Angelo) Specializes in seafood. X: Sun. eve., Mon. $$

In Trastevere:

Romolo (Via di Porta Settimiana 8, at the bottom of Via Garibaldi) A famous typical trattoria, with tables in a garden. X: Mon., Aug. $$$

Sabatini (Piazza Santa Maria in Trastevere 10 and Vicolo Santa Maria in Trastevere 18, both by the Church of Santa Maria) Two enormously popular restaurants with the same owner, both specializing in seafood. X: Wed. $$$

Taverna Trilussa (Via del Politeama 23, 3 blocks northeast of Santa Maria in Trastevere) Typical of the neighborhood, with local specialties. X: Sun. eve., Mon., Aug. $$

Corsetti—Il Galeone (Piazza di San Cosimato 27, 4 blocks south of Santa Maria in Trastevere) Specializes in seafood. X: Wed. $$

Mario (Via del Moro 53, 2 blocks northeast of Santa Maria in Trastevere) Locally popular for its low prices. X: Sun., Aug. $

TOURIST INFORMATION:

The Vatican Tourist Office, phone (06) 698-44-66, is located to the left of the steps leading into St. Peter's Basilica. For information about Rome, see this entry in the chapter "Rome—the Classical Center."

SUGGESTED TOUR:

Those coming by subway can follow the map from the nearby **Ottaviano stop** (1), the northern end of line A, to the museum entrance.

To beat the inevitable crowds, your tour should begin early at the world-renowned **Vatican Museums** (2), whose only entrance is on Viale Vaticano. One admission covers all of the museums, including the fabulous Sistine Chapel. Most of these are in the same building and all are interconnected. There is far more here than can possibly be seen in a day, let alone the two or three hours you'll probably want to devote to it, so a plan of attack is essential. Large displays inside the entrance simplify this by outlining just what is to be seen in each museum and suggesting four different color-coded routes through the maze. It is not necessary to follow any of these, of course, but they do make things much easier. Since everything is so well organized and explained, only the highlights are briefly described below. You may want to purchase an illustrated guidebook to the museums as an aid in selecting which treasures interest you the most.

The museum complex is open Mondays through Saturdays, from 9 a.m. to 2 p.m. During Easter week and in July, August, and September it remains open until 4 p.m. on Mondays through Fridays. It is also open on the last Sunday of each month, from 9 a.m. to 2 p.m., and admission is free at that time only. Some of the less important galleries may close earlier or be completely closed on certain days. The entire museum is closed on some religious holidays. These variations are posted at the entrance. Photography is permitted as long as you don't use a flash or a tripod.

Among the most outstanding galleries are: The **Pio-Clementine Museum**, whose collections of ancient Greek and Roman sculpture were assembled during the 18th century by Popes Pius VI and Clement XIV. Don't miss the **Octagonal Court** with its superb *Laocoön Group* from Nero's palace or the *Apollo Belvedere*, a Roman copy of a Greek statue from the 4th century B.C. After a long walk through other galleries you will come to the magnificent **Raphael Stanze**, four rooms decorated in the 16th century by Raphael, which were once the official residence of the popes.

Close to this is the **Sistine Chapel**, perhaps the most famous chapel in the world. The walls were mostly painted by a variety of 15th-century artists, but the real attraction is the incredible **ceiling** by Michelangelo—a supreme masterpiece depicting scenes from the *Book of Genesis*. Parts of this are covered as restoration work, begun in 1984, continues. It may be completed in 1988. Some twenty years later, Michelangelo also painted the *Last Judgement* on the altar wall. Originally, most of the figures in it were nude, but they was later clothed by another artist. When the painting is eventually restored, it is hoped that the prudish additions will be removed.

Another not-to-be-missed attraction is the **Pinacoteca**, a marvelous picture gallery near the exit and the cafeteria. Be sure to see the works by Raphael in room VIII, Leonardo da Vinci in room IX, and Caravaggio and his followers in room XII.

Scattered among these four galleries are many other museums. The most interesting of these are the rather unexpected **Modern Art Collection**, the **Etruscan Museum**, the **Map Gallery**, the **Sala dei Palafrenieri**, the **Chapel of Nicholas V**, the **Borgia Apartments**, the **Vatican Library**, and the **Pagan** and **Christian Museums**.

A special bus leaves every half-hour from the museum exit, going by way of the Vatican gardens to St. Peter's Square. Otherwise, you can easily walk the half-mile distance by following the map.

The curved colonnades of **Saint Peter's Square** *(Piazza San Pietro)* seem to reach out toward the Vatican's many visitors, embracing them in its grasp. Standing on the dark round stone in front of each of the two fountains reveals the perfection of Bernini's 17th-century design as you see the four rows of columns in the colonnade merge into one, a neat trick of perspective. The **Egyptian obelisk** in the center of the square, brought to Rome in A.D. 37 by Caligula, is topped with a cross supposedly containing a splinter of the True Cross. The large building beyond the right colonnade houses the present Pope's apartment.

On the left side of the square, near the steps to the basilica, are

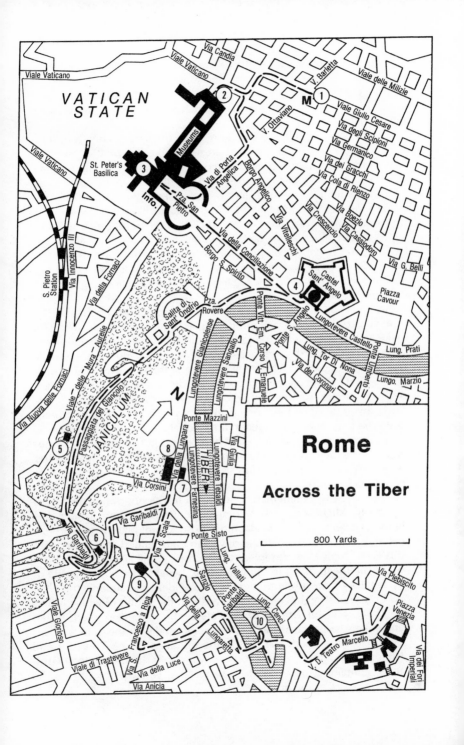

Rome

Across the Tiber

800 Yards

both the tourist information office—where you can inquire about Papal audiences and various tours—and a post office, which also sells postcards. Mail sent from here requires Vatican stamps and usually arrives at its destination more quickly than if it were sent through the Italian mails.

Saint Peter's Basilica *(San Pietro)* (3) is the largest church in the world. Begun in 1506, it replaced an earlier basilica built in the 4th century by the emperor Constantine over the supposed tomb of Saint Peter. This original church, traces of which still exist in the crypt, was no longer adequate and had already shown signs of collapse. The design of the new basilica was first entrusted to Bramante, who died eight years later. Several other architects carried on the work, including Michelangelo, who made the greatest contribution. What was to have been a Greek Cross plan was extended to the form of a Latin Cross in the early 17th century, since this layout was more suitable for the ceremonies of the Counter-Reformation. The final finishing touches were added by Bernini.

The interior is so perfectly conceived that it belies its true size—until you realize how small the people at the far end seem to be. To make a fairly thorough exploration requires several hours and is best saved for another day, perhaps joining a tour or hiring a guide. A quick probe, however, should at least cover the following highlights.

The first chapel on the right contains Michelangelo's great masterpiece, the **Pietà**, sculpted in 1499 when he was still young. It is, curiously, his only signed work. Unfortunately, it is now behind protective glass after being damaged in a 1972 attack.

Continue down the nave. Just before you get to the great dome, you will see the famous 13th-century bronze **statue of St. Peter** by the huge pier to the right. His foot is partly worn away by the kisses of countless pilgrims.

Your eyes will immediately be drawn to the enormous **dome** designed by Michelangelo but completed after his death. Under it is Bernini's utterly fantastic **baldachin**, whose 95-foot-high twisted bronze columns support an ornate canopy guarded by gilded angels. Beneath this is the **high altar**, reserved for the Pope alone. The steps in front of the altar lead down to the **confessio**, believed to be on the site of St. Peter's grave, although there is little evidence to support this.

Continue straight ahead to the apse, in the center of which is Bernini's magnificent **Throne of St. Peter**, a bronze encasement for an ancient episcopal chair traditionally associated with the saint.

Just off the south transept is the entrance to the **Treasury and Historical Museum**, which you may want to visit. The **Vatican Grottoes**, containing papal tombs, are reached via steps by one of the piers supporting the dome.

St. Peter's Basilica

Perhaps the most memorable part of a visit to St. Peter's is to make the **ascent** to the **top of the dome**, the first half of which can be done by elevator. The entrance to this is along the south aisle, near the front of the basilica. It lifts you up to the roof, from which there is a fabulous view of the square. The dome itself is actually two shells, between which a staircase leads to an interior balcony overlooking the high altar, 238 feet below. It then continues ever upward to the outdoor platform around the lantern, 394 feet above the surrounding city. The views, especially of the Vatican grounds, are stupendous and well worth the effort.

Leave the basilica and walk straight ahead through the square and back into Italy. Via della Conciliazione, a broad boulevard rammed through an ancient quarter by Mussolini in the late 1930s, leads directly to the **Castel Sant' Angelo** (4). Since this closes for the day at noon or 1 p.m., you may want to include it with the tour described in the previous chapter instead.

The massive cylindrical castle is certainly one of the more unusual sights in Rome, and its history is as strange as its appearance. Built around A.D. 135 by the emperor Hadrian as a mausoleum for himself, it was soon turned into a defensive bastion protecting the northwest approaches to Rome. In 590 Pope Gregory the Great, leading a procession to St. Peter's, saw a vision of an angel above the citadel which signified the end of a plague then decimating the city. A chapel was built on the spot and the name changed to Sant' Angelo. Its military uses increased during the Middle Ages, and it eventually became a safe residence for beseiged popes, who could reach its sanctuary via a secret passageway from the Vatican. Later used as a prison, it became a barracks during the 19th century and is now a museum. Opera fans will recognize it as the setting for the last act of Puccini's *Tosca*.

The original **Roman interior** is remarkably well preserved. Its spiral ramp leads to a staircase which in turn takes you up through the fortress to the luxurious **Papal Apartments**. A visit here will take about an hour and offers splendid views of the city in addition to the many exhibits, mostly military in nature. The castle is open Tuesdays through Saturdays, from 9 a.m. to 1 p.m., and on Sundays from 9 a.m. to noon.

Now follow the map to Piazza Rovere and climb the Salita di Sant' Onofrio steps, which soon become a street leading up the **Janiculum hill** *(Monte Gianicolo)*. The walk along the crest of the hill is mostly through a pleasant park, with views of Rome spread out before you. In about half a mile you will come to the **Giuseppe Garibaldi Monument** (5), commemorating that patriot's battle with the French, fought nearby in 1849.

The route leads downhill past the unusual Paolo Fountain to the **Church of San Pietro in Montorio** (6), erected in the 15th century on what was then thought to be the site of St. Peter's crucifixion. It contains some interesting frescoes, but is most famous for the classical **Tempietto** in the courtyard outside. This little round temple was built in 1502 by Bramante and is regarded as a masterpiece of the High Renaissance.

From here take Via Giuseppe Garibaldi steeply down to Via della Lungara. To the left is the famous **Villa Farnesina** (7), an elegant 16th-century structure filled with marvelous art. You may want to return here another day as it is only open from 9 a.m. to 1 p.m., Mondays through Saturdays. Across the street is the **Palazzo Corsini** (8), another noted art museum, which receives visitors on Mondays through Saturdays from 9 a.m. to 2 p.m., and on Sundays from 9 a.m. to 1 p.m.

The highly atmospheric **Trastevere** district now lies before you. Follow the map through narrow streets to the **Church of Santa Maria in Trastevere** (9), the first in Rome to be dedicated to the Virgin. It is allegedly built on the site of the first legal Christian church, dating from A.D. 221. The present structure was begun around 1130 and has been altered many times since. Step inside to see the wonderful **mosaics** in the apse and the massive Ionic **columns** in the nave. The church is closed between noon and 4 p.m.

You may want to stroll around some of the interesting streets in this colorful neighborhood, then continue on to the banks of the river.

View from the Top of St. Peter's Dome

The Ponte Cestio bridge, leading to **Tiber Island** *(Isola Tiberina)* (10), was built in 46 B.C. and renewed many times since. Cross it and turn left down the steps to the water's edge. A stroll to the south end of the picturesque island reveals some lovely views, including remnants of the **Ponte Rotto**—built in the 2nd century B.C. and the first arched stone bridge in Rome. Return to the square and cross the **Ponte Fabricio**, the only bridge from antiquity to survive intact. Still in excellent condition, it was erected in 62 B.C.

The walking tour is now over. You can return to the center of Rome by following the map to nearby Piazza Venezia.

EUR

You won't find ancient Roman—or even Renaissance—buildings in EUR, a modern satellite city on the southern outskirts of Rome. First begun in 1938 by the Mussolini government as the grandiose site for a world's fair that never happened, the *Esposizione Universale di Roma* of 1942, EUR has developed into a thriving commercial and administrative district. It is of interest to tourists not only for its superb and rather unusual museums, but also for its pleasant park-like atmosphere sprinkled with several outstanding examples of contemporary architecture. The original "dictator modern" buildings of the fascist era are still there, to be sure, but they've acquired a patina of age by now and no longer chill the sensibilities. EUR has in recent years become a smart residential area as well as an office, sports, and convention center.

This easy daytrip could readily be combined with one to Ostia Antica, described in the next chapter. If you do this, be sure to visit EUR first as its fascinating museums close early.

GETTING THERE:

By subway *(Metropolitana* or *M)*, take line B from beneath the Termini train station in the direction of Laurentina and get off at the **Magliana** stop. You could also board the subway at other stops en route, such as Via Cavour, the Colosseum, or the Circus Maximus. Line A intersects with line B at Termini. Tickets are sold by vending machines in the stations. Avoid traveling during the morning rush hour as half of Rome seems to work in EUR.

By bus, there are a number of routes going to EUR from various parts of Rome. Ask at your hotel for specific details. Tickets must be purchased before boarding through the rear door, and canceled in a machine once on the bus. Tickets are sold at many newsstands, bars, and tobacco shops as well as ATAC booths in front of the Termini station.

By car, take Via Cristoforo Colombo from Porta Ardeatina, just south of the Baths of Caracalla. EUR is about five miles south of the Colosseum.

WHEN TO GO:

Avoid going to EUR on a Monday or major holiday, when virtually all of its attractions are closed. An early start is recommended as the museums close by 2 p.m. (1 p.m. on Sundays). Since much of your time will be spent in them, fine weather is not especially important.

The Palazzo della Civiltà del Lavoro

FOOD AND DRINK:

Restaurants in EUR tend to be expensive and geared to business-men. In addition to those listed below you will find numerous cafeterias, snack bars, and pizzerias. For information about local specialties see the "Food and Drink" section in the chapter "Rome—the Classical Center."

Vecchia America—Corsetti (Piazza Marconi 32, right in the center) Typical of the area. X: Tues. $$

Shangri La (Viale Algeria 141, just south of the sports palace) In a small hotel. $$

Sheraton Hotel (Viale del Pattinaggio, about 6 blocks north of the center, just west of Via Cristoforo Colombo) Luxurious hotel dining. $$$

TOURIST INFORMATION:

See this entry in the chapter "Rome—the Classical Center."

SUGGESTED TOUR:

Begin your tour at the **Magliana subway station** (1), which also serves as a stop for commuter trains bound for Ostia. Follow the map slightly uphill through a park to the landmark **Palazzo della Civiltà del Lavoro** (2), a striking white marble office building of superimposed arches. Dominating a high open area surrounded by trees, it seems much more contemporary than its design date of 1938 suggests.

Now follow the map through the spacious Piazza Marconi. The tall column in its center is a memorial to Guglielmo Marconi, the inventor of radio. Stroll across the square to the **Folk Museum** (*Museo delle Arti e Tradizioni Popolari*) (3), which features a truly magnificent collection of items relating to Italian popular folk culture in years past, including costumes, furniture, farm and household implements, Nativity scenes, ex-votos, and so on. The museum has recently been rearranged, bringing it up to the most modern standards. As of this writing parts of it are still closed. Visits may be made on Tuesdays through Saturdays, from 9 a.m. to 2 p.m., and on Sundays from 9 a.m. to 1 p.m.

The star attraction of EUR, as far as tourists are concerned, is the fabulous **Museum of Roman Civilization** (*Museo della Civiltà Romana*) (4). Through models and reproductions it traces no less than the whole sweeping history of ancient Rome and its influence on the Classical world. As a special highlight, it features a gigantic model of the entire city of Rome as it was at the time of the emperor Constantine, during the 4th century A.D. Again, this has been recently renovated and some sections are still closed. The museum is open Tuesdays through Saturdays, from 9 a.m. to 2 p.m., and on Sundays from 9 a.m. to 1 p.m. On Tuesdays and Thursdays it is also open in the late afternoon and early evening.

If you're still up to museums, there are two more on the south side of Piazza Marconi. These are the **Luigi Pigorini Museum of Ethnography and Prehistory** (5), one of the best of its kind in the world, and the adjacent **Medieval Museum** (*Museo dell' Alto Medioevo*), focusing on relics from the Dark Ages. Opening times are similar to those given above.

Continue down the broad Via Cristoforo Colombo and turn right on Viale Europa, an attractive street lined with shops, banks, and restaurants. At its western end are steps leading up to the enormous **Church of SS. Peter and Paul** (6), an extraordinary structure from the late 1930s. Walk around to the terrace at its rear for a nice view across the Tiber.

The route now goes through a lovely park set around an artificial lake and continues uphill to the spectacular **Palazzo dello Sport** (7). Built for the 1960 Olympics by the noted architect Pier Luigi Nervi, one of Europe's most innovative 20th-century designers, it is over 300 feet in diameter and seats some 15,000 spectators.

Circle around it and return to the north side of the lake, where you can get a subway train (marked "Termini") to central Rome at the **EUR-Fermi stop** (8). Those heading for Ostia Antica (next chapter) should get off at the Magliana stop and transfer to the commuter train heading for "Roma Lido," sometimes marked "Ostia Lido." A separate ticket, available at Magliana, is needed for this.

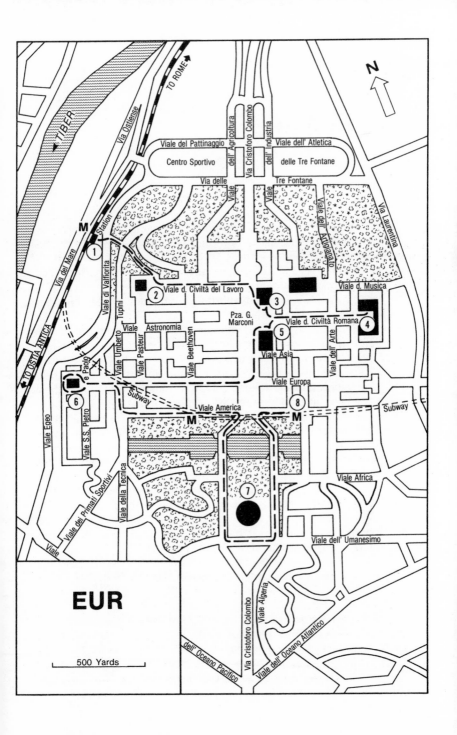

TO ROME

TIBER

N

Via Ostiense

Via del Mare

Viale del Pattinaggio

Centro Sportivo

Viale dell' Agricoltura

Via Cristoforo Colombo

Viale dell' Industria

Viale dell' Atletica

delle Tre Fontane

Via delle   Tre Fontane

Viale dell' Artigianato

Via Laurentina

M

Station

①

Viale di Valfiorita

②

Viale d. Civiltà del Lavoro

Via Tupini

Viale Umberto

Viale Pasteur

Viale Astronomia

Pza. G. Marconi

Viale Beethoven

③

Viale d. Musica

④

Viale d. Civiltà Romana

⑤

Viale Asia

Viale dell' Arte

TO OSTIA ANTICA

e Paolo

Viale S.S. Pietro

⑥

Subway

Viale America

Viale Europa

⑧

Subway

M   M

Viale Egeo

Viale dei Primati Sportivi

Viale della Tecnica

Viale Africa

⑦

Viale dell' Umanesimo

EUR

500 Yards

Viale

dell' Oceano Pacifico

Via Cristoforo Colombo

Viale Algeria

Viale dell' Oceano Atlantico

Ostia Antica

It's not necessary to go to Pompeii to see a real Roman city unearthed. In fact, the excavations at Ostia Antica are in some ways more interesting—and a lot less crowded. This was a real working place, a naval base, and a center of trade. Unlike Pompeii, which died in one cataclysmic moment, Ostia just quietly expired as the Empire declined, was slowly covered with the shifting mud of the Tiber, became farmland and was forgotten.

In Rome it was the great monuments that survived, while the dwellings of ordinary people perished long ago. Ostia is different. Here, everything is more or less intact—apartment blocks, houses, barracks, warehouses, business offices—and not just the baths, theaters, and temples. In short, it is a complete Roman city in ruin, a ghost town that your imagination can easily repopulate.

According to legend, Ostia was founded in the 7th century B.C., although archaeologists date it from about 335 B.C. Starting as a fishing village, it grew to become Rome's major port, thriving along with the Empire. After the 4th century A.D. it declined and eventually fell into oblivion, despite periodic attempts at revitalization. Silt from the Tiber caused the river to change course, creating a malarial swamp that depopulated an area already scourged by Barbarian invasions. In later years Ostia became a handy quarry for building stones, although fortunately enough of it was buried underground by then. Serious excavations started in 1909 and are still underway.

This easy daytrip can readily be combined with one to EUR, described in the previous chapter. Plan on visiting EUR first, then Ostia.

GETTING THERE:

Commuter trains operated by ACOTRAL depart frequently from the Roma-Ostia station at Porta San Paolo in Rome. This can be reached by taking subway line B in the direction of Laurentina to the **Piramide** stop, in the same building as the Roma-Ostia station. If you visit EUR first, you can board the commuter train at the Magliana subway stop. All trains are marked for Roma Lido, sometimes called Ostia Lido. Get off at the Ostia Antica station. During the summer season there may be a few commuter trains leaving directly from the subway station beneath the Termini train station in Rome and running part of the way on subway tracks. Ask about this at the subway ticket office. Return service runs at least until mid-evening. Railpasses are not accepted on either this commuter train or the subway.

Buses operated by ACOTRAL depart several times daily from Via Giolitti, next to Termini train station in Rome. Ask at their outdoor ticket booth for details.

By car, take the Via del Mare (S-8), a continuation of Via Ostiense, in the direction of Lido di Roma (sometimes called Lido di Ostia). The Ostia Antica exit, marked "Scavi," is 15 miles southwest of Rome.

WHEN TO GO:

Everything is open daily except on major holidays. Good weather is essential as you'll be outdoors all of the time. During summer it is best to visit Ostia in the late afternoon, when the sun is less strong, so have a nice, long lunch. Be sure to wear sturdy walking shoes.

FOOD AND DRINK:

There are very few restaurants at Ostia Antica, the ones listed below being the best. In addition, there is at least one pizzeria in the town and a snack bar at the Roman Theater within the excavation area. This is an exceptionally nice place for a picnic. Consult the earlier chapter "Rome—the Classical Center" for local specialties.

> **Allo Sbarco di Enea** (Via dei Romagnoli 675, between the train station and the entrance) A convenient location, with outdoor tables available. X: Mon., Feb. $$

> **Monumento** (Piazza Umberto I, in the town, just beyond the castle) Especially good for seafood. X: Mon., late Aug. to early Sept. $$

TOURIST INFORMATION:

See this entry in the earlier chapter "Rome—the Classical Center."

SUGGESTED TOUR:

Leave the **Ostia Antica train station** (1) and cross the footbridge over the highway, then continue straight ahead to the first intersection. At this point you may want to make a little side trip to the **Castle** (2) in the modern village of Ostia. Built in 1483, this outstanding example of Renaissance military architecture contains a small but interesting museum of local history and is open from 9 a.m. to noon and 3–6 p.m. daily except Mondays.

The **entrance** (3) to the excavations *(Scavi)* of the ancient Roman city is nearby. During the height of the Empire Ostia had a population of over 50,000, many of whom were foreigners who brought with them a broad variety of religions and life styles, as is readily apparent in some of the ruins. Continue straight ahead, passing an area of tombs on the left, to the Porta Romana—the main gate during Classical times.

The main street of Ostia, as in many Roman towns, was called the *Decumanus Maximus*. It begins here and continues past the forum to the far end, a distance of nearly a mile. The first major sight you will pass along it is, on the right, the **Neptune Baths** *(Terme di Nettuno)* (4). Climb up on its terrace for a view of the magnificent mosaics, especially the one depicting Neptune driving four sea horses. Just north of the baths is a gymnasium *(Palestra)* and, beyond that, the **Barracks of the Vigili** *(Caserma)*, built in the 2nd century A.D. as a home for the town's firefighters. These can both be reached by Via dei Vigili, returning on the well-preserved Via della Fontana. Where this rejoins the Decumanus Maximus there is an interesting **floor mosaic** from a former tavern advertising its wines with the words "*Dicit Fortunatus: Vinum cratera quod sitis bibe.*"

The heavily restored **Theater** (5), first erected during the reign of Augustus, is now sometimes used for outdoor performances. It has a snack bar, rest rooms, and a shop selling detailed guides to Ostia Antica—all of which you may find handy. Behind this lies the **Piazzale delle Corporazioni**, an open square lined with the remains of 70 commercial offices, whose businesses can be identified from the mosaics on the floors. In its center stand remains of the so-called **Temple of Ceres**.

Now follow the route to the **House of Diana** (6), a typical apartment building *(Insula)* of a type once common in ancient Rome. Only two floors of this survive although it may have had as many as five. You can climb upstairs for a look. Across the street is the **Thermopolium**, a neighborhood bar looking amazingly like its modern Italian counterpart.

A right on Via dei Dipinti leads to the **Museum** (7), a modern structure housing many of the art treasures found in the excavations. Continue on to the **Forum** *(Foro)* (8), the main square of the ancient city. At its north end is the **Capitol** *(Capitolium)*, erected in the 2nd century A.D. and dedicated to Jupiter, Juno, and Minerva. It was the most important temple in the city and is still quite impressive. To the south of the forum are remnants of the Temple of Rome and Augustus, noted for its two lovely but broken statues.

Leave the forum on the Decumanus Maximus, passing the House of the Larario, a combination house and shopping center, on the right. At the bend in the road turn right to the **Epagathiana Warehouses**

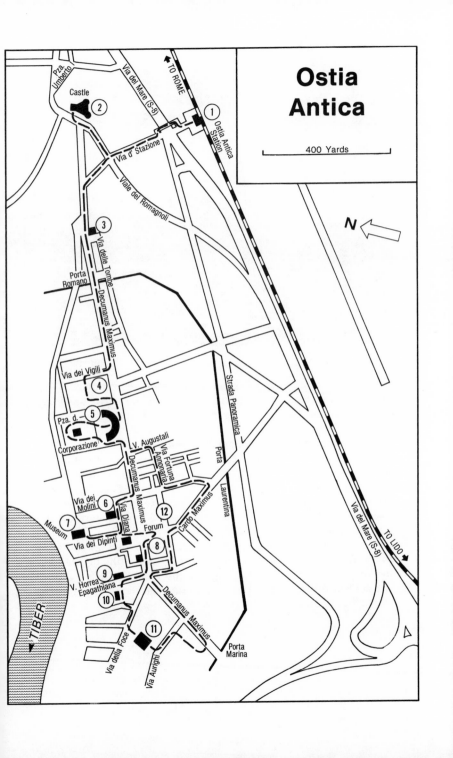

Ostia Antica

400 Yards

N ⟵

TO ROME
Pza. Umberto
Castle ②
Via del Mare (S-8)
① Ostia Antica Station
Via d' Stazione
Viale dei Romagnoli
③
Via delle Tombe
Porta Romano
Decumanus Maximus
Via dei Vigili
④
Pza. d. ⑤
Corporazione
V. Augustali
Via Fortuna Annonaria
Decumanus Maximus
Porta Laurentina
Via dei Molini ⑥
Via Diana
⑫
Cardo Maximus
Museum ⑦
Via dei Dipinti
Forum ⑧
V. Horrea Epagathiana ⑨
⑩
Strada Panoramica
Porta
Via del Mare (S-8)
TO LIDO
⑪
Decumanus Maximus
Via della Foce
Via Aurghi
Porta Marina
TIBER

The Capitol in the Forum

(Horrea) (9), a set of remarkably well-preserved commercial structures from the 2nd century A.D. Turn left here to the **House of Cupid and Psyche** *(Domus di Amore e Psiche)* (10), a luxurious private home from the 4th century A.D.

The **Baths of the Seven Sages** *(Terme dei Sette Sapienti)* (11) are decorated with marvelously satirical mosaics worth a careful examination. You are now near the western end of the city. Return via the route on the map, stopping at the **Baths of the Forum** *(Terme del Foro)* (12), the largest public baths in Ostia. On its north side are remains of a structure whose use will become immediately apparent. This is the twenty-hole public latrine.

From here, the route goes past some interesting digs and returns to the Theater (5) where you can get a snack or a drink before following the Decumanus Maximus back to the entrance. The excavation site at Ostia Antica is open daily except on major holidays, from 9 a.m. to one hour before sunset.

Tivoli

The waters of Tivoli have attracted wealthy Romans since the days of the Republic. Set on the lower slopes of the Sabine hills overlooking Rome and the *Campagna*, this ancient resort has evolved over the centuries into a magnificent wonderland of fountains, gardens, waterfalls, Roman ruins, medieval ambiance, and lovely views. It is home to both the famous Villa d'Este and the nearby Hadrian's Villa.

Today it is tourists as well as Romans who flock there by the thousands, many of them taking guided bus tours. By doing it on your own you will not only have more time to enjoy the two major attractions, but also get to explore the interesting medieval town of Tivoli itself as well as the natural splendor of Villa Gregoriana and its mighty waterfalls.

The suggested tour ends with a visit to Hadrian's Villa, an archaeological site some four miles southwest of Tivoli, then returns to Rome by bus or car. You may prefer to eliminate this and head back to Rome directly from Tivoli.

GETTING THERE:

Trains, marked for Avezzano and Pescara, depart Rome's Termini station several times in the morning for the 40-minute ride to Tivoli. At least one train leaves from Rome's Tiburtina station as well. Be careful not to get off at Bagni di Tivoli. Return service operates until late evening.

Buses operated by ACOTRAL depart frequently for the one-hour ride to Tivoli from Via Gaeta, just beyond the northeast side of the square in front of Rome's Termini station. Ask at the company's booth nearby. Get off at the stop nearest Villa d'Este in Tivoli.

By car, take Via Tiburtina (S-5) from a point east of Termini station in Rome. This goes directly to Tivoli, a distance of 19 miles, and passes Hadrian's Villa en route.

WHEN TO GO:

The attractions of Tivoli are open daily all year round. You'll be out of doors all of the time, so good weather is essential. This trip is much less attractive during the winter. Sturdy walking shoes are necessary for the Villa Gregoriana.

Detail of a Fountain in the Villa d'Este Gardens

FOOD AND DRINK:

Tivoli offers a wide selection of restaurants in every price range. Some particularly good choices are:

Del Falcone (Via del Trevio 34, in the town center, a few blocks east of Villa d'Este) Good Italian home cooking. $$

Sibilla (Via della Sibilla 50, by the Temple of Vesta northwest of Villa Gregoriana) A famous restaurant with a superb view and outdoor tables. X: Mon. $$

Cinque Statue (Largo Sant' Angelo 1, opposite the entrance to Villa Gregoriana) Home cooking in a pleasant atmosphere, outdoor tables available) X: Fri. $$

Adriano (just outside the entrance to Hadrian's Villa) Indoor or outdoor dining in a lovely setting. X: Mon. $$

TOURIST INFORMATION:

The tourist office in Tivoli, phone (0774) 21-249, is in a park at Largo Garibaldi, near Villa d'Este.

SUGGESTED TOUR:

Those arriving by train should follow the map from the **station** (1) to **Largo Garibaldi** (2), a large open square with a park overlooking the valley. The tourist office is here, and the Villa d'Este bus stop for

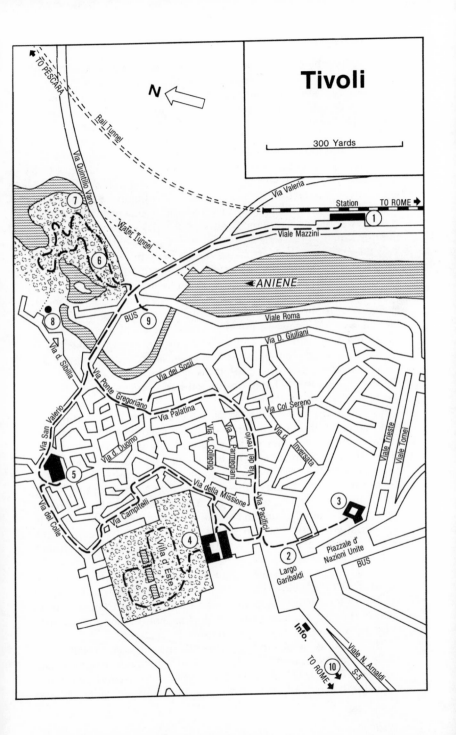

Tivoli

N

300 Yards

TO PESCARA

Rail Tunnel

Via Quintilio Varo

Water Tunnel

Via Valeria

Station

TO ROME →

Viale Mazzini

ANIENE

Viale Roma

BUS

Via D. Giuliani

Via d. Sibilla

Via Ponte Gregoriano

Via dei Sosii

Via Col Sereno

Via San Valerio

Via Palatina

Via d. Duomo

Via d. Collegio

Via A. Parmegiani

Via del Trevio

Via d. Università

Via della Missione

Via Pacifici

Via Campitelli

Villa d'Este

Via del Colle

Largo Garibaldi

Piazzale d'
Nazioni Unite

BUS

Viale Trieste

Viale Tomei

Info.

TO ROME

Viale N. Arnaldi

S-5

those coming by bus from Rome is nearby in Piazzale delle Nazioni Unite. While in the area you may want to visit the **Rocca Pia** (3), a 15th-century castle built by the Pope to keep the citizens of Tivoli in line. It is usually open from 9 a.m. to 12:30 p.m. and 3–6:30 p.m. Adjacent to it are the ruins of an ancient Roman amphitheater.

Stroll over to the **Villa d'Este** (4), whose entrance is next to the Romanesque Church of Santa Maria Maggiore. Converted from a former Benedictine convent in the 16th century by Cardinal Ippolito II d'Este, the villa itself is sumptuously decorated and well worth exploring. The main attraction here, however, is the **luxuriant garden** with its hundreds of astonishing **fountains** and magnificent panoramic **views**. A delightful place of sublime beauty (as long as you get here before the bus tours), it has long been one of the great sights of Italy. The Villa d'Este is open daily, from 9 a.m. to 6:45 p.m., closing one hour before sunset during the off season. During the summer it is also sometimes open in the evenings, with illuminations.

Leave the villa and thread you way through the picturesque medieval quarter to the **Cathedral** *(Duomo)* (5). You'll probably get lost in the maze of passageways, but that's part of the fun. Rebuilt in 1650 while retaining a fine 12th-century bell tower, the cathedral is noted for its superb 13th-century carved wooden figures depicting the *Descent from the Cross*. These are located in the fourth chapel on the right, while the third chapel on the left has a precious triptych from the 12th century.

Continue on to the **Villa Gregoriana** (6), a steep hillside natural park laid out in the 19th century around the magnificent **waterfalls** (7) of the Aniene river. The woodland paths, leading first to the cascade, descend into a deep ravine and then climb a bit to a rock gallery and a cave. Return the way you came in, ignoring signs (marked *Uscita*) to the exit on the other side of the gorge—which is often locked. At the top of the far side you will see the **Temple of Vesta** (8), a circular structure with ten Corinthian columns, dating from the late Republican era. If you wish, you can visit it from the town by asking at the adjacent Sibilla restaurant. The Villa Gregoriana is open daily, from 9 a.m. to one hour before sunset.

Amble over to the nearby Tivoli **bus terminal** (9), where you can board an ACOTRAL bus to Bivio Villa Adriana, four miles southwest of Tivoli and the nearest stop to Hadrian's Villa. If you decide not to include this last attraction in your daytrip, you can return to Rome either by bus from here or by train from the station (1).

Those taking the bus to Bivio Villa Adriana will have to walk about a mile to **Hadrian's Villa** *(Villa Adriana)* (10). Built by the emperor Hadrian between A.D. 125 and 134 as a retreat from the rigors of court life, it was the largest and most lavish imperial villa of antiquity. Hadrian

In the Gardens of the Villa d'Este

was an accomplished architect himself, and he designed the many structures as scaled down re-creations of places that had impressed him during his travels throughout the Empire. As these are in a state of ruin today, you should begin your visit by studying the scale model next to the bar by the parking lot. You may also want to buy an illustrated guide to make sense of the broken structures. Among the many buildings, be certain not to miss the **Poikile** *(Pecile)*, the **Maritime Theater**, the **Canopus**, and the **Imperial Palace**.

Hadrian's Villa is open daily, from 9 a.m. until one hour before sunset. You can get a ride back to Rome from the bus stop.

Viterbo

Many towns in Italy claim to be the most perfectly preserved holdover from the Middle Ages, but in the area near Rome that honor almost surely belongs to Viterbo. Calling itself the "City of the Popes" because no fewer than five of them lived there during the 13th century, the town has kept its splendid old buildings and highly atmospheric medieval quarter almost totally intact.

Viterbo began as a settlement of the ancient Etruscans, those enigmatic people about whom so little is known, and was later conquered by the Romans. Its great period of development was during the Middle Ages, when it rivaled Rome itself. After the papacy moved to Avignon the town declined, ultimately becoming the minor provincial capital that it remains today.

GETTING THERE:

Trains depart Rome's Termini station several times in the morning for Orte, where you change to a local for Viterbo's Porta Fiorentina station. The total trip takes about two hours. There is also direct railcar service from Rome's San Pietro station, just south of the Vatican. This takes about the same time. Return service on both routes operates until mid-evening. Check the schedules carefully.

Buses operated by ACOTRAL depart from Via Lepanto in Rome, north of Castel Sant' Angelo, reached by subway line A to Lepanto. The ride to Viterbo is about two hours. ACOTRAL also operates infrequent commuter trains from the Roma-Viterbo station north of Piazza del Popolo in Rome, reached by subway line A to Flaminio. All of these go to the Roma-Nord station in Viterbo. Railpasses are not accepted by ACOTRAL.

By car, take the Via Cassia (route S-2) north from Rome to Viterbo, a distance of 50 miles.

WHEN TO GO:

Some sights in Viterbo are closed on Sundays, Mondays, and major holidays. Good weather will make this trip more enjoyable.

FOOD AND DRINK:

Viterbo has essentially the same cuisine as Rome. The local wine is the famous *Est! Est!! Est!!!*, a slightly sweet white from nearby Montefiascone. Some good restaurant choices are:

La Zaffera (Piazza San Carluccio, at the west end of Via San Pellegrino) In the medieval San Pellegrino quarter, with a garden, X: Mon. $$$

Il Richiastro (Via della Marrocca 18, 3 blocks west of the Municipal Museum) Well hidden, but worth searching for. X: Mon. to Wed. $$

Il Grottino (Via della Cava 7, 3 blocks southwest of San Francesco church) A popular trattoria. X: Tues, $$

Trattoria Tre Re (Via Macel Gattesco 3, 2 blocks north of Pza. del Plebiscito) Very popular with local businessmen. X: Thurs. $

TOURIST INFORMATION:

The local tourist office, phone (0761) 22-66-66, is at Piazza Verdi 4; while the provincial office, phone (0761) 23-47-95, is at Piazza dei Caduti 16, 2 blocks northwest of Piazza del Plebiscito.

SUGGESTED TOUR:

Leave the **Porta Fiorentina train station** (1) or the **Roma-Nord station** (2) and follow the map through a gate in the well-preserved medieval walls to Piazza Verdi, where the local tourist office is located. Continue on through a succession of narrow streets to the **Municipal Museum** (*Museo Civico*) (3), which you should see before its afternoon closing. Housed in a former convent around an elegant 13th-century cloister, the museum is noted for its wonderful collection of **Etruscan objects** and sarcophagi from nearby digs. Some of these, dating from as far back as the 7th century B.C., are inscribed in the strange alphabet of the still-undeciphered Etruscan language. There are also early Roman works on display. The art gallery upstairs has among its treasures a magnificent *Pietà* and a *Flagellation,* both by Sebastiano del Piombo, as well as the *Incredulity of St. Thomas* by Salvator Rosa. Visits may be made from 8 a.m. to 1:30 p.m., daily except on holidays. During the summer season it is also open from 3:30 to 6 or 7:30 p.m., except on Sundays and holidays.

While at the museum, be sure to also visit the adjacent **Church of Santa Maria della Verità**. First built in the 12th century and later altered, it is beautifully decorated with 15th-century frescoes by Lorenzo da Viterbo, restored after suffering bomb damage during World War II. The church is closed between noon and 3 p.m.

The route now leads through the Porta Romana gate, rebuilt in 1653, to the **Fontana Grande** (4). Easily the most beautiful fountain in Viterbo, it has been merrily bubbling away since the 13th century. A left turn on Via delle Fabbriche brings you into the unspoiled San Pellegrino district, where time has stood still since the Middle Ages.

In the San Pellegrino district

The utterly delightful **Piazza San Pellegrino** (5) is one of the most picturesque little squares in Italy. The stark Alessandri Tower beyond its western end dates from the 13th century, as do many of the unusual structures around it.

Pick your way through the maze and continue on past the shady Piazza della Morte, crossing the historic Ponte del Duomo bridge with its scanty Etruscan remains. Piazza San Lorenzo, another splendid medieval square, was built on the site of the ancient Etruscan acropolis, somes of whose stones are incorporated in surrounding houses. At the western side of this is the 12th-century **Cathedral** *(Duomo)* (6), with a later façade and a 14th-century bell tower. The restored Romanesque interior has some interesting columns, floor mosaics, and remnants of 12th-century frescoes.

Viterbo's most impressive piece of architecture is undoubtedly the **Papal Palace** *(Palazzo Papale)* (7), built in the 13th century as a home for the popes who stayed there to avoid troubles in Rome. Its Gothic loggia, outside staircase, massive arches, and battlements make a dramatic sight against the clear Italian sky. A conclave of cardinals, meeting here in 1268 to select a new pope, was unable to reach a decision

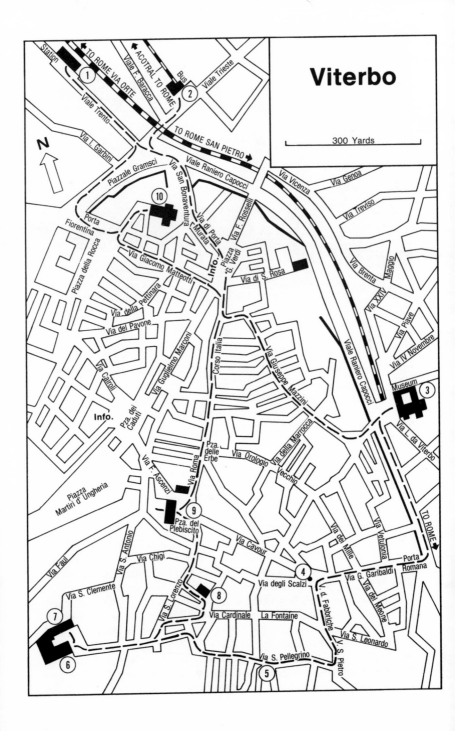

Viterbo

300 Yards

Station

TO ROME VIA ORTE
ACOTRAL TO ROME
Viale F. Baracca
Bus
Viale Trieste

① ②

Viale Trento
Via I. Garbini
TO ROME SAN PIETRO
Viale Raniero Capocci
Via Vicenza
Via Genoa

N

Piazzale Gramsci
Via San Bonaventura
Via Treviso

Porta
Fiorentina

⑩

Via di Porta
C. Murata
Via F. Rosselli
Piazza
G. Verdi

Piazza della Rocca

Via Giacomo Matteotti
Info.

Via di S. Rosa

Via Brenta
Maggio

Via della Pettinara

Via del Pavone

Corso Italia

Via Giuseppe Mazzini

Via XXIV
Maggio
Via Piave

Via Guglielmo Marconi

Viale Raniero Capocci

Via IV Novembre

Via Cairoli

Info.

Pza. dei
Caduti

Museum ③

Via L. da Viterbo

Via della Marrocca

Pza.
delle
Erbe
Via Orologio Vecchio

Via Roma

Via F. Ascenzi

Piazza
Martiri d'Ungheria

⑨

Pza. del
Plebiscito

Via Cavour

Via del Mille

Via Vetulonia

TO ROME

Porta
Romana

Via Faul

Via S. Antonio

Via Chigi

Via S. Clemente

Via S. Lorenzo

⑧

④
Via degli Scalzi

V. d. Fabbriche

Via G. Garibaldi
Via del Meone

⑦

Via Cardinale La Fontaine

Via S. Leonardo

V. S. Pietro

⑥

Via S. Pellegrino

⑤

The Palazzo Papale

for over two years. Tired of the procrastination, the local ruler first locked them in, then removed the roof, and finally cut off the food supply. Hunger did the trick, and soon a new pope, Gregory X, was elected. From this incident came the rules by which popes are elected to this day in the Vatican. The palace may usually be visited on Mondays through Saturdays, from 10 a.m. to 12:30 p.m.

Return to Piazza della Morte and stroll over to the **Church of Santa Maria Nuova** (8), a 12th-century church of great charm. The tiny outdoor pulpit on its left façade was once used by St. Thomas Aquinas for preaching. Walk behind this and turn right on Via San Lorenzo, a street lined with interesting buildings.

The **Piazza del Plebiscito** (9) is the busy center of the Old Town. On its west side stands the 15th-century Palazzo Comunale, whose exquisite **courtyard** can be reached through a passage, revealing some very nice views. To the north is the 13th-century Palazzo del Podestà with its beautiful 15th-century clock tower.

The route now leads past the animated Piazza delle Erbe and down the long Corso Italia, a favorite street for strolling. When you reach Piazza Verdi, turn left and follow Via Matteotti uphill to the **Church of San Francesco** (10). Built in the Gothic style in 1237, it has an interesting outdoor pulpit on the façade. Step inside to see the tombs of two popes who died in Viterbo, Ardian V and Clement IV. From here it is an easy walk through the Porta Fiorentina back to the train station.

Orvieto

The first sight of Orvieto never fails to astonish visitors. Perched high atop a rocky mound overlooking the rich Umbrian countryside, this ancient town is famous throughout the world for both its delicious white wine and its spectacular cathedral. These attractions plus its convenient location mid-way on the main highway and rail line between Rome and Florence act as a magnet for tourists, who come by the thousands. The pity is that so few of them ever venture beyond the cathedral square to explore the magnificently well-preserved medieval town itself. The walking tour described here probes deeply into this and leads you to some rather intriguing sights.

Orvieto's history was determined by its easily defended site, a natural fortress if ever there was one. Although it was already inhabited during prehistoric times, it was those mysterious Etruscans who developed the first real settlement there around 800 B.C. This was destroyed by the Romans in the 3rd century B.C., after which the population—protected by the Empire—moved down to the green valleys. Orvieto again served its defensive role during the Barbarian invasions and the troubled period that followed. In the Middle Ages it became a stronghold of the popes, who often had to flee Rome. Today, the modern part of Orvieto lies in the valley, while the Old Town retains its medieval character.

In addition to being an exciting daytrip destination, Orvieto makes a fine stopover for travelers en route between Rome and Florence.

GETTING THERE:

Trains depart Rome's Termini station several times in the morning for the 1½-hour run to Orvieto. Most of these are marked for Milan or Venice. Return service operates until mid-evening.

By car, take the A-1 Autostrada north to the Orvieto exit. The distance from Rome is 75 miles. There are several parking lots in the upper town near the cathedral.

WHEN TO GO:

Orvieto may be visited at any time, but note that the two small museums are closed on Mondays. Clear weather is essential for the magnificent views.

FOOD AND DRINK:

The heart cuisine of Umbria leans heavily to meats. Orvieto's white wine, available either dry *(secco)* or slightly sweet *(abboccato)*, is world famous. Some good restaurant choices are:

Le Grotte del Funaro (Via Ripa di Serancia 41, midway between Pza. Repubblica and San Giovenale church) Umbrian specialties in an underground grotto. X: Mon. $$

Maurizio (Via del Duomo 78, a block northwest from the cathedral) A long-time favorite in a great location. X: Tues., Jan. $$

Dell' Ancora (Via di Piazza del Popolo 7, just off the west end of Pza. del Popolo) Real country cooking. X: Thurs., Jan. $$

Del Cocco (Via Garibaldi 4, just south of Pza. della Repubblica) A favorite with the locals. X: Fri. $

Co-op CRAMST "San Francesco" (Via Maitani 17, 1 block west of the cathedral, hidden in an alleyway) Combination restaurant, cafeteria, and pizzeria. Popular with the young crowd. X: Sun. $

TOURIST INFORMATION:

The local tourist office, phone (0763) 41-772, is directly opposite the cathedral.

SUGGESTED TOUR:

The **train station** (1) is, naturally, down in the valley. Take one of the frequent buses, marked "Duomo," to the upper town. Tickets are sold in the station's bar and must be canceled on board the bus. It would be convenient to buy a return ticket at the same time for use later. The bus may go directly to the cathedral (3), or take you to Piazza XXIX Marzo (2) instead—in which case you can follow the map to the cathedral.

The flamboyant façade of the Orvieto's **Cathedral** *(Duomo)* (3) is literally covered with dazzling multicolored mosaics and splendid bas-reliefs. Whether you admire the effect or consider it a study in wretched excess, there is no doubt that it is certainly impressive. The structure itself, a perfect example of the Italian Gothic style, was begun in 1290 to house the relics of the Miracle of Bolsena. The amount of money lavished on its construction was surely due to the fact that many of the popes of that time took refuge in Orvieto, safe from the deadly plots of Rome. Building continued until the early 17th century, and the solid bronze doors were not added until 1970.

Compared to the façade, the simple interior seems uncluttered and almost restrained—although the alternating layers of black and white stone lend a strange spatial effect. In the north transept is the **Corporal Chapel**, where the relics of the Miracle of Bolsena are kept

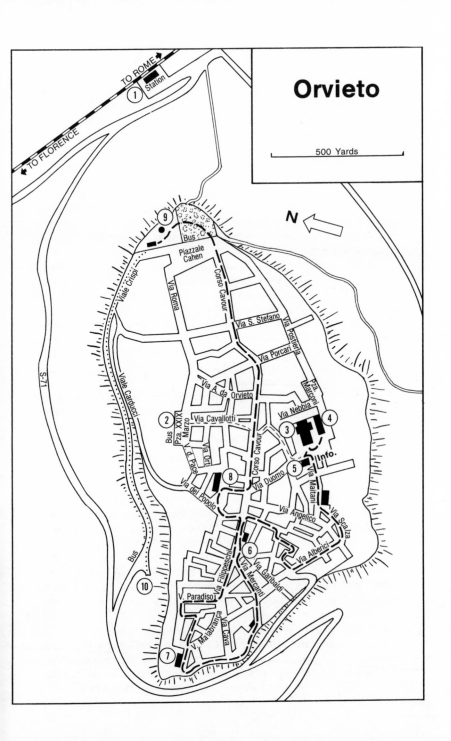

Orvieto

500 Yards

N

TO ROME
TO FLORENCE
Station
①

⑨
Bus
Piazzale
Cahen

Viale Crispi
Via Roma
Corso Cavour
Via S. Stefano
Via Posterla
Via Porcari

Via A. da Orvieto
Pza. Marconi
Via Nebbia

S-71
Viale Carducci
② Bus
Pza. XXIV Marzo
P. N.
Via Cavallotti
Via Pace
Via Orti
③ ④
⑤ Info.
Via Maitani

Via del Popolo
⑧
Corso Cavour
Via Duomo
Via Angelico
Via Scalza

Bus
⑥
Via Alberici

Via Filippeschi
Via Garibaldi
Via Mercanti
Via Cava

⑩
V. Paradiso
V. Malabranca
⑦

in a sumptuous 14th-century reliquary within a tabernacle. It seems that in 1293 a priest in nearby Bolsena, plagued by doubts, was convinced of the presence of Christ in the host as it dripped blood onto the altar linen. Pope Urban IV, residing in Orvieto at the time, considered this to be a true miracle and ordered the construction of the cathedral to shelter the blood-stained cloth.

The greatest art treasures of the cathedral are in the **New Chapel**, sometimes called the Chapel of San Brizio, occupying the south transept. These are the incomparable frescoes depicting the *Apocalypse*, begun in 1447 by Fra Angelico and completed in 1504 by Luca Signorelli. Among the greatest masterpieces of the Renaissance, they supposedly provided the inspiration for Michelangelo in his painting of the Sistine Chapel ceiling in the Vatican. The cathedral is closed between 1 and 2:30 p.m.

Standing next to the cathedral is the 13th-century **Papal Palace** *(Palazzo dei Papi)* (4), also called the *Palazzo Soliano*. This stark, monumental Gothic structure, built as a residence for the popes, now houses the **Cathedral Museum** *(Museo dell' Opera del Duomo)*. Climb the outside staircase and step inside to see a magnificent collection of religious art associated with the cathedral, the most impressive of which is the *Madonna* polyptych by Simone Martini. The museum is open daily except Mondays, from 9:30 a.m. to 12:30 p.m. and 2:30–4, 5, or 6 p.m., depending on the season.

Across the square from the cathedral is the **Claudio Faina Archaeological Museum** *(Museo Civico Archeologico)* (5), specializing in Etruscan antiquities from the local area. This outstanding collection is a must if you have an interest in the subject. It is open every day except Mondays, from 9 a.m. to 1 p.m. and 3–6:30 p.m. (2:30–4:30 p.m. in winter).

The route now follows a complicated path through a colorful old neighborhood, with several places where you can look out across the valley. Follow it to **Piazza della Repubblica** (6), the heart of the Old Town. In the center of this is the 16th-century town hall, while to the east is the 12th-century **Church of Sant' Andrea** with its strange 12-sided bell tower. It was in this church that Pope Innocent III announced the Fourth Crusade in 1216. Excavations beneath it have revealed the remains of a 6th-century church on top of Etruscan and Roman ruins. These can be seen by asking the caretaker.

Continue down Via Loggia dei Mercanti and enter a world that has hardly changed since the Middle Ages. By carefully following the map you will come to the 11th-century **Church of San Giovenale** (7), a very primitive structure of immense charm. Enter via the side door to admire the cool simplicity of its frescoed interior, a treat not to be missed.

The route leads ever onwards through more delightful medieval

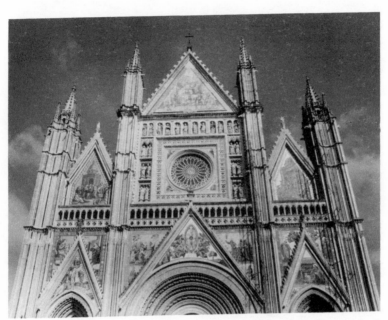

The Cathedral's ornate façade

streets back to Piazza della Repubblica (6), then continues on to the **Piazza Capitano del Popolo** (8). The **People's Palace** *(Palazzo del Popolo)*, an immense structure from the 12th century, was first built as an ecclesiastical seat and later used as a palace for the Captain of the People. It has long dominated the square, where outdoor markets are held on Saturdays.

Stroll down the main street, Corso Cavour, to Piazzale Cahen and the ruins of an old fortress, now a public park. Just beyond this is **St. Patrick's Well** *(Pozzo di San Patrizio)* (9), dug in 1527 on orders from Pope Clement VII as a precaution against the town's water supply being cut off by a siege. It is over 200 feet deep and lined with two remarkably intertwined staircases that never meet except at the bottom. You can have the somewhat eerie experience of going down it, but remember that what goes down must come up. Descents may be made any day from 9 a.m. to 7 p.m. (6 p.m. in winter). Only a few yards to the west of this are the ruins of an Etruscan temple.

To return to the train station take one of the frequent buses from the stop in front of the Funicular, a fantastic 19th-century device that has recently been restored. Those interested in exploring the ancient

Piazza della Repubblica

Etruscan Necropolis (10) can do so by walking downhill along the road to the station, a distance of nearly a mile. Dating from at least the 4th century B.C., this well-preserved area of chamber tombs is utterly fascinating. The strange inscriptions above the burial entrances are probably the names of the deceased, although the language has never been deciphered. The tomb area is open until sunset and there is no charge. You can get on the bus to the station at the stop *(Fermata)* opposite the tombs.

Assisi

Few places are as completely permeated with the memory of a single person as Assisi is with Saint Francis. Miraculously, the steady stream of pilgrims and tourists who come in veneration or out of curiosity have not managed to undo the gentle tranquility of this ancient Umbrian hill town.

Assisi began as an Umbrian settlement strongly influenced by the nearby Etruscans, and later developed into the Roman town of *Asisium*. After the usual destruction by the Barbarians, it became subject to the duchy of Spoleto and eventually, in the 12th century, was a republic in its own right. From the beginning of the 16th century until the unification of Italy in the mid-19th, it was a peaceful part of the Papal States.

Saint Francis was born in Assisi in 1182, the son of a wealthy merchant and his French wife. After a dissolute youth and a year's imprisonment during a war with Perugia, he became disenchanted with the worldly life and embraced absolute poverty. Through his personal example and teachings, a new religious order was founded with the blessings of the pope, in time becoming known as the Franciscans. According to tradition, he received the stigmata during a vision on September 14, 1224. Two years later he died in a nearby village. His simple faith, kindness, and love of nature has made him one of Christendom's most cherished saints.

GETTING THERE:

Trains marked for Ancona depart Rome's Termini station several times in the morning. Take one of these as far as **Foligno** and change there to a local train for Assisi. The total trip takes about 2½ hours. Check the schedules carefully as a change at Orte instead of Foligno may be required. Return service operates until early evening.

By car, take the A-1 Autostrada north to Orte, then the S-3 past Spoleto to Foligno, and finally the S-75 into Assisi. The total distance from Rome is 110 miles. There are parking lots near the gates to the Old Town.

WHEN TO GO:

Assisi may be visited at any time, but expect crowds on holy days, especially the Feast of St. Francis in early October. Some minor sights are closed on Mondays.

FOOD AND DRINK:

There is no shortage of restaurants in Assisi. Some good choices are:

Il Frantoio (Via Fontebella 25, 3 blocks southeast of the basilica) Luxurious dining, with an outdoor terrace. X: Mon. in winter $$$

Buca di San Francesco (Via Brizi 1, 2 blocks west of Pza. del Comune) In a basement wine cellar, with outdoor tables on a terrace. X: Mon., July $$

Medio Evo (Via Arco dei Priori 4, just south of Pza. del Comune) A highly romantic ambiance. X: Wed., Jan. $$

Umbra (Vicolo degli Archi 6, just south of Pza. del Comune) In a small hotel, with a garden terrace. X: Tues. $$

La Fortezza (Vicolo della Fortezza 2, just north of Pza. del Comune) Good food in an atmospheric setting. X: Thurs. $$

Pallotta (Via San Rufino 4, just east of Pza. del Comune) A nice place for an inexpensive meal. X: Tues. $

TOURIST INFORMATION:

The local tourist office, phone (075) 81-25-34, is at Piazza del Comune 12.

SUGGESTED TOUR:

The Assisi **train station** (1) is located in the village of Santa Maria degli Angeli at the foot of the Subasio mountain. Buses depart about every 30 minutes for the three-mile journey uphill to the walled town of Assisi. Tickets can be purchased at the bar or newsstand in the station, and must be canceled on board the bus. It would be convenient to buy a return ticket at the same time.

Get off the bus at **Porta San Pietro** (2) and walk uphill to the **Basilica of St. Francis** (San Francesco) (3), the main attraction of Assisi and the goal of countless pilgrimages. It was begun as early as 1228, just two years after the saint's death, and already consecrated by 1253. There are actually two churches, one on top of the other, and both built over a crypt containing the tomb of St. Francis.

Begin your visit in the **Lower Church**, whose dark vaulted interior is lined with magnificent frescoes. Artists came from all over Italy to add their contributions, bringing about a new kind of naturalistic art imbued with the Franciscan spirit. Be sure you bring along plenty of

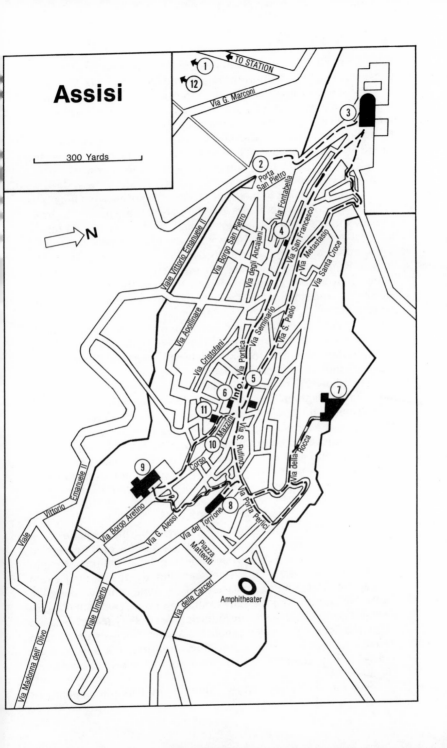

Assisi

300 Yards

N

TO STATION

1
12

Via G. Marconi

Porta San Pietro
2

3

Via Fontabella

4

Viale Vittorio Emanuele II

Via Borgo San Pietro

Via degli Ancajani

Via San Francesco

Via Metastasio

Via Santa Croce

Via Apollinare

Via Cristofani

Via Seminario

Via S. Paolo

Via Portica

Info.

5

6

11

Mazzini

Via S. Rufino

10

Corso

7

Via della Rocca

9

Via Borgo Aretino

Via G. Alessi

8

Via del Torrione

Via Porta Perlici

Vittorio

Viale

Emanuele II

Viale Umberto

Via Madonna dell' Olivo

Piazza Matteotti

Via delle Carceri

Amphitheater

coins for the light switches, otherwise you may miss some of the best treasures. The most famous of these is the *Madonna with St. Francis* by Cimabue, on the wall of the right transept, from which the often-reproduced portrait of the saint is derived. Other noted artists represented are Giotto, Simone Martini, Pietro Lorenzetti, and Andrea da Bologna. In the middle of the nave are steps leading down to the **crypt** where St. Francis is buried. Return to the lower church and take the steps from the right transept up to the main cloisters, from which you can visit the **Treasury** and the well-stocked bookstore.

Continue climbing to the **Upper Church**, whose well-lit interior is in complete contrast to the lower. The transepts are lined with badly damaged **frescoes** by Cimabue, although his *Crucifixion* still retains much of its intense power. The walls of the nave are decorated with a famous cycle of 28 frescoes, mostly by Giotto, depicting the *Life of St. Francis*. Begin at the right transept to see them in chronological order. Above these are two cycles of frescoes, those on the north wall showing scenes from the Old Testament, and on the south wall the New Testament.

The Basilica of St. Francis is open to tourists from 8 a.m. to 7 p.m., but not on Sunday mornings or some holy days. From November through March it closes for lunch between noon and 2 p.m. Proper dress is required, as in most Italian churches.

Now follow the colorful Via San Francesco, perhaps stopping at the delightful **Pilgrims' Oratory** *(Oratorio dei Pellegrini)* (4), a tiny chapel embellished with 15th-century Umbrian frescoes. Continue on to remnants of the former Church of San Nicolò, whose crypt now houses the small **Museo Romano Comunale** (5) with its displays of Etruscan and Roman antiquities. A tunnel from here gives access to the old Roman Forum beneath the present-day piazza. The museum is open daily 9:30 a.m. to 8 p.m. in summer; 10:30 a.m. to 1 p.m. and 3–6:30 p.m. in winter.

The Piazza del Comune, just steps away, is the main square of Assisi. On its north side stands the remarkable **Temple of Minerva**, dating from the reign of Augustus and now serving as a church. Next to it is the tall 13th-century *Torre Comunale* and, to the left, the *Palazzo del Capitano del Popolo*, a palace from the same century. Along the south side you will find the tourist office and the **Town Hall** *(Palazzo dei Priori)* (6), which houses the **Municipal Art Gallery** *(Pinacoteca)* on its ground floor. This small museum has a good collection of Umbrian frescoes and other art works. It is open daily from 9:30 a.m. to noon and 3–7 p.m. in summer; and in winter from 10:30 a.m. to 1 p.m. and 3–6:30 p.m.

Leave the square on Via San Rufino and follow the complicated

The Basilica di San Francesco

route uphill through picturesque streets to the **Castle** *(Rocca Maggiore)* (7). First built in the 12th century, it was reconstructed in the 14th and is still in fine condition. The views in all directions from its summit are spectacular. You may explore its interior from 9 a.m. to 8 p.m. in summer, and 10 a.m. to 4 p.m. in winter. On the way down you may want to go a little out of the way to see the scanty remains of a Roman amphitheater.

The **Cathedral of San Rufino** (8) was begun in 1140 and has some interesting carvings around its doors and windows. Step inside to see the font, at the beginning of the right aisle, where St. Francis, St. Clare, and the emperor Frederick II Hohenstaufen were baptized. The small museum, crypt, and a Roman well may be seen on request.

Continue downhill to the **Church of Santa Chiara** (9), erected in the 13th century to house the remains of St. Clare, the companion of St. Francis. Its plain façade, embellished with a lovely rose window, is supported by monumental buttresses. Inside, be sure to visit the **Chapel of San Giorgio** on the south side. This contains the famous Byzantine crucifix which is said to have spoken to St. Francis, revealing to him his mission in life.

On the way back to Piazza del Comune you will pass the **Oratorio of San Francesco Piccolino** (10), a simple stone structure believed to be the birthplace of St. Francis. Nearby is the **New Church** *(Chiesa*

The Rocca Maggiore

Nuova) (11), built in the 17th century on the supposed site of St. Francis's parents' house.

Head back to the Basilica of St. Francis (3) via the interesting route on the map, then continue down to the bus stop at Porta San Pietro (2). Take a look at the adjacent **Chiesa di San Pietro,** a 13th-century abbey church with an unusual façade, before boarding a bus back to the train station. If you have a wait there, you may want to visit the **Basilica of Santa Maria degli Angeli** (12, off the map), just a few blocks south of the station. Within its nave is the *Cappella della Porziuncola,* a small 4th-century chapel used by St. Francis, and the *Cappella del Transito,* where he died in 1226.

Perugia

Oh, what a strange city is Perugia! Perched high atop a mountain with its head in the clouds, remote, reserved, it still looks down on its ancient enemies. A quirky and moody place that scarcely resembles any other Umbrian hill town, its violent past is still echoed in its forbidding architecture. Yet, Perugia is as sophisticated as any city its size, and even stylishly elegant in spots. Certainly one of the most interesting towns in Italy, it is home to two universities—one reserved solely for foreign students.

Perugia was always an important place, even in prehistoric times. The Etruscans, defeating the Umbrians, made it one of their 12 great city-states. In 310 B.C. it fell to the Romans, and was destroyed again during the civil wars of the 1st century B.C. Augustus rebuilt it and called it *Augusta Perusia*. The Dark Ages were darker here than elsewhere, with nearly continuous sieges and strife. Even during periods of peace, the ruling families were kept busy murdering each other. It was not until the 16th century, when Pope Paul III seized the town and built a massive fortress, that order was established. After that, it belonged to the Papal States until 1860, when a bloody popular insurrection ended with unification into the new Kingdom of Italy.

GETTING THERE:
Trains marked for Ancona depart Rome's Termini station several times in the morning. Take one of these as far as **Foligno** and change there to a local for Perugia. Do not get off at the Perugia-Ponte San Giovanni stop, but wait for the main station, Fontivegge. There may be another train—marked for a different destination—that requires a change at Orte instead of Foligno. The total trip takes nearly three hours. Return service operates until early evening.

By car, take the A-1 Autostrada north almost to Orte, then the S-3 and the S-3-bis north to Perugia. The total distance from Rome is 107 miles. Park in the big lot south of the Carducci Gardens and take the underground escalator up to the town.

WHEN TO GO:
Most of the sights are open daily; a few close on Mondays and holidays, and some earlier on Sundays.

FOOD AND DRINK:

Some of the specialties of Perugia are *Porchetta* (roast suckling pig), *Scaloppine alla Perugina* (tiny veal cutlets), and game dishes. The city is also famous for its cakes and cookies, and especially for its chocolate—the best in Italy. Two local wines are the golden white *Grechetto* and the dark red *Sagrantino,* both slightly on the sweet side.

Perugia has many good restaurants, some of which are listed below—more or less in trip sequence.

La Taverna (Via delle Streghe 8, 1 block east of Pza. della Repubblica) Well hidden but worth the search. X: Mon., late July. $$

Del Sole (Via Oberdan 28, just south of Pza. Matteotti) With a great view and an outdoor terrace in summer. X: Sat. $$

Ricciotto (Piazza Danti 19, just east of the cathedral) A friendly and somewhat rustic place. X: Sun., June. $$

Falchetto (Via Bartolo 20, 1 block north of the cathedral) Umbrian specialties in a medieval atmosphere. X: Mon. $$

La Bocca Mia (Via Rocchi 36, 2 blocks north of the cathedral) A delightful place for local dishes. X: Sun. $$

Dal Mi' Cocco (Corso Garibaldi 12, 2 blocks north of the Etruscan Arch) A very popular local institution with a delicious fixed-price menu and little choice of dishes. X: Mon. $

TOURIST INFORMATION:

The local tourist office, phone (075) 23-327, is at Piazza IV Novembre 3, in the Palazzo dei Priori.

SUGGESTED TOUR:

It is a long, steep climb from the Perugia **train station** (1, off the map) to the city itself. Take a bus going to *"Centro"* from the front of the station and get off at Piazza Italia, the first large square at the top of the hill. Tickets are sold at the outdoor booth by the bus stop and must be canceled aboard the bus. For convenience you should buy a return ticket at the same time.

From Piazza Italia walk around to the **Carducci Gardens** (2) for a wonderful view across the countryside. The gardens and the adjacent government offices are built over the ruins of the former **Rocca Paolina**, a fortress erected in 1540 by the pope to keep the unruly citizens in line. It was demolished in 1860 by the Perugians after they finally overthrew the pope's rule. What lies below it is utterly fantastic, and well worth visiting. When the castle was first erected in the 16th century there was no time to demolish the houses and streets then on the site, so it was raised right on top of them, the spaces being filled with rubble. Long forgotten, this buried part of town was

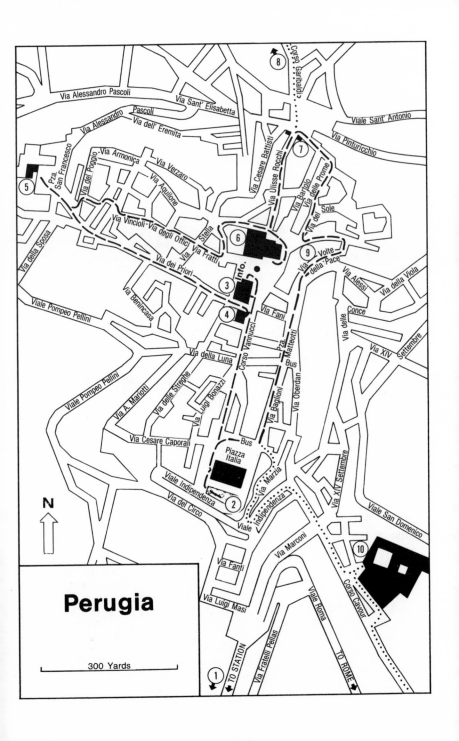

Via Alessandro Pascoli

Via Sant' Elisabetta

Corso Garibaldi

⑧

Viale Sant' Antonio

Via Alessandro Pascoli

Via dell' Eremita

Via Pinturicchio

Via Armonica

Via Verzaro

Pza. San Francesco

Via del Poggio

Via Aquilone

Via Cesare Battisti

Via Ulisse Rocchi

Via Bartolo

Via delle Prome

⑦

⑤

Via della Sposa

Via Vincioli-Via degli Offici-Via Fratti

Stella

Via del Sole

⑥

⑨

Via delle Volte della Pace

Via Alessi

Via dei Priori

Info.

③

Via della Viola

Viale Pompeo Pellini

Via Benincasa

④

Via Fani

Conce

Via delle

Via XIV Settembre

Via della Luna

Corso Vannucci

Pza. Matteotti

Bus

Via Baglioni

Via Oberdan

Viale Pompeo Pellini

Via A. Mariotti

Via delle Streghe

Via Luigi Bonazzi

Via Cesare Caporali

Bus

Piazza Italia

Via Marzia

Via XIV Settembre

Viale San Domenico

Viale Indipendenza

②

Via del Circo

Viale Indipendenza

⑩

Via Fanti

Via Marconi

N

Via Luigi Masi

Corso Cavour

Perugia

Viale Roma

300 Yards

① TO STATION

Via Fratelli Pellas

TO ROME

rediscovered in the 1950s and excavated. The present-day escalators connecting the upper and lower town, opened in 1983, pass right through this ghostly subterranean world. Complete medieval streets, shops, houses, and even the palace of the leading rebel family are still there among the foundations of the former fortress. Take the escalator from the southwest corner of the government building down into this strange, eerie place and probe its arched passageways. The main street, Via Baglioni Sotteranea, leads downhill to the ancient Etruscan town gate, the **Porta Marzia**, which opens into the daylight on Via Marzia.

Return on the escalator to Piazza Italia and stroll down the pedestrians-only **Corso Vannucci**, a busy shopping street, passing Piazza della Repubblica en route. The very heart of old Perugia is the picturesque Piazza IV Novembre, enlivened with the **Fontana Maggiore**, a 13th-century fountain of extraordinary beauty. Its superlative carvings are by Nicolò Pisano and his son, Giovanni.

At the south end of the square stands the massive, crenelated **Palazzo dei Priori** (3), begun in the 13th century as a palace for the prior. Its arched main doorway is surmounted by the bronze griffin of Perugia and the proud lion of the papist party. From these two sculptures hang chains stolen from the city gates of Siena after a Perugian victory in 1358. Now serving as the town hall and tourist office, the palace also contains the fabulous **National Gallery of Umbria**, an art museum that should not be missed. Use the side entrance on Corso Vannucci and take the elevator to the third floor. Specializing in the entire scope of Umbrian art and culminating in works by the local painter Pietro Vannucci, usually known as Perugino, this beautiful gallery also displays works by Fra Angelico and Piero della Francesca—among many others. It is open Mondays through Saturdays, from 8:45 a.m. to 1:45 p.m. and 3–7 p.m.; and on Sundays from 9 a.m. to 1 p.m.

Adjoining the palace is the **Collegio del Cambio** (4), built in the 15th century as a hall for bankers. Anyone interested in Perugino's art should not miss his frescoes in the audience chamber (Sala dell' Udienza), which are probably his most important works. Included in the scenes are a self-portrait and the grouped frieze of Prophets and Sibyls—thought by critics to have actually been painted by Perugino's young pupil, Raphael. Visits may be made on Tuesdays through Saturdays, from 9 a.m. to 12:30 p.m. and 2:30–5:30 p.m., and on Sundays from 9 a.m. to 12:30 p.m.

Now stroll down the colorful Via dei Priori to the **Oratory of San Bernardino** (5), a tiny jewel of a 15th-century church with an exquisite façade by Agostino de Duccio. The altar inside is formed from a 3rd-century Christian sarcophagus.

Continue on, following the map through medieval streets to the

The Palazzo dei Priori and the Fontana Maggiore
(Photo Courtesy of Perugia Tourist Office)

Cathedral (6), a 15th-century structure whose façade was never completed. Its dark interior is quite imposing and contains, in the front chapel in the right, a superb *Descent from the Cross* by Barocci. The first chapel on the left aisle is revered for a wedding ring kept in a gilded reliquary with 15 locks. This allegedly belonged to the Virgin Mary and was stolen by a Perugian monk from the Franciscans at Chiusi. The small Cathedral Museum has an outstanding *Madonna with Saints* by Luca Signorelli. The cathedral itself is closed between 12:30 and 4 p.m.

Via Ulisse Rocchi leads north and passes through the highly unusual **Etruscan Arch** (7), which represents three different eras in history. The lower section, easily identified, was part of the original Etruscan walls. On top of this the Romans under Augustus added another layer, and above that is a lovely 16th-century Renaissance loggia. The building on the west side of the square houses the Italian University for Foreigners, an institution that adds much verve to Perugian life.

At this point you could, if you feel ambitious, take a half-mile walk north on Corso Garibaldi to the ancient **Church of Sant' Angelo** (8, off the map). Dating from the 5th century, this strange circular church—the oldest in Perugia—contains columns from earlier Roman structures.

Along the Corso Vannucci

Return by the route on the map to the cathedral and continue on through Piazza Piccinino to the **Via Volte della Pace** (9), an arched street along the ancient Etruscan walls. Charged with the atmosphere of the Middle Ages, it leads down to Piazza Matteotti, from which you take Via Baglioni back to the bus stop at Piazza Italia.

Time and energy permitting, you may want to see a bit more before leaving Perugia. Via Marzia goes past the outside of the Etruscan town gate which opens into the previously visited underground city. Continue on by Via Indipendenza and Corso Cavour to the 14th-century **Church of San Domenico** (10), the largest in Umbria. Step inside for a look at the marvelous tomb of Pope Benedict XI. Directly adjacent to the church, in the former convent, is the noted **National Archaeological Museum of Umbria**, which unfortunately is open only until 2 p.m. About a half-mile farther down the street stands the delightful **Church of San Pietro**, founded in the 10th century but many times rebuilt. Its balcony, beyond the choir, has a remarkable view across the countryside to Assisi.

Spoleto

Spoleto is best known today for its annual Festival of Two Worlds, founded in 1958 by the Italian-American composer Gian-Carlo Menotti. The same qualities that first attracted the festival should bring you here, too. A small Umbrian hill town of great antiquity and unspoiled character, Spoleto has the additional merit of being easy to reach. Although it possesses no great sights as such, its exceptionally well-preserved core does contain a large number of remarkable Roman and medieval structures of more than passing interest. As a bonus, the town is blessed with a truly cosmopolitan ambiance—a blend of rural Italy with a touch of international sophistication. In short, Spoleto is a delightful destination for a relaxed and thoroughly enjoyable daytrip.

An ancient Umbrian center of unknown origin, *Spoletium* became a Roman colony in 242 B.C. Twenty-five years later it successfully repelled an attack by Hannibal, giving Rome the needed time to reorganize its defenses and save the republic. During the Middle Ages it was the seat of a fairly large duchy, and in the 14th century became part of the Papal States, yielding to the new Kingdom of Italy in 1860.

GETTING THERE:

Trains, usually marked for Ancona, depart Rome's Termini station several times in the morning for the under-two-hour ride to Spoleto. One of these requires a change at Orte. Return service operates until mid-evening.

By car, take the A-1 Autostrada north almost to Orte, then the S-3 past Terni and into Spoleto. Park as close to Piazza della Libertà as possible. The total distance from Rome is 81 miles.

WHEN TO GO:

Spoleto is crowded during the Festival of Two Worlds, held annually between mid-June and mid-July. Good weather is essential as almost all of this trip is out of doors.

FOOD AND DRINK:

The major gastronomic experience of Spoleto is the black truffle (*Tartufo*), found on local hillsides. Other specialties are a pasta called *Stringozzi*, and a variety of game dishes. The local wine is *Trebbiano*

Spoleto, a rather strong white.

Some choice restaurants are:

Il Tartufo (Piazza Garibaldi 24, between the train station and the upper town) Considered to be the best restaurant in Spoleto. X: Wed., late July $$$

Sabatini (Corso Mazzini 52, 2 blocks north of Pza. della Libertà) A traditional restaurant with Umbrian specialties. X: Mon., Jan. $$

La Barcaccia (Piazza Fratelli Bandiera 3, just west of the town hall) A good choice in the heart of the Old Town. X: Tues., Jan. $

Il Panciolle (Largo Muzio Clemente 4, 3 blocks west of the cathedral) A charming local restaurant on a quiet, shady little square. X: Wed. $

TOURIST INFORMATION:

The local tourist office, phone (0743) 28-111, is at Piazza della Libertà 7.

SUGGESTED TOUR:

Spoleto's international flavor becomes apparent the moment you step outside the **train station** (1, off the map) and confront the overpowering 1962 sculpture by Alexander Calder. From there it is a pleasant one-mile walk to Piazza della Libertà, fairly level most of the way until you get to the steep Via Porta Fuga. Just go straight ahead and follow the route on the map. There is also a frequent bus service from the station if you'd rather ride.

The **Piazza della Libertà** (2) is the real start of this walk. On its east side is the tourist office, while the west opens onto the ancient **Roman Theater**, built in the 1st century A.D. Unearthed in recent years, it has been restored and is once again used for performances.

Via Brignone leads east towards the **Roman Arch**, a relic from the 3rd century B.C. which still spans the road. Just before this turn left onto Via Arco de Druso. The small **Arch of Drusus** (3), dating from A.D. 23, commemorates the victories of the great military leader Drusus—the adopted son of Augustus—over the Germanic tribes. To the right of it is the interesting small **Church of Sant' Ansano**, built around the walls of a 1st-century Roman temple. In its crypt is the Chapel of Sant' Isacco, a primitive Christian church within the old temple.

Continue on through the **Piazza del Mercato**, where an open-air market is held Mondays through Saturdays on the site of the ancient Roman forum. The route now leads through some quaint old streets to the Bishop's Palace, in whose courtyard is the lovely 12th-century **Church of Sant' Eufemia** (4). Step inside to see the unusual women's

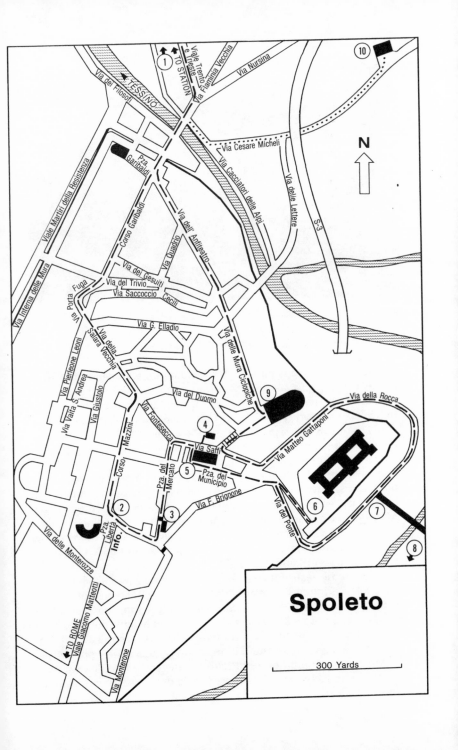

The Bridge of Towers

galleries above the aisles and the 15th-century triptych behind the altar.

Via di Visiale leads past the **Casa Romano**, a Roman house from the 1st century A.D. supposedly owned by the mother of the emperor Vespasian. Its restored interior may usually be seen by inquiring at the adjacent **Town Hall** *(Palazzo Comunale)* (5) on Piazza del Municipo. The town hall also houses the **Pinacoteca**, a small art museum displaying mostly Umbrian works. It is open on Wednesdays through Mondays, from 10 a.m. to 1 p.m. and 3–7 p.m.

Now walk uphill to the massive 14th-century **Fortress** *(Rocca)* (6), built as a stronghold for the popes' representatives. In the late 15th century it was home to none other than the notorious Lucrezia Borgia. After the unification of Italy it became a prison and remained so until 1982. It is now open to the public, and may be visited on Mondays through Saturdays, from 10 a.m. to 7:30 p.m. As of this writing it was undergoing restoration and might be closed.

Around the rear of the castle, spanning a narrow valley, is the remarkable **Bridge of Towers** *(Ponte delle Torri)* (7). Erected in the 14th century over Roman foundations, this 755-foot-long bridge and aqueduct is supported by pillars up to 262 feet in height, the center two of which are hollow for use as defensive towers. A stroll across it offers breathtaking views and the opportunity for a short country walk to the nearby **Church of San Pietro** (8). Begun in the 5th century, it later acquired a lavish 12th-century façade depicting strange narrative folk fables.

The Cathedral

Return around the other side of the fortress. Along the way you will see little signs reserving the harvest rights for truffles on the hillside. Back in town, you will soon come to the top of the spectacular stairway that leads down to the **Cathedral** *(Duomo)* (9), a very beautiful and unusual sight. Consecrated in 1198 and altered over the years, it has a marvelous Renaissance porch, eight rose windows, and a majestic tower. Inside, there are some wonderful 15th-century **frescoes** in the apse by Filippo Lippi, whose tomb is in the chapel to the right. The first chapel on the south aisle, nearest the entrance, contains a splendid *Madonna Enthroned* by Pinturicchio, while the interior west façade is decorated with a bust of Pope Urban VIII by Bernini. The cathedral is closed between 1 and 3 p.m.

Your tour is now really over. Those returning to the train station can follow the map back past Piazza Garibaldi and cross the river. From here you may want to make an easy side trip to the nearby **Church of San Salvatore** (10), one of the oldest Christian churches in Europe. It was begin as early as the 4th century and altered in the 9th. The interior is extremely atmospheric and contains several excellent Roman columns.

Gubbio

Time has stood still in Gubbio ever since the 14th century, when its prosperity peaked and then suddenly declined. What may well be the best-preserved of the Umbrian hill towns now lives mainly on its memories. Relatively few foreign tourists get to savor this holdover from the Middle Ages—at least compared to the hordes that descend on Orvieto or Assisi—and one look at the map tells why. Gubbio is located quite a distance from any rail line or major highway, and is somewhat difficult to reach. Making the extra effort is, however, well worthwhile as it gives you a rare chance to probe the mysteries of a real medieval town in peace.

Beginning as the Umbrian settlement of *Iguvium*, Gubbio became the flourishing Roman town of *Eugubium* as early as the 3rd century B.C. During the Middle Ages it was an independent city-state of some stature, but in the 14th century voluntarily surrendered its freedom to the powerful dukes of Urbino. From the 17th until the 19th century the town was a minor part of the Papal States, and in 1860 joined the Kingdom of Italy.

In addition to its intriguing ambiance, Gubbio has long been a center for exquisite ceramics, and is noted for a few architectural eccentricities such as the *Porta del Morto* doorways in many of the old houses, allegedly sealed to prevent the return of evil spirits after dead bodies were passed through. Another legend has it that in the 13th century the surrounding countryside was terrified by a gigantic wolf, who was made tame through the kindness of St. Francis.

GETTING THERE:

Trains marked for Ancona depart Rome's Termini station at least twice in the morning. Take one of these as far as **Fossato di Vico**, a trip of nearly three hours. From there it is a 12-mile, 30-minute ride on a connecting ASP bus into Gubbio. Tickets are sold at the bar in the Fossato train station and canceled on board the bus. Buy a return ticket at the same time. Check both the bus and train return schedules carefully so you don't wind up with a long wait at Fossato, not exactly a very exciting place. Return trains operate until mid-evening.

By car, Gubbio is 135 miles north of Rome. Take the A-1 Autostrada almost to Orte, then the SE-7 past Terni and Perugia to Bosco, and the S-298 into Gubbio.

WHEN TO GO:
Gubbio can be visited at any time in nice weather, although the Ducal Palace is closed on Mondays and some holidays. Folklore festivals are held on May 15th and also the last Sunday in May.

FOOD AND DRINK:
The hearty cooking of Gubbio can be enjoyed in a number of good restaurants, among which are:

Alla Fornace di Mastro Giorgio (Via Mastro Giorgio 2, 2 blocks southeast of the Consuls' Palace) An atmospheric place in a medieval building. X: Mon., Feb. $$

Taverna del Lupo (Via Ansidei 21, near Via della Repubblica and Via Baldassini) Local specialties in an ancient setting. X: Mon., Jan. $$

Federico da Montefeltro (Via della Repubblica 35, 2 blocks northeast of Pza. 40 Martiri) Authentic regional dishes. X: Thurs. between Oct. and Mar. $$

Grotto dell' Angelo (Via Gioia 47, a block southwest of the tourist office) Local dishes in a homey setting. X: Tues. $$

San Francesco e Il Lupo (Via Cairoli 24, around the corner from the tourist office) Both a restaurant and a pizzeria, locally popular. X: early July $

TOURIST INFORMATION:
The local tourist office, phone (075) 92-20-693, is at Piazza Oderisi on the Via Garibaldi.

SUGGESTED TOUR:
Begin your walk at the **Piazza 40** *(Quaranta)* **Martiri** (1), where the bus stop and parking lot are located. This lovely square has a fine view of the town, and a very unusual mossy fountain in its center. On its northeast side is the 14th-century **Weavers' Gallery**, once used by wool makers to protect their cloth from the sun.

Enter the Old Town by the picturesque Via Piccardi, turning left at the top of the hill onto Via Baldassini. At the intersection of Via dei Consoli stands the elegant 13th-century **Palace of the Bargello**, a medieval police headquarters. Turn right on Via dei Consoli and follow it up to Piazza della Signoria, a gorgeous public square with outstanding views.

On the north side of this rises the magnificent **Consuls' Palace** *(Palazzo dei Consoli)* (2), built in the 14th century and still a highly impressive sight. Its massive interior now houses the **Civic Museum and Art Gallery**, whose greatest treasures are the fascinating *Tavole Eugubine*, seven bronze tablets discovered in 1444 near the Roman

Via dei Galeotti

theater. Dating from around 250–150 B.C., they are inscribed in the mysterious Umbrian language, using both the Etruscan and Latin alphabets, and are a priceless source of information about that era. Other important exhibits include ancient coins, pottery, local artifacts, and a nicely balanced art collection. Don't miss seeing this treat, which is open daily from 9 a.m. to 12:30 p.m. and 3:30–6 p.m. in summer, and from 9 a.m. to 1 p.m. and 3–5 p.m. in winter.

Before having lunch you may want to continue up to the nearby **Ducal Palace** (3), which closes for the day at 1 or 2 p.m. Erected in the 15th century for the ruling Duke of Urbino, it is noted for its splendid arcaded courtyard, frescoes, and impressive fireplaces. Visits may be made on Tuesdays through Saturdays, from 9 a.m. to 2 p.m., and on Sundays from 9 a.m. to 1 p.m.

Across the street is the 13th-century **Cathedral** *(Duomo)* (4), a rather plain structure whose façade has a rose window framed by bas-reliefs of the Apostles. The uncluttered interior has some remarkable stone vaulting and several fine frescoes along the side walls.

Return to Via XX Settembre and follow it to the lower **cable car station** *(Funivia)* (5), from which you can get an open-air ride up the side of Mount Ingino for a truly glorious panorama. A short climb from the upper station brings you to the **Basilica and Monastery of**

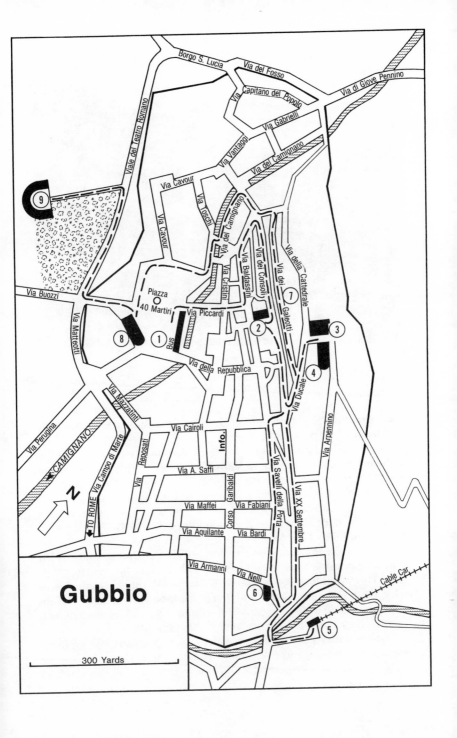

Borgo S. Lucia
Via del Fosso
Via Capitano del Popolo
Via di Giove Pennino
Via Gabrielli
Via Vantaggi
Via del Camignano
Viale del Teatro Romano
Via Cavour
Via Toschi
Via del Camignano
Via Cavour
9
Via Baldassini
Via dei Consoli
Via della Cattedrale
Via dei Galeotti
Via Cristini
Via Buozzi
Piazza
40 Martiri
7
Via Piccardi
Via Matteotti
8
1
Bus
2
3
Via della Repubblica
4
Via Ducale
Via della Repubblica
Via Mazzatinti
Via Cairoli
Info.
Via Arpennino
Via Perugina
CAMIGNANO
Via Campo di Marte
Via Reposati
Via A. Saffi
TO ROME
N
Via Maffei
Corso Garibaldi
Via Fabiani
Via Savelli della Porta
Via XX Settembre
Via Aquilante
Via Bardi
Via Armanni
Via Nelli
6
Cable Car
Gubbio
5

300 Yards

The Weavers' Gallery
(Photo by Franco Gavirati, Gubbio)

Sant' Ubaldo, the patron saint of Gubbio. The cable car operates daily from 8 a.m. to 1 p.m. and 2–8 p.m.

Back in town, pass through the Porta Romana gate and stop at the 13th-century **Church of Santa Maria Nuova** (6), noted for its excellent *Madonna of the Belvedere* fresco by the local 15th-century artist, Ottaviano Nelli. Continue on Via Savelli and turn right, crossing Via XX Settembre. Heading back toward the cathedral on Via Ducale, make a left into the dark and strangely arcaded **Via dei Galeotti** (7) heavy with the atmosphere of the Middle Ages.

Now follow the route on the map to **Via del Camignano**, which follows alongside a mountain torrent with ancient houses on either side. This will return you to Piazza 40 Martiri (1), on the south side of which is the medieval **Church of San Francesco** (8), the finest in Gubbio. Step inside to see the early-15th-century cycle of frescoes depicting the *Life of the Madonna,* again by Ottaviano Nelli.

If time permits before your bus departure, you can make an interesting little side trip to the **Roman Theater** (9). Dating from the 1st century A.D., this large and well-preserved theater is still used for performances.

North Central Italy

To many tourists, Tuscany *(Toscana)* is the very heart and soul of Italy. Boasting the oldest culture in the land and speaking the purest form of Italian, this gently mountainous region was the birthplace of the Renaissance. Its splendid capital of Florence, along with the ancient, unspoiled towns and villages to the south and west, attracts countless visitors in search of art, beauty, and just plain good living. This section also includes a foray into neighboring Emilia-Romagna, whose urbane capital of Bologna is reputed to have the best cooking in all Italy.

Tuscany was named after its early inhabitants, the Etruscans, an enigmatic people of unknown origin whose written language remains undeciphered to this day. Their highly developed civilization evolved around 800 B.C., and ultimately spread as far north as Milan and south to Rome before being defeated by the growing Roman Empire in the 4th century B.C. You will be meeting up with these remarkable people, or at least their artifacts, in several of the daytrips that follow, especially those to Fiesole and Arezzo.

The natural center for daytrips in North Central Italy is Florence, which lies at the junction of major rail and highway routes, and is itself one of the three most important tourist attractions in the nation. A one-day "get acquainted" walking tour of this intriguing city is described in the pages that follow. Although Florence is extremely well endowed with hotels and restaurants in every conceivable price range, some travelers may prefer to stay outside the city itself. An excellent choice for this is nearby Fiesole, with Pisa being a workable but less convenient alternative.

Ferrara, described in Section V, can also be seen on a daytrip from Florence. Centrally located Bologna is easily visited from either Milan (Section IV) or Venice (Section V), as well as from Florence.

Florence

(Firenze)

Few cities on earth have contributed more to Western civilization than Florence. Renowned as the birthplace of the Renaissance, that ill-defined era that marked the end of the Middle Ages and the beginning of humanism, the city is a treasure house of great art and architecture. This, after all, was home to such luminaries as Leonardo da Vinci, Michelangelo, Raphael, Botticelli, Fra Angelico, Giotto, Donatello, Brunelleschi, Cellini; not to mention Dante, Machiavelli, Savonarola, and, of course, the ruling Medici family. Despite this, Florence is not just a museum—it remains as always a vital, highly attractive city with a zest for good living. Just about everyone who goes there enjoys the experience, and many continue to return year after year.

A settlement existed at this site since Etruscan times, but it was not until the Romans bridged the Arno river that a town, then called *Florentia*, developed. This was a relatively unimportant place, invaded periodically by both barbarian tribes and disease. As trade began to flourish during the Middle Ages, the town, lying then and now at the junction of major transportation routes, slowly became a wealthy mercantile center. Prosperity attracts talent, and by the 15th century the Renaissance, one of the major turning points in history, was off and running. For nearly two centuries the city enjoyed a golden age of artistic brilliance. Gradually, however, the focus turned to Rome, and Florence was left with its memories and its incomparable store of art. For a brief period, from 1865 to 1870, it was the capital of the new Kingdom of Italy.

It is presumptuous to pretend that anyone can see Florence in a single day, or even a month. Yet, a start must be made somewhere. The suggested walking tour in this most walkable of cities is designed to give you a quick impression of the whole, while allowing enough time for brief visits to some of the more famous sights. It also takes into account the opening times of the various museums along the route.

GETTING THERE:

Trains connect Florence's main station (S.M.N.) with other towns in North Central Italy at fairly frequent intervals. Typical running times are: Arezzo—1 hour, Siena—90 minutes, Pisa—55 minutes, Lucca—90 minutes, and Bologna—70 minutes. For more details consult the chapters for those specfic towns. There are also convenient schedules from Rome (2 hours), Milan (3 hours), and Venice (3 hours).

Buses link Florence with other towns throughout North Central Italy, and are especially recommended for trips to and from Fiesole, San Gimignano, Siena, and possibly Lucca. Practical details are given in the chapters on those towns.

By car, Florence is 172 miles from Rome, 185 miles from Milan, and 158 miles from Venice, all by Autostrada. Distances from towns in North Central Italy are: Fiesole—5 miles, Arezzo—50 miles, San Gimignano—34 miles, Siena—42 miles, Pisa—57 miles, Lucca—46 miles, and Bologna—65 miles. Recommended routes are shown in the chapters for those towns.

By air, Florence has direct flights from London, Paris, and Frankfurt via the Pisa airport, as well as service to other Italian cities.

WHEN TO GO:

The best time to visit Florence is in the late spring or early fall—it is always crowded and often hot during the summer. The local patron saint's day is June 24, honoring St. John the Baptist. Good weather is not really necessary for this walking tour as much of your time will be spent indoors. There are so many things to see that an early start, preferably before 9 a.m., is strongly advised. Try to hold back your hunger pangs and not have lunch until after visiting the Pitti Palace (7), which closes for the day at 2 p.m. Avoid making this trip on a Monday or certain holidays, when nearly everything is closed. Most of the attractions close at 1 p.m. on Sundays.

FOOD AND DRINK:

The cooking in this agricultural region tends to be simple and wholesome, with the prize dish being *Bistecca alla Fiorentina,* a large charcoal-broiled steak. *Chianti* is the local wine, whose quality ranges from magnificent to terrible. The variety known as *Chianti Classico,* in a straight-sided Bordeaux-type bottle, is usually regarded as the best, and is still quite inexpensive. Avoid anything in a straw-wrapped *fiasco* bottle.

Some choice restaurants in Florence, in the order that you will pass or come close to them along the walking route, are:

Enoteca Pinchiorri (Via Ghibellina 87, 2 blocks north of Santa Croce) Considered to be the best restaurant in town, famous for wines. Reservations needed, phone (055) 242-777. X: Sun., Mon. lunch, Aug. $$$

Il Fagioli (Corso dei Tintori 47, 1 block south of Santa Croce) Typical Tuscan dishes. X: Sat., Sun., Aug. $$

Celestino (Piazza Santa Felicita 4, near south side of Ponte Vecchio) A fashionable trattoria. X: Sun., Aug. $$

Birreria Borgo Antico (Piazza San Spirito 6, 3 blocks west of Pitti Palace) Popular neighborhood place. X: Sun., Mon. Lunch. $

Cammillo (Borgo Sant' Jacopo 57, 3 blocks west of south side of Ponte Vecchio) A favorite trattoria. X: Wed., Thurs., late Dec. to mid-Jan., early to mid-Aug. $$$

Mama Gina (Borgo Sant' Jacopo 37, 1 block west of south side of Ponte Vecchio) Typical local dishes. X: Sun., Aug. $$

Il Cavallino (Via delle Farine 6, north side of Piazza della Signoria) A good choice in an area notorious for tourist traps. X: Tues. eve., Wed., Aug. $$

Paoli (Via dei Tavolini 12, 3 blocks southeast of Piazza della Repubblica) Elegant decor. X: Tues. $$

Al Campidoglio (Via Campidoglio 8, 2 blocks northwest of Piazza della Repubblica) A popular, old-fashioned establishment. X: Thurs., Aug. $$

Giannino (Borgo San Lorenzo 31, 1 block north of Baptistry) The self-service cafeteria, not the restaurant. X: Thurs. $

Buca Lapi (Via del Trebbio 1, 5 blocks west of Duomo) A friendly cellar restaurant with local specialties. X: Sun., Mon. lunch. $$

Sabatini (Via de' Panzani 9, 1 block southeast of Santa Maria Novella) A famous old traditional favorite. X: Mon. $$$

You will pass many less expensive restaurants along the route, but beware the "bargain" tourist traps—take a look and see who's eating there first.

TOURIST INFORMATION:

The local tourist office (*Azienda di Promozione Turistica Firenze—APT*), phone (055) 24-78-141, is located at Via Manzoni 16, about one-half mile east of the Duomo (3), a block north of Piazza Beccaria. Convenient branches are located at Via Cavour 1r (a block north of the Duomo entrance) and Chiasso Baroncelli 17 (near the rear exit of the Uffizi Gallery). There is also a small office just outside the train station, and an accommodations booking office by Track 16 in the station.

SUGGESTED TOUR:

The real start of this walk is at the cathedral square, but those coming from out of town will want to begin at the main **train station** (Firenze S.M.N.) (1), adjacent to the various bus terminals and a large parking lot. Continue down Via de' Panzani and Via de' Cerretani, both busy commercial streets, to the cathedral group arranged around Piazza del Duomo.

Consisting of three major buildings, the cathedral complex lies at the very heart of Florence. The oldest structure here is the **Baptistry** (Battistero) (2) of St. John the Baptist, once thought to be of Roman construction. Much altered over the years, this magnificent octagonal building may originally have been erected as far back as the 5th century A.D., although the green-and-white marble sheathing was added during the 11th century. Its most famous feature, the three sets of exterior **bronze doors**—which merit a very careful examination—date from the 14th and 15th centuries. Those on the east side, facing the cathedral itself and sculpted between 1425 and 1452 by Lorenzo Ghiberti, were dubbed the "Gates of Paradise" by Michelangelo, who certainly knew good carving when he saw it. They depict ten scenes from the Old Testament. Although some of the panels are periodically removed for restoration, the overall effect is a triumph of the emerging Renaissance style over the Gothic. The slightly older north doors, also by Ghiberti, were the result of a competition held in 1401 in which the young sculptor won out over such esteemed artists as Brunelleschi and Donatello.

Enter the Baptistry through the south doors, created in 1336 by Andrea Pisano, which illustrate both the life of St. John the Baptist and the eight virtues. The vault is covered with marvelous 13th-century **mosaics** of the Last Judgement and other Biblical stories, while the floor is inlaid with Oriental motifs. Don't miss the **tomb** of the Antipope John XXIII, a splendid 15th-century joint effort by Donatello and Michelozzo. The Baptistry is usually open Mondays through Saturdays from 1–7 p.m., and on Sundays and holidays from 9 a.m. to 1 p.m. If it is closed in the morning, you will have another opportunity for a visit near the end of the walk.

Just opposite the entrance to the Baptistry is the charming 14th-century **Loggia del Bigallo**, a porch where abandoned children were displayed for adoption. The nearby **Bell Tower** (Campanile), to the right of the cathedral façade, offers the best possible view of Florence—a treat well worth the 269-foot climb to its summit. Begun in 1334 by Giotto and continued by Pisano, the tower was completed in 1359 by Francesco Talenti. Ascents, on foot, give you an ever-changing panorama as you go higher and can usually be made any day between 9 a.m. and 7:30 p.m., closing at 5:30 p.m. in winter. You must begin

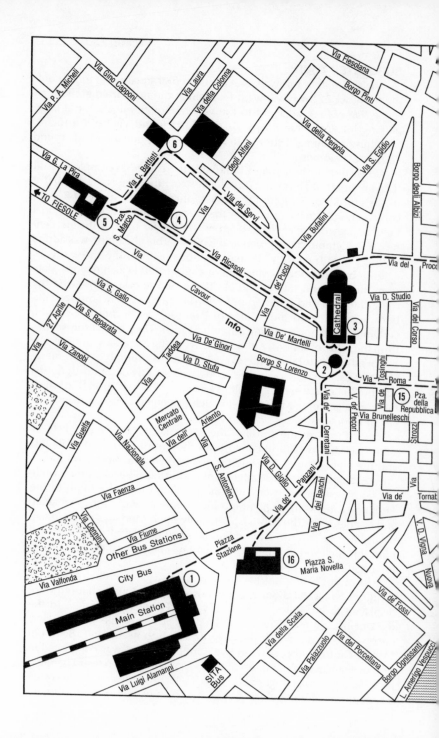

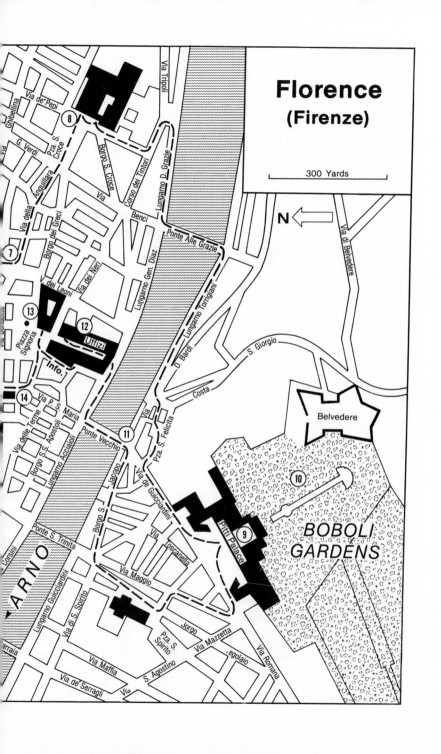

Florence
(Firenze)

300 Yards

N

Via Tripoli
Via de' Pepi
Ghibellina
G. Verdi
Pza. S. Croce
Via della Anguillara
Borgo S. Croce
Borgo dei Greci
Via
Corso dei Tintori
Via dei Neri
Benci
Lungarno D. Grazie
Ponte Alle Grazie
Via di Belvedere
Lungarno Gen. Diaz
Lungarno Torrigiani
V. dei Leoni
D. Bardi
S. Giorgio
Piazza Signoria
Uffizi
Info.
Costa
Belvedere
Via delle Terme
Via P. S. Maria
Borgo S.S. Apostoli
Lungarno Acciaioli
Ponte Vecchio
Via P. S. Felicita
Pza. S. Felicita
Via de' Guicciardini
Lungarno Guicciardini
Ponte S. Trinita
Via di S. Spirito
Borgo S. Iacopo
Via Toscanella
Via Maggio
Via Mazzetta
Via Romana
Pza. S. Spirito
Jorgo
Iegolalo
Pitti Palace
BOBOLI GARDENS
ARNO
Corsini
arraia
Via Maffia
Via de' Serragli
Via
S. Agostino

(1)
(7)
(8)
(9)
(10)
(11)
(12)
(13)
(14)

the climb at least 45 minutes before the closing time. Again, you will have another chance to do this near the end of the walking tour, when the sun is perhaps lower and the cityscape etched in deeper relief.

The **Cathedral of Santa Maria del Fiore** *(Duomo)* (3), next to the bell tower, is one of the largest churches on earth. It was begun in 1296 on the site of a former cathedral dedicated to St. Reparata, remains of which can be seen in the crypt. Begin your visit by strolling around the massive exterior, resplendent in its red, white, and green marble facing. The enormous **dome**, seeming far too large for the building it caps and visible for miles around, is the very symbol of Florence. Designed by the great Brunelleschi in 1420, it was the first monumental dome erected since the Roman era and pioneered a construction principle later used in such great domes as St. Peter's in Rome and St. Paul's in London. It is actually two domes, one inside the other, with interconnecting ribs in which stress is concentrated in the hollow space, thus greatly reducing the amount of weight that must be borne by the cathedral walls. As a crowning ornament, the dome is capped with an elegant marble lantern.

Enter through the flamboyant west façade, a late-19th-century addition in what can only be termed a Victorian Gothic style. Compared to the grandiose exterior, the interior may seem a bit barren, but there are some real treasures to be found. Along the north aisle you will see three particularly interesting paintings, the first two being *trompe l'oeil* equestrian **frescoes** honoring the *condottieri* mercenary captains Niccolò da Tolentino and John Hawkwood, both from the mid-15th century. The third, closer to the crossing, depicts Dante explaining his *Divine Comedy*. The inside of the dome is decorated with a fresco of the Last Judgment, under which there is a magnificent octagonal choir enclosure.

You can climb to the very top of the great **dome** itself via a maintenance stairway between the two shells. Along the way there is a remarkable view of the cathedral interior, and at the peak—actually higher than the adjacent bell tower—a sweeping panorama across Florence and the surrounding countryside. Ascents begin near the north transept and may usually be made any day except Sunday, up to one hour before the cathedral closes. If you only have the energy for one climb, however, remember that the previously mentioned view from the bell tower is more attractive as it takes in the whole of the cathedral.

Excavations in the 1960s unearthed the remains of earlier churches beneath the cathedral, some possibly dating as far back as the 5th century A.D., along with the tomb of the architect Brunelleschi. These may be seen by going down into the **Crypt of Santa Reparata** via a staircase near the south side of the nave.

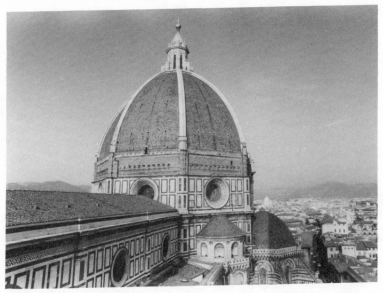

The Cathedral Dome from the Bell Tower

Now follow Via Ricasoli to the **Galleria dell' Accademia** (4), an art museum that attracts countless tourists. Most of them come to see only one work, Michelangelo's world-famous **statue of *David***. Splendidly displayed in its own rotunda, this gigantic early-16th-century masterpiece stood outdoors in the Piazza della Signoria until 1873, when it was replaced by a good copy. While in the museum, you should take a look at some of the other works of art, especially Michelangelo's four unfinished statues called the *Slaves,* set against a backdrop of Renaissance tapestries. Other statues on display by the master include the *Palestrina Pietà* and the *St. Matthew.* There are also several galleries of excellent Florentine paintings. The Accademia is open Tuesday through Saturday, from 9 a.m. to 2 p.m., and on Sunday and some holidays from 9 a.m. to 1 p.m. It is closed on Mondays and a few major holidays.

Continue across the square to the **Fra Angelico Museum** *(Museo dell' Angelico* or *Museo di San Marco)* (5) in the San Marco Convent. Devoted almost entirely to the works of the revered, gentle early-15th-century artist who was also a Dominican monk, this small museum is one of the most satisfying places to visit in Florence. The convent and its cloisters were rebuilt around 1438 by Michelozzo and paid for by Cosimo de' Medici, the noted ruler who kept his own cell (numbers 38 and 39) here for private meditation. Sometimes considered the last of the great medieval painters, Fra Angelico (*Beato Angelico* in Italian), a resident of the convent, was called upon to create the inspirational frescoes which bring so much life to the structure. Since it was converted into a museum in 1869, other outstanding works by him have been brought here from churches and galleries—including the Uffizi—all over Florence. There are also a few major paintings by other artists, notably Ghirlandaio and Fra Bartolommeo.

Another famous resident of the convent was Girolama Savonarola (1452–1498), the religious zealot who preached the strictest morality and eventually set up a theocratic state in Florence with Christ as King and himself as political leader. The people soon tired of his demagoguery and dragged him from here, hung him, and burned his body in the Piazza della Signoria. You can visit his **cell** (number 11), decorated with his portrait by Fra Bartolommeo. While there, stop in at the **library** between cells 42 and 43. Its lovely interior was designed by Michelozzo. The museum is open Tuesday through Saturday, from 9 a.m. to 2 p.m., and on Sunday from 9 a.m. to 1 p.m. It is closed on Mondays and some major holidays.

A short stroll along Via Battisti brings you to the delightful **Piazza della S.S. Annunziata** (6), graced with a fine equestrian statue of Ferdinand I and two baroque fountains. On the north side is the Church of S.S. Annunziata, noted for its beautiful frescoes and baroque interior. The **Foundling Hospital** *(Ospedale degli Innocenti)* on the east side of the square has a marvelous early-15th-century loggia by Brunelleschi, sometimes regarded as the first true Renaissance structure. Inside, there is a small art gallery with some notable works, which you can visit.

Via dei Servi leads to the rear of the Cathedral (3), opposite which is the **Cathedral Museum** *(Museo dell' Opera del Duomo)*. You may want to stop in for a look at some art treasures belonging to the cathedral, including an unfinished *Pietà* by Michelangelo, intended for his own tomb. If so, the hours are from 9 a.m. to 7:30 p.m., Mondays through Saturdays, closing at 6 p.m. in winter. Since the walking tour will bring you back this way in the afternoon, it is probably best to wait until then.

Continue down Via del Proconsolo to the **Bargello Museum** *(Museo Nazionale del Bargello)* (7), housed in a forbidding 13th-century palace once used as a police headquarters and prison. The great bell in its tower announced executions in the courtyard, a practice that lasted until 1848. A few years later it was converted into what is now perhaps Italy's greatest museum of Renaissance sculpture. Surprisingly, the interior of this grim structure is actually quite elegant, and makes a fine home for the many outstanding works of art on display. Be sure to see, in the ground floor gallery, Michelangelo's somewhat drunken *Bacchus,* along with his *Brutus* and *Pitti Tondo.* There are also magnificent statues by Cellini and others. Upstairs, the star attractions are Donatello's *St. George* of 1416 and his noted bronze *David* of 1430, the first freestanding nude since ancient times. Continuing upwards, the second floor features another *David,* this one by Verroccio. Some other major works are Cellini's *Ganymede* and Bernini's *Constanza Bonarelli,* along with a great many portrait busts. A display of arms and armor rounds out the collection. The Bargello may be visited between 9 a.m. and 2 p.m., Tuesdays through Saturdays, and 9 a.m. to 1 p.m. on Sundays. It is closed on Mondays and some holidays.

Now follow the map to the **Church of Santa Croce** (8), widely regarded as the most beautiful in Florence. Begun by the Franciscans in the late 13th century, its enormous interior contains the **tombs** of several leading citizens, including Michelangelo, Machiavelli, Galileo, and Ghiberti. There is also an empty monument to Dante, whose body the city of Ravenna still refuses to part with. Most of the **chapels** are exceptionally well decorated, especially the Castellani and Baroncelli chapels facing the south transept. Also make a careful examination of Bardi and Peruzzi chapels, to the right of the altar, both late works by Giotto. The 15th-century **pulpit**, along the side of the nave, is carved with scenes from the life of St. Francis, while along the same wall there is a masterful *Annunciation* by Donatello. Close to this is the tomb of Leonardo Bruni, one of the greatest funerary monuments of the Renaissance.

The **Cloisters**, to the right of the church, lead into the wonderful **Pazzi Chapel**, a 15th-century masterpiece by Brunelleschi. While there, be sure to visit the small **Museum of Santa Croce**, noted for its *Crucifixion* by Cimabue and Donatello's bronze *St. Louis of Toulouse.* The cloisters and museum are usually open daily except on Wednesdays, from 10 a.m. to 12:30 p.m. and 2:30–6:30 p.m., closing at 5 p.m. in winter.

From here it is a delightful stroll along the banks of the Arno and across a bridge into the charming Oltrarno district, the Left Bank of Florence. Some of the city's most enjoyable restaurants—in all price ranges—are to be found here, but try to hold off having lunch until after the next attraction as it closes for the day at 2 p.m. After that, everything along the remaining part of the walking tour is open until much later.

The **Pitti Palace** (9) is one of the top tourist attractions in Florence, and for good reason. Begun by the mid-15th century by Luca Pitti, a political rival of the ruling Cosima de' Medici, the palace was sold a century later to the Medici family, who greatly expanded it and used it as a grand ducal residence. In 1865 it became the royal palace of

Victor Emmanuel, the first King of Italy, who lived here until the government moved to Rome in 1870. Today, this enormous palace houses several museums, all of which are at least interesting. Since you can't possibly see everything in the very short amount of time available, it is suggested that you make a brief visit to the Palantine Gallery—the number one attraction—and plan on returning another day.

Purchase your ticket for the **Palantine Gallery** (Galleria Palatina) on the right side of the inner courtyard, then climb the long staircase to the first floor. The sumptuously appointed rooms are filled with hundreds of masterpieces displayed in the old-fashioned manner of a private royal collection, which this of course is. You really get the feeling of not being in a museum at all, but of having stepped into an opulent 17th-century palace. Some of the artists represented, not all Florentine or even Italian, include Titian, Tintoretto, Van Dyck, Rubens, Raphael, Valázquez, Caravaggio, Filippo Lippi, and Botticelli. The Palantine Gallery is open Tuesdays through Saturdays, from 9 a.m. to 2 p.m., and on Sundays from 9 a.m. to 1 p.m. It is closed on Mondays and some holidays.

While in the neighborhood, you might want to stroll through the pleasant **Boboli Gardens** (10), a public park just behind the Pitti Palace. Laid out in the 16th century, its quiet paths are adorned with classical statuary. There is a nice outdoor café halfway up the hill, where you can sit down for a welcome drink or even have a sandwich. The **Belvedere Fortress**, nearby, offers a splendid view of Florence across the Arno.

Now follow the map to the **Ponte Vecchio** (11), one of the most famous bridges on earth. Built in 1345 on the site of earlier spans, this is the only bridge in Florence to have escaped destruction by the retreating German army in 1944, although its access roads were totally blocked by rubble. It even survived the great flood of 1966 which brought vast devastation to the city. The Arno is a peculiar river, ranging from a mere trickle to a torrent according to precipitation. The shops that line the sides of the bridge have been there since the beginning, although they were originally occupied by butchers and related trades. This was deemed unsuitable for a bridge linking two great palaces, so in 1593 they were forced out and replaced by the classier goldsmiths, a tradition that lives on today. Unknown to most visitors, there is an enclosed corridor, the Corridoio Vasariano, above the shops on the east side of the span, which passes through various buildings and over streets all the way from the Pitti Palace to the Uffizi. Lined with art, it may be visited on guided tours by prior arrangement with the Uffizi Gallery.

Cross the bridge, reserved for pedestrians only, and turn right to the **Uffizi Gallery** (Galleria degli Uffizi) (12), whose entrance is adja-

The Ponte Vecchio

cent to Piazza della Signoria. This U-shaped building was erected in the mid-16th century to house government offices, hence the name. Today, it is mostly occupied by one of the greatest art museums on earth, and by the thousands of tourists who come each day. You could easily spend a great deal of time here, but the museum is laid out so logically that a quick "get acquainted" visit is both easy and enjoyable. You can always come back for more.

Enter the museum and purchase your ticket. Before mounting the stairs, however, be warned that it is a long climb to the picture galleries. The elevator adjacent to the entrance will take you directly there. While waiting for the lift you can study the famous *Annunciation* by Botticelli on the wall opposite.

The art on display throughout the museum was largely collected by the Medici family during their centuries of rule. Once scattered among the various palaces, the best works gradually found their way to the top floor of the Uffizi, where they remain today, high above any possible flood damage from the unpredictable Arno. Fearing that the treasures might wind up in foreign hands, the last of the Medici bequeathed the whole lot to the city in 1737, on the condition that they never be removed.

The exhibition rooms of the gallery are conveniently numbered. Begin with room 2, just off the main corridor, where you will find the three altarpieces of the *Maestà* which illustrate the beginnings of Renaissance painting. The one created by Giotto in 1310, only a few decades after the other two, already shows a realistic sense of modeling and depth. Room 3 features Sienese Gothic painting—especially noteworthy is the *Annunciation* by Martini. Skip over room 4 and take a careful look at the *Adoration of the Magi* by Gentile da Fabriano, almost a final summation of the Gothic age, comparing it with the other paintings in rooms 5 and 6.

Passing through rooms 7 through 9—remember, this is a *quick* trip—stop at rooms 10–14, a combined gallery of captivating paintings by Botticelli, unquestionably the most famous treasures of the Uffizi. The greatest of these are his *Primavera* from 1480 and the *Birth of Venus*, completed around 1485. Examine the other Botticellis, then take a look at Hugo van der Goes' *Adoration of the Shepherds*, also known as the *Portinari Altarpiece*, in the same gallery.

Leonardo da Vinci is represented by some of his earliest works, especially the *Adoration of the Magi* and the *Annunciation*, both in room 15. Continue on through the other rooms, pausing to study works by Signorelli, Cranach, Dürer, Bellini, Holbein, Altdorfer, Correggio, and other greats. Upon reaching the south corridor, which has nice views across the Arno, turn right to the west wing of the Uffizi.

Florence possesses several great sculptures by its native son, Michelangelo, but very few paintings. One of these is the *Doni Tondo*, also known as the *Holy Family*, in room 25. Moving on to room 26, you will be treated to two magnificent works by Raphael, his *Madonna of the Goldfinch* and the powerful *Portrait of Leo X*. Skip to room 28, where Titian's *Venus of Urbino* will delight you with its sensuality. Next door, in room 29, the 16th-century Mannerist style is well represented by Parmigianino's *Madonna of the Long Neck*.

The rooms beyond, leading off the west corridor, feature works by Tintoretto, El Greco, Rubens, Van Dyck, Caravaggio, Rembrandt, Canaletto, Tiepolo, and others. At the far end there is a bar and restrooms, both of which you may be in need of by now. Leave the museum via the stairs leading off the west corridor. The Uffizi is open Tuesdays through Saturdays, from 9 a.m. to 7 p.m., and on Sundays and holidays from 9 a.m. to 1 p.m. It is closed on Mondays and certain holidays.

Return to **Piazza della Signoria**, the main square of Florence since the late 14th century. Near its center stands the **Neptune Fountain** of 1576, ringed by some elegant bronze figures. The very spot where Savonarola was hanged and burned in 1498 is marked by a plaque in the pavement, just steps from the fountain. The fine equestrian statue of Cosima I, to the left, was done in 1594 by Giambologna.

On the south side, adjacent to the west wing of the Uffizi, is the magnificent **Loggia dei Lanzi**, a 14th-century arcade once used for public ceremonies. It is now filled with statues. Take a look at Cellini's

The Palazzo Vecchio and the Loggia dei Lanzi

masterful *Perseus with the Head of Medusa*, in the left arch, completed in 1553 after a difficult casting described in his *Autobiography*. Another outstanding work is Giambologna's *Rape of the Sabines*, this under the right arch. Michelangelo's statue of *David*, in front of the Palazzo Vecchio, is of course a copy—the original was moved to the Accademia in 1873 to protect it from both the elements and bird droppings.

The massive, imposing **Palazzo Vecchio** (13), also known as the *Palazzo della Signoria*, has been Florence's city hall since the beginning of the 14th century—a function it still serves. At that time, members of the governing cabinet, known collectively as the *Signoria*, were virtually imprisoned here during their two-month terms of office— safely sequestered from any corrupting contact with outsiders, much as a jury is today. In 1540 some of the upper floors were remodeled to serve as the ducal palace of Cosima I. This only lasted until 1550, when the court moved to the larger Pitti Palace, but the **State Apartments** are still luxuriously decorated. You can visit them Mondays through Fridays, from 9 a.m. to 7 p.m., and on Sundays and some holidays from 8 a.m. to 1 p.m. They are closed on Saturdays and a few holidays. Whether you have time for this or not, at least step into the lovely **courtyard**, designed in 1453 by Michelozzo and graced with a splendid 16th-century fountain.

Now follow the map past the 16th-century **Mercato Nuovo** (14), an open loggia which was once the venue of Florence's merchants. Today the trade is mostly in crafts and souvenirs, but a short visit can be fun. Don't miss the statue of a bronze boar, known as "Il Porcellino." Continue up Via Calimala to **Piazza della Repubblica** (15), laid out in the late 19th century on the site of the ancient Roman forum. Although there is nothing to see here, the large outdoor cafés make it an excellent place to sit down for some welcome refreshment.

Via Roma leads back to the Baptistry (2), the Bell Tower, the Cathedral (3), and the Cathedral Museum, which can be seen now if you missed the opportunity earlier. Indefatigable tourists, or those heading back to the station (1), may want to make a stop at the **Church of Santa Maria Novella** (16). Begun in the mid-13th century by the Dominicans, this Gothic church with a Renaissance façade is one of the two or three most interesting in Florence. Step inside to admire Masaccio's *Holy Trinity* fresco in the third bay of the left aisle. The Gondi Chapel, to the left of the main choir, has a famous *Crucifix* by Brunelleschi, while the Strozzi Chapel in the left transept is noted for its altarpiece of *Christ with Saints Peter and Thomas* as well as its frescoes depicting the *Last Judgement*. The chancel behind the high altar is decorated with some fascinating **frescoes** in which Biblical stories are shown in a Renaissance context. There are several other excellent works in the right transept, after which you might want to visit the adjacent **cloisters** with their outstanding Old Testament frescoes, and the Spanish Chapel.

Although your whirlwind tour of Florence is now over, you have only scratched the surface of what this remarkable city has to offer. Perhaps, between your daytrips to the other great attractions of North Central Italy, you can find time to explore in greater depth with the aid of a specialized local guide book. The adventures have only begun!

Fiesole

Long before there was a Florence, there was a Fiesole. This ancient settlement, located high on a hill overlooking the City of the Renaissance, has for centuries been a favorite retreat for Florentines longing to escape the heat. You will probably be more attracted to its Etruscan and Roman ruins, splendid vistas, and delightfully unpretentious small-town atmosphere. Easy to get to, it makes a perfect half-day excursion and a wonderful place for dinner.

Although its origins are clouded in the mists of prehistory, Fiesole was an important Etruscan village as far back as the 6th or 7th century B.C. Later conquered by the Romans, it became known as *Faesulae* by the 1st century B.C. The subsequent development of Florence deprived it of economic activity, and it eventually took on a new role as a wealthy suburb, which it remains to this day.

Fiesole and its surroundings has a number of excellent inns, which combined with the frequent bus service makes it a good alternative base for those who would rather not stay in Florence. The name, incidentally, is pronounced *FYE zaw le.*

GETTING THERE:

Perched high atop a hill, Fiesole is of course not served by rail.

City bus #7 departs frequently from the plaza on the east side of Florence's main (S.M.N.) train station, and can also be boarded at Piazza del Duomo and Piazza San Marco en route. The ride to Fiesole, the end of the line, takes about 25 minutes. Purchase your ticket (and another for the return) at the booth by the train station bus stop in Florence, or from a nearby tobacco shop, and cancel it on board the bus. Return service operates until late evening.

By car, Fiesole is five miles northeast of downtown Florence. From Piazza della Libertà take Viale Don G. Minzoni, Viale Alessandro Volta, and Via San Domenico, then follow signs.

WHEN TO GO:

Fiesole can be visited in any season, and makes a fine half-day trip, preferably in the afternoon. This leaves your morning free for more sightseeing in Florence. Good weather is essential, both for the stunning view and for the archaeological excavations. The Bandini Museum is closed on Tuesdays.

FOOD AND DRINK:

There are a number of restaurants and cafés around the main square, Piazza Mino da Fiesole, and some truly exquisite establishments in the nearby countryside. This is a particularly fine place for an evening dinner. Some choices are:

Aurora (Piazza Mino da Fiesole 39) An inn with a nice view. X: Sun. eve., Mon. $$

Etrusca (Piazza Mino da Fiesole 2) Pizzeria with other Italian dishes, has outdoor tables on the piazza. X: Fri. $

Il Lordo (Piazza Mino da Fiesole 13) Family-run, with a quaint interior. X: Mon. $

Cappello di Paglio (Piazza Mino da Fiesole 40) A pizzeria with regular meals as well. X: Wed. $

Villa San Michele (Via di Doccia 4, less than one-half mile downhill southeast of the main square, leave by Via Verdi) World-famous, extremely luxurious, in a 14th-century villa. Phone (055) 594-51. X: Dec. through Feb. $$$

TOURIST INFORMATION:

The tourist information office (Azienda Autonoma), phone (055) 598-720, is located at Piazza Mino da Fiesole 37, near the bus stop. They offer an exceptionally useful free booklet in English.

SUGGESTED TOUR:

Begin your walk at the bus stop in **Piazza Mino da Fiesole** (1), built on the site of the ancient Roman forum and named for the noted 15th-century sculptor. This large tree-lined main square is ringed with several attractive outdoor cafés and restaurants. Stop at the tourist office, then stroll over to the **Archaeological Excavations** (Zona Archeologica), whose most prominent feature is the **Roman Theater** (2). Built around 80 B.C., it seats 2,500 people in an outdoor semi-circle and is still used for the annual Estate Fiesolana, a summer festival of theater, music, and films. For many hundreds of years the theater remained buried under earth, being excavated only in the late 19th century.

Continue around to the remains of a **temple** originally erected by the mysterious Etruscans around the 3rd century B.C. and modified by the Romans two centuries later. Next to this runs a section of the

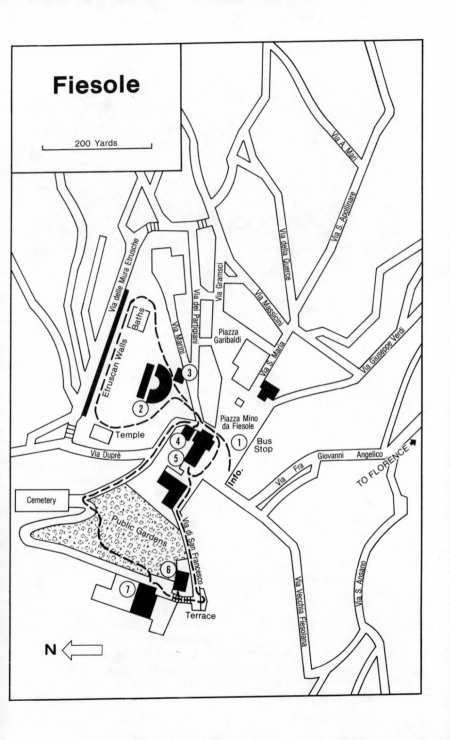

The Roman Theater

massive **Etruscan town walls**, which lead to the ruined **Roman Baths**.
Dating from the 1st century A.D. and later enlarged during the reign
of the emperor Hadrian, they have a remarkable set of three arches
dividing several pools. The more time you spend poking around this
area, the more fascinating discoveries you will come across—such as
a Roman gravestone and an Etruscan tomb.

The **Archaeological Museum** (3), next to the theater, has recently
been modernized and features a splended collection of prehistoric,
Etruscan, and Roman artifacts, most of which were found locally. Don't
miss the famous *Stele Fiesolana,* a marvelously carved Etruscan stone
from the 5th century B.C. The excavation site, including the museum,
is open every day, from 9 a.m. to 7 p.m., closing at 5 p.m. between
October and March. One entrance fee covers everything.

Step across the street to the **Bandini Museum** (4), a small but highly
interesting collection of medieval and Renaissance art displayed along
with other items. Note in particular the della Robbia terracottas, the
Annunciation by Taddeo Gaddi, and the *Triumphs of Petrarch,* at-
tributed to Jacopo del Sallaio. It is open from 10 a.m. to 1 p.m. and
3–7 p.m. (until 6 p.m. in winter), every day except Tuesdays.

Now amble back to the Piazza Mino and visit the **Cathedral** *(Duomo)*
(5). Dedicated to Saint Romolo, it was begun in 1028 and later enlarged, with a tall bell tower being added in the 13th century. Although quite plain on the outside, its interior is unusual and contains

some excellent works of art. Foremost of these is the glazed terracotta statue of St. Romolo above the main door, a 16th-century work by Giovanni della Robbia. The **Salutati Chapel**, upstairs and to the right of the high altar, is decorated with outstanding 15th-century carvings by Mino da Fiesole along with frescoes by Cosimo Rosselli. Other things to look for are the antique Roman capitals atop the supporting columns and the tempera *triptych* of the *Virgin in Majesty* above the high altar by Bicci di Lorenzo. Step down into the **crypt** before leaving. The Cathedral is usually closed between noon and 4 p.m.

From here it is a steep climb up Via di San Francesco, starting between the 17th-century seminary on the left and the Bishop's Palace, originally from the 11th century, on the right. At the top you will come to a **terrace** with an unbelievably beautiful view of Florence nestled in the valley below, well worth the effort of reaching.

A few steps beyond this is the **Church of Sant' Alessandro** (6), first built in the 6th century A.D. on the site of a Roman temple to Bacchus, which itself replaced an earlier Etruscan temple. Much modified and rebuilt over the centuries, the church is plain on the outside but intriguing within, and makes use of columns and Ionic capitals taken from ancient Roman buildings.

Continue up the steps to the delightful 14th-century **Monastery of San Francesco** (7), located at the top of the hill where once an ancient acropolis stood. Step inside the church, and take a look at its charming cloisters. A few steps lead down into the strange **Missionary Museum**, a weird assemblage of bits and pieces collected over the years, including an Egyptian mummy, Roman coins, and Chinese tourist souvenirs from the early part of this century—all jammed into a tiny space. It is open every day from 10 a.m. to noon and 3–6 p.m.

Now follow the map through some lovely public gardens and return the back way to Piazza Mino (1), where you can rest at a café before having dinner or returning to Florence.

Arezzo

Somewhat off the beaten tourist trail, the well-preserved medieval town of Arezzo has its roots in a long-forgotten Etruscan past, when it was one of the 12 major centers of that mysterious civilization. It remained prosperous under Roman rule and later became a free republic, finally submitting to Florence in the late 14th century.

Long noted as a crafts center, especially in metalworking and pottery, Arezzo was the birthplace of some of Italy's most creative minds. These included Maecenas, a minister of the Roman emperor Augustus and the patron of Virgil and Horace; Guido d'Arezzo, who invented our musical scale in the 11th century; the 14th-century poet Petrarch; Pietro Aretino, the outspoken satirist of the late Renaissance; and Giorgio Vasari, the 16th-century painter, architect, and art historian. While most of their achievements occurred elsewhere, the town they left behind is still haunted with their spirit, its medieval aspect surprisingly intact.

GETTING THERE:

Trains leave Florence's main station frequently for the one-hour run to Arezzo, a major stop on the way to Rome. Return service operates until late evening.

By car, take the superb *Autostrada del Sole* (A-1) direct to the Arezzo exit, then follow signs into town. It is 50 miles from Florence to Arezzo.

WHEN TO GO:

Arezzo may be enjoyed at anytime, but some sights are closed on Mondays.

FOOD AND DRINK:

Some choice restaurants, more or less in the order that you will pass or come close to them, are:

Buca di San Francesco (Piazza San Francesco 1) A longtime favorite, with a colorful 14th-century ambiance. X: Mon. eve., Tues., July. $$

Le Tastevin (Via de Cenci 9, 2 blocks south of San Francesco church) Contemporary and traditional cuisine. X: Mon. $$

Spiedo d'Oro (Via Crispi 12, near the amphitheater) Tuscan specialties in a trattoria. X: Thurs., July. $

Othello (Piazza Risorgimento 16, near the tourist office) A modern place for inventive food. X: Tues. $

TOURIST INFORMATION:

The provincial tourist office (EPT), phone (0575) 239-52, is located on the second floor at Piazza Risorgimento 116, three blocks northeast of the station.

SUGGESTED TOUR:

Leave the **train station** (1) and follow the map past the tourist office to the **Archaeological Museum** (2), which occupies a former 16th-century convent built into the scanty remains of a 2nd-century **Roman Amphitheater**. There is a wonderful collection of artifacts from the Stone and Bronze Ages as well as the Etruscan and Roman periods. Some of the highlights include a group of coralline **vases** from between 100 B.C. and 100 A.D. in room VII; many ancient coins; and, on the upper floor, the marvelous Etruscan **bronze figures** dating as far back as the 7th century B.C. The museum is open from 9 a.m. to 2 p.m., Tuesdays through Saturdays, and from 9 a.m. to 1 p.m. on Sundays and holidays. It is closed on Mondays.

Now continue on, threading your way through the colorful market place at Pizza Sant' Agostino, to the 14th-century **Church of San Francesco** (3), dedicated to St. Francis of Assisi. The most famous attraction in Arezzo, it contains in its choir the fabulous 15th-century *Legend of the True Cross* by Piero della Francesca, possibly the greatest **cycle of frescoes** to have come out of the Renaissance. Among the scenes depicted are the *Death of Adam,* the *Queen of Sheba Received by Solomon, Constantine's Dream,* the *Torture of Judas,* and *Heraclius Restores the Cross to Jerusalem.* If possible, bring a pair of binoculars for a close-up examination. You may want to return here in the late afternoon, when the light is better. The church is closed between noon and 2 p.m.

Via Cavour leads to the **Museum of Medieval and Modern Art** (4) in the Palazzo Bruni-Ciocchi on Via San Lorentino. The entire development of art in Arezzo, from the Middle Ages to modern times, is well displayed in this lovely 15th-century palace. Don't miss the remarkable collection of Renaissance **ceramics** in rooms VI through VIII.

The Church of San Domenico

Visits may be made between 9 a.m. and 7 p.m., Mondays through Saturdays, and from 9 a.m. to 1:30 p.m. on Sundays and holidays.

The **House of Vasari** (5), just a short stroll up Via XX Settembre, was acquired by the great painter, architect, and art historian Giorgio Vasari in 1540. It is exceptionally well decorated and certainly merits a visit, which may be made between 9 a.m. and 7 p.m., Mondays through Saturdays, and from 9 a.m. to 1 p.m. on Sundays and holidays.

Now follow the map to the rather austere 13th-century **Church of San Domenico** (6), noted for its *Crucifix* over the high altar, an early work by Cimabue. There are also some splendid 14th- and 15th-century fragmentary frescoes by local painters. The church is closed between noon and 3:30 p.m.

Continue on to the **Cathedral** *(Duomo)* (7), begun in the 13th century but not completed until the early 20th. Among the art works on view is a fresco of *St. Mary Magdalen* by Piero della Francesca, near the far end of the north aisle. Immediately left of this stands the magnificent 14th-century **tomb** of Bishop Guido Tarlati, thought to have been designed by Giotto. Step into the large **Chapel of the Madonna**, off the north aisle, for a look at some admirable 15th-century terracottas by Andrea della Robbia and his school. The Cathedral is closed between noon and 3:30 p.m.

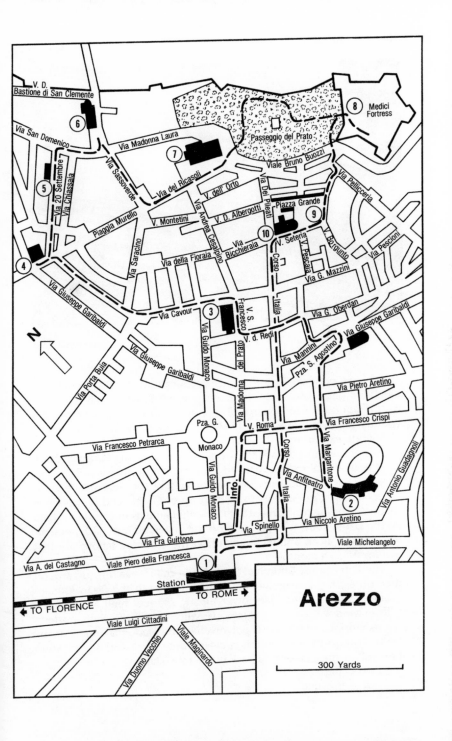

V. D.
Bastione di San Clemente

⑥

Via San Domenico

Via Madonna Laura

⑦

Passeggio del Prato

⑧ Medici
Fortress

Via 20 Settembre

⑤

Via Chiassaia

Via Sassoverde

Via del Ricasoli

Via dell' Orto

Viale Bruno Buozzi

Via Pellicceria

Piaggia Murello

V. Montetini

Via Andrea Cesalpino

V. D. Albergotti

Via Dei Pileati

Piazza Grande
⑨

Via Borgunto

Via Pescioni

④

Via della Fioraia

Via Bicchieraia

⑩

N. Seteria

V. Pescaia

Corso Italia

Via G. Mazzini

Via Giuseppe Garibaldi

Via Cavour

Via Guido Monaco

V. S. Francesco

V. d. Redi

③

Via G. Oberdan

Via Porta Buia

Via Giuseppe Garibaldi

Via Madonna del Prato

Via Mannini

Pza. S. Agostino

Via Giuseppe Garibaldi

N

Via Pietro Aretino

Pza. G.
Monaco

V. Roma

Via Francesco Crispi

Via Francesco Petrarca

Via Margaritone

Via Antonio Guadagnoli

Corso Italia

Via Anfiteatro

②

Info.

Via Guido Monaco

Via Spinello

Via Niccolo Aretino

Viale Michelangelo

Via Fra Guittone

Via A. del Castagno

Viale Piero della Francesca

①

Station

◀ TO FLORENCE

TO ROME ▶

Arezzo

Viale Luigi Cittadini

Via Duomo Vecchio

Viale Maginardo

300 Yards

The Piazza Grande

You are now close to the town fortifications. Stroll through the delightful park, known as the Passeggio del Prato, which is graced with a monument to Petrarch. There are extensive views across the countryside from here. The old **Medici Fortress** (8), or what's left of it, is worth exploring.

It is only a short distance downhill to the charming **Piazza Grande** (9), the medieval main square of Arezzo. The northeast side is bordered by Vasari's impressive loggia, the west by the elegant Palazzetto della Fraternità dei Laici with its mixture of Gothic and Renaissance styles. A jousting tournament with mounted knights in costume is held on the last Sunday in August and on the first Sunday of each September, as well as an antiques market on the Saturday before the first Sunday of each month.

The 12th-century **Church of Santa Maria della Pieve** (10), just around the corner, has a magnificently ornate façade in the Pisan Romanesque style. Its **campanile tower**, nearly 200 feet high and pierced with 40 windows, is the most famous symbol of Arezzo. Step inside to see its glorious altarpiece, a polyptych of the *Madonna and Saints* by Pietro Lorenzetti. The church is closed between 1 and 3 p.m. From here follow the Corso Italia back to the train station.

San Gimignano

Perched high atop a hill and completely surrounded by its ancient walls, the small town of San Gimignano is an incredibly well-preserved holdover from the Middle Ages. It is famous throughout the world for the 13 surviving medieval towers which give its skyline the startling appearance of a miniature Manhattan. There were once more than 70 of these, built around the 12th and 13th centuries both as status symbols and for family defense during those violent times.

The Etruscans probably had a settlement on this site, but there are no actual references to San Gimignano prior to the Middle Ages. Its location, overlooking fertile farmland and near the old road linking Rome with the north, brought a measure of prosperity until, unable to defend itself, it fell under the rule of Florence in 1353. A backwater ever since, it has remained practically unchanged to this day.

Located seven miles from the nearest rail station or highway, San Gimignano is not quite as easy to reach as most of the other daytrip destinations, but its allure is so extraordinary that a little extra effort is well worthwhile. Its name, by the way, is pronounced *Sahn Gee-meen-YAHN-oh*.

GETTING THERE:

Trains, bound for Siena, depart Florence's main station several times in the morning. Some of these require a change at Empoli. Get off the train at Poggibonsi, about 70 minutes from Florence, and continue by local TRA-IN bus to San Gimignano's Porta San Giovanni stop, a 20-minute ride. Bus tickets are sold at the newsstand in the Poggibonsi station, and canceled on board. You may have a little wait as there is no coordination of the train and bus schedules. Return service operates until mid-evening, but check the posted schedules in San Gimignano's Piazza del Duomo to be certain.

Buses depart several times in the morning from the SITA terminal near the west side of Florence's main train station. Some of these go direct to San Gimignano while others require a change at Poggibonsi, as above. Tickets must be purchased before boarding the bus and canceled when on board. Buy a return ticket at the same time. The average run is a bit over one hour, considerably faster than the train/bus combination above. Check the return schedules as above.

By car, San Gimignano is 34 miles from Florence. Take the *Superstrada del Palio* in the direction of Siena and get off at the Poggibonsi exit. From there it is seven miles on local roads to San Gimignano. Park in the lot at Porta San Giovanni.

WHEN TO GO:

San Gimignano may be visited at any time, but avoid coming on a Monday between October and March, when some major sights are closed. Clear weather is essential for the glorious views.

FOOD AND DRINK:

Being an important tourist attraction, the town has quite a few restaurants and cafés. Some excellent choices are:

Le Terrazze (Piazza della Cisterna 23) A country-inn atmosphere with a view, in the La Cisterna hotel. X: Tues., Wed. lunch, Winter. $$$

Bel Soggiorno (Via San Giovanni 91, near Porta San Giovanni) A medieval ambiance with a view of the town. X: Mon. $$

La Griglia (Via San Matteo 34, near Piazza del Duomo) Grilled foods in a nice atmosphere. X: Thurs., Jan., Feb. $$

La Stella (Via San Matteo 75, on the way to Porta San Matteo) Home grown foods. X: Wed. $

Taverna Paradiso (Via San Giovanni 6, just off Piazza della Cisterna) Pizza and a range of other foods. X: Mon. $

A favorite dessert in these parts is *Panforte,* a dense concoction of nuts, candied fruits, and honey. The local wine is, of course, Chianti. The *Classico* variety is usually considered the best. Another interesting wine, this one a white, is *Vernaccia di San Gimignano.*

TOURIST INFORMATION:

The tourist office, phone (0577) 94-00-08, is on Piazza del Duomo. You can confirm the return schedules there.

SUGGESTED TOUR:

Begin your walk at the **Porta San Giovanni** (1), a magnificent town gate erected in 1262. It is right next to the bus stop and the parking lot. Before entering, take a look at the impressive guard room perched above the gate.

Via San Giovanni is a colorful old street lined with medieval buildings, a taste of things to come. Follow it past the **Becci Arch**, an opening in the original 11th-century inner walls which leads to the **Piazza della Cisterna** (2). Named for the beautiful 13-century fountain in its center, this delightful square is paved with bricks in a herringbone pattern. It is said that if you walk around the fountain you will surely

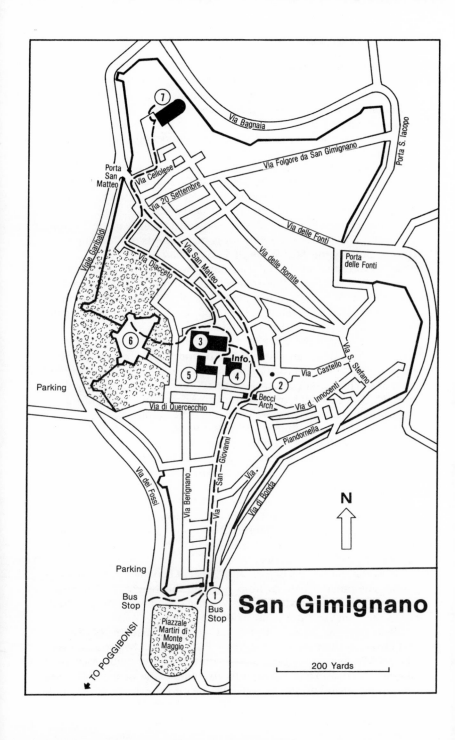

San Gimignano

7

Via Bagnaia

Porta S. Iacopo

Via Folgore da San Gimignano

Porta San Matteo

Via Cellolese

Via 20 Settembre

Via delle Fonti

Via San Matteo

Via Diacceto

Via delle Romite

Porta delle Fonti

Viale Garibaldi

6

3

Info.

5

4

2

Via S. Stefano

Via Castello

Becci Arch

Via d. Innocenti

Via di Quercecchio

Piandornella

Parking

Via del Fossi

Via Berignano

Via San Giovanni

Via .

Via di Bonda

N

Parking

Bus Stop

1

Bus Stop

Piazzale Martiri di Monte Maggio

TO POGGIBONSI

200 Yards

return to San Gimignano, a very likely prophecy. The famous **towers** rise all around you, a legacy of times when height meant safety. Many Italian towns were once graced with these fascinating structures, but most of them were torn down as the cities developed, a progress which happily bypassed sleepy old San Gimignano. Take a look at the Palazzo Tortoli at number 7, an elegant 14th-century house in the Sienese manner.

Now stroll into the adjacent Piazza del Duomo, whose name is somewhat of a misnomer. The **Collegiate Church of Santa Maria Assunta** *(Collegiata)* (3), dominating the west side, is often referred to as the Cathedral *(Duomo)* although it never was one. Begun in the 13th century, the church has been enlarged and greatly modified over the years. The Romanesque interior is noted for its outstanding frescoes, especially the *Martyrdom of St. Sebastian* by Benozzo Gozzoli, a mid-15th century work on the inside of the entrance wall flanked by two wooden statues of the *Annunciation*. Above this there is a fine *Last Judgement* by Taddeo di Bartolo. Covering the length of the right aisle are **frescoes** depicting scenes from the New Testament, while the left aisle tells stories from the Old Testament.

Be sure to visit the **Chapel of Saint Fina** at the end of the right aisle. Dedicated to San Gimignano's patron saint, a young girl who died in 1253 at the age of 15 after years of suffering, it is widely regarded as a high point of Renaissance art. An admission is charged for this, which is also valid for the Torre Grossa and the town's museums. The church is closed between 12:30 p.m. and 3 p.m.

To the left of the church stands the **People's Palace** *(Palazzo de Popolo)* (4), which has been the Town Hall since the 13th century. It has the highest tower in town, the **Torre Grossa** *(Fat Tower)*, which you can climb for a truly enchanting panorama. On the way up stop at the **Council Chamber** *(Sala del Consiglio)*, where Dante argued the case for a Tuscan alliance in 1300. In the same room there is a vast fresco of the *Maestà* by Lippo Memmi, painted in 1317. Continue up to the **Municipal Museum** *(Museo Civico)* on the second floor, where you will see a fine collection of Sienese and Florentine paintings from the 13th to the 15th centuries.

Now the climb really begins, all 177 feet of it. A medieval ordinance forbid any other structures from reaching this height, and as this is the only tower open to the public, you can put all your energy into it. The view from the top is really worth it.

Returning to earth, stroll over to the **Museum of Sacred Art/Etruscan Museum** (5) in the lovely Piazza Pecori. Religious art from the Middle Ages is featured along with a small but quite fascinating display of Etruscan and Roman artifacts found in the vicinity. All of the museums, including the People's Palace and the Torre Grossa, are

View from the Rocca di Montestaffoli

open daily between April and September, from 9:30 a.m. to 12:30 p.m. and 3–6 p.m. From October through March they are open every day except on Mondays and major holidays, from 9:30 a.m. to 12:30 p.m. and 2:30–5:30 p.m. There is a joint ticket for all of them, including the Chapel of Saint Fina.

Now follow the map to the ruined **Fortress of La Rocca** (6), built by the Florentines in 1353 but later demolished. It is now a public park, the perfect spot for a picnic, and offers the most unforgettable view of San Gimignano's skyline.

Via Diacceto leads, down steps, from the north side of the church to the Porta San Matteo, another main gateway into the town erected in 1262. Just beyond this is the **Church of Saint Augustine** *(Sant' Agostino)* (7), a rather plain 13th-century structure containing some remarkable art. Among the most noted works here are the frescoes in the choir depicting the *Life of Saint Augustine*, a lively cycle of 15th-century masterpieces by Benozzo Gozzoli. While there, don't miss the lovely **cloisters** to the left of the church, which closes between noon and 3 p.m.

Return on Via San Matteo to the Piazza della Cisterna, where you can sit down at an outdoor café for some well-earned refreshment before heading back to Florence.

Siena

While Florence is the embodiment of the Renaissance, its ancient rival is resolutely rooted in the Middle Ages. One of the great sights of Italy, Siena is built atop the convergence of three clay hills whose soil yields the pigment *Burnt Sienna*. A complete circuit of medieval walls still encloses the perfectly preserved buildings and narrow, twisting streets which thread their way to the magnificent Piazza del Campo, one of the very finest public squares in the world.

Siena's origins go back to the time of the Etruscans, later being established as a Roman military colony, *Saena Julia,* under the emperor Augustus. It was not until the 12th century that the town became a free republic and assumed a position of importance rivaling that of Florence. The period preceding the mid-14th century saw great prosperity and an unprecedented building boom. Then, in 1348, the plague struck. It was again decimated in 1555 by the Spaniards and became a part of Tuscany, an arrangement which lasted until the unification of Italy in the 19th century.

Unlike the other great tourist centers of Italy, Siena has largely insulated itself from a changing world, remaining inward-looking, reserved, and just a little bit aloof. Its speech is the purest, most musical Italian spoken anywhere; its art and architecture a superlative example of unspoiled Gothic.

Siena is divided into 17 wards, or *Contrade,* to which individual citizens devote an almost fanatical allegiance. Twice every year, on July 2nd and August 16th, these districts compete in a spectacular medieval horse race called the *Palio,* an event that draws huge crowds from all over the globe. No mere tourist attraction, this is the real thing—as it has been for many centuries.

Looking at a map, you may be tempted to combine a visit to Siena with one to nearby San Gimignano. That would be a mistake, as Siena requires every bit of a full day to sample its treasures.

GETTING THERE:

Trains depart Florence's main station several times in the morning for the 1½-hour ride to Siena. Some of these require a change at Empoli, others are direct. Not all carry first-class cars, but on such a minor line this is unimportant. Return service operates until mid-evening.

Buses are considerably faster than the train on this route. Departures, almost hourly, are from Florence's SITA terminal near the west side of the main train station. The *Rapida* buses take about one hour, the locals a bit longer. Purchase tickets before boarding and cancel them on board. Return buses leave from Siena's Piazza San Domenico (11) until mid-evening.

By car, Siena is 42 miles south of Florence by way of the *Superstrada del Palio.* Park near Piazza Gramsci (2) as driving is forbidden in the historical center.

WHEN TO GO:

Siena is truly a town for all seasons. Its main sights are open for unusually long hours every day of the week, except for the Palazzo Pubblico which closes on Sunday afternoons and a few holidays. The Pinacoteca Nazionale is also closed on Mondays. Mass insanity rules during the *Palio* races, held every year on July 2nd and August 16th.

FOOD AND DRINK:

Chianti is, naturally, the local wine, of which the *Classico* variety is considered to be the best. Oenophiles will enjoy a visit to the Enoteca Italica (12), where Italy's best vintages may be sampled. Siena is famous for its *Panforte,* a sinfully rich concoction of nuts, candied fruits, and honey. Being a major tourist center, the town is well endowed with restaurants and cafés in all price ranges. Some outstanding choices, in the sequence that you will pass or come close to them along the walking route, are:

Guido (Vicolo Pettinaio 7, between Piazza Tolomei and Piazza del Campo) Dining in a medieval atmosphere. X: Wed. $$

Al Mangia (Piazza del Campo 42) Overlooking one of Europe's most beautiful squares, with outdoor tables. X: Mon., Feb. $$

Il Campo (Piazza del Campo 50) Opens onto the main square with outdoor tables available. X: Tues. $$

Nello-La Taverna (Via del Porrione 28, just off the northeast corner of Piazza del Campo) A traditional old tavern. X: Sun. eve., Mon. $$

Mariotti da Mugolone (Via dei Pellegrini 8, between Piazza del Campo and the rear of the Cathedral) A popular restaurant in the Old Town. X: Thurs. $$

Al Marsili (Via del Castoro 3, between the Palazzo Chigi-Sara-cini and the Cathedral) Famous for pasta and steak. X: Mon. $$

Le Logge (Via del Porrione 33, a block east of the Torre del Mangia) Rustic Tuscan cuisine. X: Sun. $$

Grotta Santa Caterina (Via della Galluzza 26, near the house of St. Catherine) A rustic decor, popular with locals. X: Mon. $$

TOURIST INFORMATION:

The local tourist office, phone (0577) 28-05-51, is located at Piazza del Campo 56.

SUGGESTED TOUR:

The **train station** (1) is down in the valley and off the map. Buy a bus ticket in the station and board the bus to town, canceling the ticket on board. Disembark at **Piazza Gramsci** (2). Those coming by bus from Florence will get off at Piazza San Domenico (11), just a short stroll away.

Continue along Via Pianigiani to Piazza Salimbeni. Here the flavor of the city begins in earnest. The building at the center of the piazza, the Gothic-styled **Salimbeni Palace**, dates from the 14th century and is flanked by two equally impressive palaces from the 15th and 16th centuries. All three are occupied by a bank which has been here since 1624. Via Banchi di Sopra, the main street of Siena, now leads to Piazza Tolomei and its marvelous **Palazzo Tolomei**. Built in 1205 and altered in 1267, this elegant Gothic structure is the oldest private mansion in town. Keep walking straight ahead until you come to the **Loggia della Mercanzia**, a 15th-century open arcade which once sheltered a commercial tribunal.

You are now just steps from one of Europe's most compelling sights, the **Piazza del Campo** (3). Popularly known as *Il Campo*, this magnificent public square in the shape of a sloping shell is the very hub of Siena. It is here that the twice-yearly *Palio* race is held, and here that citizens have gathered since medieval times. At its highest point the **Fountain of Joy** *(Fonte Gaia)* splashes merrily while locals and tourists alike refresh themselves at the many outdoor cafés. The open area, bordered by exquisite buildings, is divided by paving stones into nine segments representing the Council of Nine, merchants who governed Siena in the 13th and 14th centuries.

Dominating the scene is the 334-foot-high **Torre del Mangia**, built in the 14th century, and the adjoining Palazzo Pubblico (4), begun in 1297. At the base of the tower stands the Renaissance arches of the **Cappella di Piazza**, a chapel commemorating the end of the plague

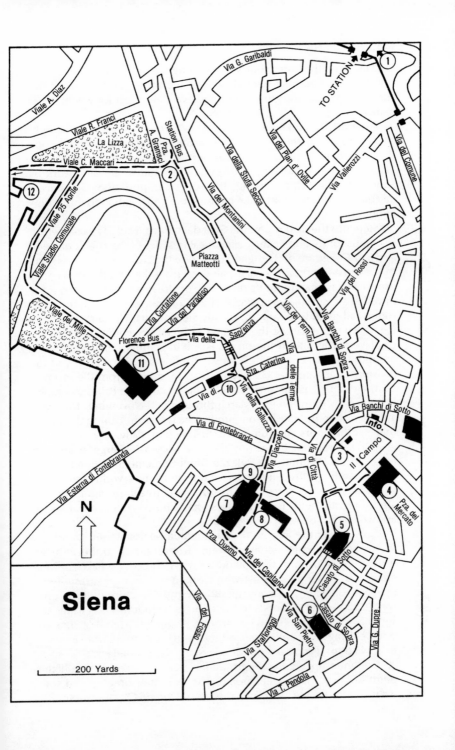

in 1348. From the inner courtyard to its right *(Cortile del Podestà)* you can get a wonderfully framed view of the tower, and a look at the statue of Mangia, the gluttonous medieval bell-ringer for whom it was named.

Enter the Palazzo Pubblico *(Town Hall)* from a doorway to the right and climb up to the first floor. The **Sala del Mappamondo** *(Globe Room)*, where the city council once met, has among its treasures a *Maestà* fresco of the Virgin surrounded by saints, an early work by Simone Martini. Opposite this, the equestrian portrait of *Guidoriccio da Fogliano* was thought to be by the same artist, although this is now in doubt.

Step into the next room, the **Sala della Pace** *(Hall of Peace)*, which is famous for its 14th-century allegorical frescoes of the *Effects of Good and Bad Government*. Designed to inspire the civic leaders, this is one of the most important secular paintings from the Middle Ages and is especially fascinating for its rendering of street scenes in Siena, many of which are surprisingly recognizable. Continue on through the other rooms, all filled with superb, mostly Sienese, art. Upstairs, there is a loggia where pieces of the original 15th-century Fountain of Joy are displayed. The one in the piazza is a 19th-century copy. Wandering around, you will come to a doorway leading to the tower. If you can possibly negotiate the 332 steps, do so—the **view** from the top presents a dramatic panorama of the medieval city. The Palazzo complex is open daily between mid-March through mid-November, from 9:30 a.m. to 7:45 p.m., closing on Sundays at 1:30 p.m. During the rest of the year the hours are from 9 a.m. to 1:45 p.m. daily.

Leave the square by the tiny alleyway, Vicolo del Bargello, and turn left onto Via Di Città. The **Palazzo Chigi-Saracini** (5) at number 89 is an outstanding 14th-century palace now housing a world-famous musical academy. Step into its courtyard, where free impromptu concerts are frequently held. The school also has a noted collection of Tuscan art, which may be seen on request.

Now follow the map to the **Pinacoteca Nazionale** (6), an art museum specializing in Sienese painting from the 12th to the 16th centuries. It is housed in the splendid early-15th-century Palazzo Buonsignori. Virtually every artist who worked in Siena is represented in the vast collection, all conveniently arranged in chronological order so you can better understand the stylistic evolution. Visits to the museum may be made Tuesdays through Saturdays, from 8:30 a.m. to 7 p.m. (closing at 2 p.m. in mid-winter), and on Sundays from 8:30 a.m. to 12:45 p.m. It is closed on Mondays and some holidays.

Continue up Via San Pietro and Via del Capitano to the highest point in town, Piazza del Duomo. The extremely ornate—and somewhat fussy—façade of the **Cathedral** *(Duomo)* (7) overwhelms this

Looking into the Piazza del Campo

square with its intricate designs. Although begun in the Romanesque style in 1196, it evolved into Tuscan Gothic during the two centuries of its construction, and remains perhaps the best example of that genre.

When a larger cathedral was started in rival Florence, the Sienese, not to be outdone, decided to use the present building as the transept of a truly enormous church. The plague of 1348, however, soon put an end to that scheme and the work was never resumed. You can see the remains of the huge, unbuilt nave in the small piazza on the right by the bell tower.

Inside, the cathedral is every bit as interesting as its exterior promises. The **floor** is unique, illustrating Biblical and other scenes with inlaid marble executed by more than 40 leading artists between the mid-14th and mid-16th centuries. Some of the better sections are usually covered for protection, but are generally on view in late summer. The magnificently carved octagonal marble **pulpit**, borne on nine columns, was created in the late 13th century by Nicola Pisano and his pupils.

Be sure to visit the **Libreria Piccolomini**, just off the left aisle. One of the most beautifully decorated rooms in Italy, it is renowned for its ten early-16th-century frescoes depicting the life of Pope Pius II. The famous statue of the *Three Graces,* in the center of the room, is a 3rd-century Roman copy of a Greek original.

Siena's Cathedral is unusual in that it does not close during the noon meal period during the summer.

Now stroll over to the **Museo dell' Opera del Duomo** *(Cathedral Museum)* (8), housed in what remains of the 14th-century attempt to add a gigantic nave to the cathedral. Nearly all of the works on display here come from the cathedral and represent an enormous treasury of religious art. Don't miss the original carvings from the cathedral façade (most of the present ones are copies), done in the late 13th century by Giovanni Pisano—easily among the best Gothic statuary in Italy. On the upper floors are the noted early-14th-century *Maestà* by Duccio, which marked a new era in Sienese painting, and the *Blessed Agostino with Four of his Miracles* by Simone Martini. You can climb out on the roof for excellent views. The museum is open daily from 9 a.m. to 7:30 p.m., closing in winter at 1:30 p.m.

The steps at the rear of the cathedral lead to the **Baptistry** *(Battistero)* (9), noted for its remarkable 15th-century baptismal font designed by Jacopo della Quercia. Another work to look for is Donatello's dramatic *Feast of Herod,* one of the earliest uses of perspective. The baptistry is dark, so make sure you have coins for the light switches. It is open every day from 9 a.m. to 1 p.m. and 3–6 p.m.

Continue along Via di Diacceto and turn left into **Via della Galluzza**, one of the most picturesque streets in Siena. Here the Middle

Ages come alive in a dark, narrow and mysterious setting, with many arches connecting the ancient buildings.

This leads to the **Sanctuary of St. Catherine** *(Santuario Caterini-ano)* (10), a place of pilgrimage since 1464. St. Catherine of Siena, a patron saint of Italy, was born here in 1347 and took the veil at the age of eight. Her life and works are celebrated in this small complex of buildings, open daily from 9 a.m. to 12:30 p.m. and 3–6 p.m.

Now follow the map to the **Church of San Domenico** (11), a rather austere brick structure begun in the 13th century. This is where St. Catherine worshipped, and several of the works inside are devoted to her. Don't miss the **Cappella di Santa Caterina**, a chapel on the right side of the nave with two masterpieces by Sodoma and a reliquary containing the head of the saint. There is a nice view of Siena from the terrace beyond the apse.

A delightful way to end your stay in Siena is to visit the **Enoteca Italica Permanente**, a national wine museum and tasting cellar in the 16th-century **Medici Fortress of Santa Barbara** (12). You can sample the best of Italian vintages by the glass here, either on an outdoor terrace or in the atmospheric old dungeons. The wines flow every day from 3 p.m. until midnight.

A short walk along Viale Cesare Maccari brings you to Piazza Gramsci, where you can get a local bus to the train station. Those going all the way to Florence by bus should return to Piazza San Domenico (11).

Pisa

Millions of tourists come to Pisa to see the Leaning Tower, have their pictures taken propping it up, buy some tacky souvenirs—and then leave. What a pity! This proud old city, once among the greatest in Europe, has much more to offer than that. The better part of a day could be spent enjoying its glorious medieval buildings and fine museums.

Pisa was probably founded by the Greeks around the 7th or 6th century B.C. Later occupied by the Etruscans, it became a Roman colony in 180 B.C. and by the year 1000 had evolved into a major trading and maritime power. Its Golden Age was during the 12th and 13th centuries. Badly defeated by Genoa in 1284, it neglected its harbor, which slowly silted up and now lies some six miles to the west. World War II brought terrible devastation, followed by a lackluster rebuilding program. Much of the city is rather dull, but with its university it remains a lively intellectual center and, fortunately for us, a treasury of the surviving monuments from the Middle Ages.

Pisa could be used as an alternative base for daytrips in North Central Italy as it has frequent trains to Lucca and Florence. Visits to San Gimignano and Siena can be made by changing trains at Empoli. The Galileo Galilei Airport, just outside Pisa (connected by an excellent rail service which continues on to Florence), has convenient flights to London, Paris, and Frankfurt—a real boon to travelers who wish to bypass Rome or Milan.

This trip could be combined in the same day with one to Lucca, the subject of the next chapter, by cutting the walking tour short. If you decide on this option, it is probably best to do Lucca first since some of its sights close early. There is very good train service between the two towns.

GETTING THERE:

Trains depart Florence's main station fairly frequently for the 55-minute ride to Pisa Centrale. Most of these are second class only, but the modern cars are usually uncrowded. Return service operates until late evening.

146

By car, Pisa is 57 miles from Florence via the A-11 Autostrada to Lucca followed by the S-12 road into Pisa. There is a shorter but slower route following the S-67 all the way, a distance of 52 miles. Parking is available near the train station.

WHEN TO GO:

Pisa may be visited at any time, although fine weather makes the view from the tower much more exciting. The National Museum of San Matteo is closed on Mondays.

FOOD AND DRINK:

The area adjacent to the Learning Tower is, of course, infested with tourist restaurants. You will do much better to dine elsewhere. Some reliable choices, in walking tour sequence, are:

Spartaco (Piazza Vittorio Emanuele 22, 2 blocks north of the station) A large trattoria with outdoor tables. X: Sun. $$

Emilio (Via Roma 28, near the river, south of the Cathedral) An elegant dining room with traditional Italian cuisine. X: Mon. $$

Trattoria da Bruno (Via Luigi Bianchi 12, 4 blocks northeast of the Leaning Tower) An old favorite with hearty local dishes. X: Mon. eve., Tues., Aug. $$

Al Castelletto (Piazza San Felice 12, 2 blocks southeast of Pza. dei cavalieri) Excellent pizza and simple Italian dishes. X: Sun. $

Sergio (Lungarno Pacinotti 1, on the river) Pisa's leading restaurant, reservations needed, phone (050) 48-245. X: Sun.. Mon. lunch, Jan., July. $$$

TOURIST INFORMATION:

The provincial tourist office, phone (050) 56-04-64, is located on Piazza del Duomo, next to the Leaning Tower. There is also an office by the train station.

SUGGESTED TOUR:

Leave the **train station** (1) and follow the map to the Arno River. The small, lovely **Church of Santa Maria della Spina** (2), clinging to the quay, represents the last great triumph of the Pisan Gothic style. Named for a thorn *(spina)* believed to be from Christ's crown, this early-14th-century structure was raised several feet in 1871 to prevent further flood damage. Its richly decorated interior, well worth a visit, can usually be seen between 8 a.m. and noon and 3:30–7 p.m.

Cross the bridge and continue along Via Roma to the world-famous **Field of Miracles** *(Campo dei Miracoli)*, surely one of the most stunning architectural groups to be found anywhere. More prosaically known as Piazza del Duomo, the large open area attracts thousands of tourists a day. Join them and amble over to the **Leaning Tower** *(Torre Pendente)* (3). Begun in 1174, this *campanile*, or bell tower, was cursed from the start. It began leaning to one side before the third floor was even completed, and continued to tilt as successive architects attempted corrections, all of which resulted in a tower that not only leans, but is also twisted. Completed around 1350, it still continues to sink—ever so slightly—despite the tons of concrete injected into its base. Tradition holds that native-son Galileo Galilei used it in the late 16th century in his experiments on the effect of gravity.

While it hasn't toppled over yet (keep your fingers crossed!), the tower is now considered unsafe and has been closed to visitors until a solution is found. It's still a great sight, though.

Now stroll over to the **Cathedral** *(Duomo)* (4), begun in 1063 and regarded as one of the most important Romanesque buildings in Italy. Its style was frequently emulated by other churches throughout Tuscany. You can usually enter through the doorway closest to the Leaning Tower, a portal graced with marvelous **bronze doors** cast around 1180 and depicting scenes from the life of Christ.

Step inside and take a look at the **Tomb of Emperor Henry VII** in the south transept, a 14th-century masterpiece by Tino di Camaino. The cathedral is filled with magnificent works of art, but perhaps its greatest treasure is the **pulpit** in the nave, near the crossing. Carved in the early 14th century by Giovanni Pisano, it is richly decorated with scenes from the New Testament. Close to this hangs the famous **bronze lamp** which, according to legend, stimulated Galileo in his discovery of the pendulum. Some doubt has been cast on its true age, but it is entirely possible that an earlier lamp was the actual source of inspiration. The cathedral is open daily from 7:45 a.m. to 1 p.m. and 3–7 p.m., closing earlier in winter. Visits are restricted during services.

Upon leaving the cathedral, be sure to take a careful look at its wonderfully detailed **west façade**, rich in hidden surprises. The early-17th-century bronze doors are by the school of Giambologna. Just a few steps away is the **Baptistry** *(Battistero)* (5), a rather ornate circular marble structure from the 12th and 13th centuries, with a remarkable dome from the 14th topped by a statue of St. John the Baptist. Inside, its most famous feature is the superb hexagonal **pulpit**—the earliest known work by Nicola Pisano—with its five panels in bold relief of the Nativity, Adoration of the Magi, Presentation, Crucifixion, and Last Judgement, all resting on pillars depicting the Virtues. Also note the 13th-century marble font and, especially, the peculiar **acoustics** which leave notes hanging in mid-air, a phenomenon frequently demonstrated by the guards. Visits may be made from 9 a.m. to 1 p.m. and

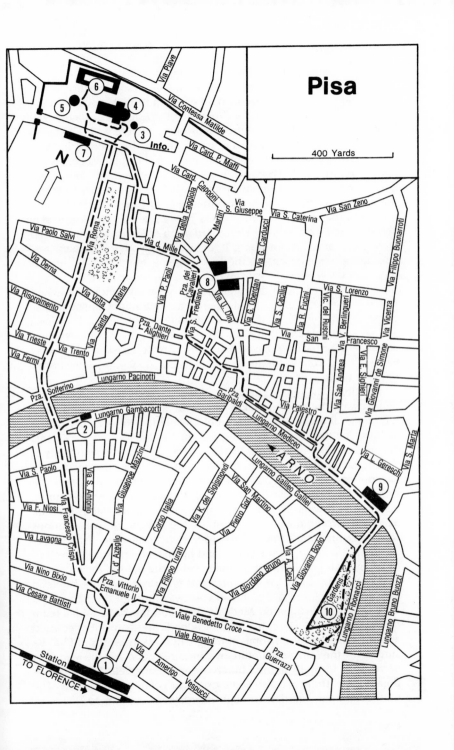

Pisa

400 Yards

N

Via Prave
Via Contessa Matilde
Via Card. P. Maffi
Info.
Via Card. Capponi
Via della Faggiola
Via d. Mille
Via Martiri
Via S. Giuseppe
Via S. Caterina
Via San Zeno
Via G. Carducci
Via Paolo Salvi
Via Roma
Via P. Paoli
Pza. dei Cavalieri
Via S. Frediano
Via U. Dini
Via G. Oberdan
Via S. Cecilia
Via R. Fucini
Vic. del Ruschi
Via V. Berlingueri
Via S. Lorenzo
Via Vicenza
Via Filippo Buonarroti
Via Derna
Via Volta
Via Santa Maria
Pza. Dante L. Alighieri
San Francesco
Via San Andrea
Via Giovanni de Simone
Via Risorgimento
Via Trieste
Via Trento
Via Fermi
Lungarno Pacinotti
Pza. Garibaldi
Via Palestro
Via E. Sighieri
Pza. Solferino
Lungarno Gambacorti
Lungarno Mediceo
Via L. Gereschi
Via S. Marta
ARNO
Lungarno Galileo Galilei
Via S. Paolo
Via S. Antonio
Via Giuseppe Mazzini
Corso Italia
Via K. del Sigismondi
Via San Martino
Via Pietro Gori
Lungarno Bovio
Via F. Niosi
Via Lavagna
Via Francesco Crispi
V. d' Azeglio
Via Filippo Turati
Via Giordano Bruno
Via A. Ceci
Via Giovanni Bovio
Gardens
Lungarno Fibonacci
Lungarno Bruno Buozzi
Via Nino Bixio
Via Cesare Battisti
Pza. Vittorio Emanuele II
Viale Benedetto Croce
Viale Bonaini
Pza. Guerrazzi
Station
TO FLORENCE
Via Amerigo Vespucci

5 6 4 3 7 8 2 9 1 10

3–7 p.m., closing earlier in winter.

The **Sacred Field** *(Camposanto)* (6), a cloistered cemetery immediately to the north, is allegedly built on earth brought back from the Hill of Calvary by 13th-century Crusaders. Its beautiful porticoed galleries are paved with interesting tombstones, and the walls lined with outstanding frescoes which were badly damaged by bombs in 1944. During the course of restoration the original preliminary sketches under the plaster, called *Sinopie*, were discovered and are now exhibited in the Sinopia Museum described below. The actual **frescoes** themselves are being pieced together, with the best on display in a room near the northwest corner. These have a strangely haunting quality about them. Don't miss the famous *Triumph of Death*, which inspired Liszt to compose his disturbing *Totentanz*. Some other intriguing frescoes in the same gallery are the *Last Judgement* and *Hell*. The cemetery complex is open daily, from 8 or 9 a.m. until early evening.

A fascinating look at the original sketches found under the famed frescoes of the *Camposanto* can be had at the **Sinopia Museum** *(Museo delle Sinopie)* (7), on the south side of the Field of Miracles. These are particularly interesting since they were done by the artists themselves—the actual fresco overlay was often left to assistants. They may be seen daily from 9 a.m. to 12:30 p.m. and 3–6:30 p.m., with shorter hours in winter.

Now leave the tourists behind and explore some other parts of Pisa by following the map to **Piazza dei Cavalieri** (8), the main square of the medieval town. The **Palazzo dei Cavalieri**, a 16th-century palace by Vasari on the northeast corner, was the headquarters of the Knights of the Order of St. Stephen. Its richly decorated façade with busts of the six grand dukes of Tuscany is quite handsome. The adjacent **church**, also designed by Vasari but with a later façade, belonged to the same order and is decorated with banners captured from the infidels during Pisa's Turkish wars. On the north side of the square stands the **Palazzo dell' Orologio** which incorporates the remains of two notorious towers. Dante, in his *Inferno*, passionately recounts the 13th-century incident in which Count Ugolino and his male heirs were starved to death by their political rivals in the tower to the right of the entrance.

Continue on along a route which gets progressively more medieval as you approach the river. Thread your way through the narrow old alleyways to the Lungarno Mediceo quay and the **National Museum of San Matteo** (9). Here, in a former Benedictine convent once used as a prison, are housed some of the greatest art treasures of Pisa. Be sure to see the *Dancer* sculpture by Giovanni Pisano and the *Madonna of the Milk*, formerly in the Church of Santa Maria della Spina, by Andrea Pisano. There are also some excellent paintings on display. The museum is open Tuesdays through Saturdays, from 9 a.m. to 7:30 p.m.,

The Cathedral and the Leaning Tower

and on Sundays from 9 a.m. to 1:30 p.m.

Cross the bridge and return to the station by way of a delightful **public park** *(Giardino Scotto)* (10) and the remains of the Bastion of Sangallo.

Lucca

Often overlooked in favor of the more famous towns of Tuscany, Lucca is a refreshing escape from the tourist hordes and yet remains every bit as fascinating as the rest. It is completely encircled by massive 16th-century ramparts which offer delightful opportunities for strolls with a view. The streets within the well-preserved medieval center are both level and uncrowded, making this one of the most eminently walkable of cities. Although it has no major tourist sights, such as Pisa's Leaning Tower, Lucca is filled with a magical charm that never fails to enchant discriminating visitors.

Originally settled by the Ligurians and later the Etruscans, Lucca became a Roman colony in 180 B.C. Despite incessant wars with Pisa and Florence during the Middle Ages, the town has always been prosperous, a happy situation reflected by its splendid buildings. In 1805 Napoleon gave it to his sister as a principality, and in 1847 it was incorporated into the Grand Duchy of Tuscany, soon to become part of the Kingdom of Italy.

This trip could be combined in the same day with one to Pisa, just 14 miles away, as there is excellent transportation between the two towns. If you do this, you may prefer to visit Lucca first since some of its attractions close early.

GETTING THERE:

Trains, mostly bound for Viareggio, depart Florence's main station several times in the morning. The average time to Lucca is about 90 minutes. Return service operates until late evening. Most trains are second class only but largely uncrowded, except when the Florentines are heading for the beach. There is also good train service between Lucca and Pisa.

Buses leave from the Lazzi terminal just opposite the east side of the main train station in Florence. The ride to Lucca takes about 70 minutes. Buy your ticket before boarding. The bus station in Lucca is at Piazzale Verdi at the west end of the ramparts.

By car, Lucca is 46 miles west of Florence via the A-11 Autostrada. The most convenient parking inside the walls is at Piazza Napoleone, near the tourist office. Don't attempt to drive in the old part of town.

WHEN TO GO:

Lucca may be enjoyed at any time, but remember that its major museum is closed on Mondays and some major holidays.

FOOD AND DRINK:

The restaurants of Lucca offer unusually good dining for your money. Some excellent choices, in the order that you will pass or come close to them on the walking tour, are:

> **Giglio** (Piazza del Giglio, near Piazza Napoleone) A traditional restaurant in an old building. X: Tues. eve., Wed. $$

> **Margherita** (Via Sant' Andrea 8, near the Guinigi Tower) Home cooking, low prices. X: Sun. $

> **Antica Locanda dell' Angelo** (Via Pescheria 21, a block southeast of Pza. San Michele) A nice, quiet restaurant with outdoor tables in season. X: Sun. eve., Mon. $$

> **Buca di Sant' Antonio** (Via della Cervia, near Piazza San Michele) The most famous restaurant in Lucca, specializes in game dishes. Reservations advised, phone (0583) 55-881. X: Sun. eve., Mon., July $$

> **Da Giulio** (Via San Tommaso 29, near the northwest corner of the ramparts) Very popular with the local crowd, an exceptional value. X: Sun., Mon., Aug. $$

There are two good local wines, the red *Colline Lucchesi* and the white *Montecarlo*. Lucca is world famous for its superb olive oil.

TOURIST INFORMATION:

The local tourist office, phone (0583) 49-36-39, is at Via Vittorio Veneto 40, just south of Piazza Napoleone.

SUGGESTED TOUR:

Leaving the **train station** (1), follow the map through the Porta San Pietro gate and into the Old Town. Via Vittorio Veneto leads past the tourist office to the main square, **Piazza Napoleone**, dominated on the west by the handsome 16th-century Palazzo della Provincia (or *Ducale*). Continue on to the **Cathedral** *(Duomo)* (2), an 11th- to 13th-century Romanesque structure which appears to be leaning against its bell tower. Its richly decorated façade with three tiers of arches somewhat resembles that of Pisa, although a top pediment was never added.

The interior, rebuilt in the Gothic style during the 14th century, has a fine inlaid marble floor. The cathedral's greatest treasure, from a religious point of view, is the **Holy Face** *(Volto Santo)*, a wooden effigy of Christ on the Cross housed in its own little temple in the middle of the north aisle. There is an utterly fantastic story associated with this, one which drew pilgrims to Lucca for many years. According to this legend, the figure was carved by Nicodemus shortly after the Crucifixion, and remained hidden for centuries. Through a vision, an Italian bishop found it in Lebanon and cast it adrift on an unmanned boat. Miraculously, it appeared off the Italian shore at Luni, near La Spezia. Naturally, there was a dispute as to which town got it. To solve this, the Crucifix was placed on a cart drawn by two untamed oxen who would go wherever God willed them. They went to Lucca. The flaw in the tale is that the figure seems to be of 11th-century origin. In any case, the people of Lucca love their statue and take it for a ride around town every September 13th. The temple which houses it was built in 1484 by Lucca's own Matteo Civitali.

The cathedral has several other art treasures, foremost of which is the celebrated **tomb of Ilaria del Carretto**, an early 15th-century masterpiece by Jacopo della Quercia in the north transept. To the right of this, in a chapel, is a famous painting of the *Madonna with St. Stephen and St. John the Baptist*. Returning towards the west end, the third chapel in the south aisle has a marvelous *Last Supper* by Tintoretto. Just before exiting, note the sculpture near the center door of *St. Martin and the Beggar*. The cathedral is open daily from 7:30 a.m. to noon and 3–7 p.m.

Now wind your way through the ancient streets to a most peculiar sight, the 14th-century **Guinigi Tower** (3). There is nothing unusual about medieval Italian town palaces with towers, but this one is topped by full-grown trees and, what's more, you can climb up and sit in the shade under them. The view is absolutely marvelous and well worth the effort. Ascents may be made daily, April through September, from 9 a.m. to 7 p.m., and from 10 a.m. to 4 p.m. between October and March.

Continue on, following the map, past the 13th-century Church of Santa Maria Forisportam, so named because it was then outside the gate of the original Roman walls. Via del Fosso, divided by a small canal, is all that remains of a medieval defensive moat. Stroll along it to the statue of the Madonna atop a column, then turn right on Via della Quarquonia.

The **National Museum**, housed in the impressive 15th-century **Villa Guinigi** (4) just outside the Old Town, contains a rich collection of art and artifacts. The ground floor rooms are filled with Roman, Etruscan, and even Ligurian items found locally, along with Lucchese sculpture from the 8th through the 14th centuries. The painting galleries, upstairs, include among their treasures two large major works by Fra Bartolommeo. There is also some interesting furniture, textiles, and inlay work. The museum is open from 9 a.m. to 2 p.m., with shorter hours in winter. It is closed on Mondays and some major holidays.

Retrace your steps and continue on to Via dell' Anfiteatro, which

Atop the Guinigi Tower

follows the walls of the **Roman Amphitheater** (5), or what's left of it.
Built in the 2nd century A.D. to house ten thousand spectators, the
arena became a quarry after the fall of the empire, many of its stones
being used in church construction. Some remained, however, and
medieval dwellings were built incorporating the original walls with
newer masonry. As you walk down the street you will be able to pick
out clearly the Roman stones and arches from the later fabric. Enter
the first archway into Piazza del Mercato, an outdoor market place in
the center of the former arena. The atmosphere here is charged with
ancient memories, especially after the last vegetable sellers have gone
home.

The **Church of Saint Frediano** (6), nearby, was built in the 12th
century on the site of a 6th-century basilica. Its rather austere façade
is topped with a wonderful mosaic depicting Christ and the Twelve
Apostles. Inside, there is a magnificent 12th-century **font** in the right
aisle, carved with the story of Moses, the Good Shepherd, and the
Apostles. The **Trenta Chapel**, on the left, has some fine reliefs by Jacopo della Quercia. Also on the left aisle is the Chapel of St. Augustine with a fresco illustrating the transport of the Holy Face to Lucca,
a legend you already came across on your visit to the cathedral.

Just a few steps away stands the elegant 17th-century **Palazzo
Pfanner** (7). Enter the simple doorway and wander around the delight-

ful 18th-century statuary gardens, built up against the town's ramparts. The splendid galleried staircase leads to a small exhibit of local costumes.

Now follow the map down Via Fillungo, a narrow pedestrian street steeped in the atmosphere of the Middle Ages. The **Torre delle Ore**, a 13th-century clock tower on the left, is one of the few medieval towers which survive in a town once full of them. A right on Via Roma brings you to the Piazza San Michele, a large open square on the site of the Roman forum. Note the open Renaissance loggia of the Palazzo Pretorio at the southwest corner.

The **Church of San Michele in Foro** (8) has an absolutely marvelous oversized façade, easily the most impressive in town. Crowned with an enormous statue of the Archangel Michael, it was built in the 13th century for a planned enlargement of the 12th-century church— which never took place. Step inside to see, on the first altar in the south aisle, the terracotta *Madonna and Child* by Andrea della Robbia and, in the north transept, a panel painting of *Four Saints* by Filippo Lippi.

It is now only a few steps to the **House of Giacomo Puccini** (9) on Via di Poggio. Born here in 1858, the renowned composer studied music in Lucca before moving on to Milan. Opera lovers will, of course, want to go upstairs to see the small museum devoted to his life. It is open on Tuesdays through Sundays from 10 a.m. to 6 p.m.; but closed on some holidays.

Continue straight ahead to the **National Gallery** *(Pinacoteca Nazionale)* (10) in the 17th-century Palazzo Mansi. Its sumptuous interior houses an excellent collection of paintings, primarily from the Renaissance through the 19th century, which may be seen Tuesdays through Sundays, from 9 a.m. to 7 p.m., closing at 4 p.m. on holidays.

Now wander past the bus terminal at Piazzale Verdi and head uphill onto the 16th-century **fortifications** which encircle the Old Town. These tree-shaded ramparts offer wonderful views as well as a delightful route back to the train station.

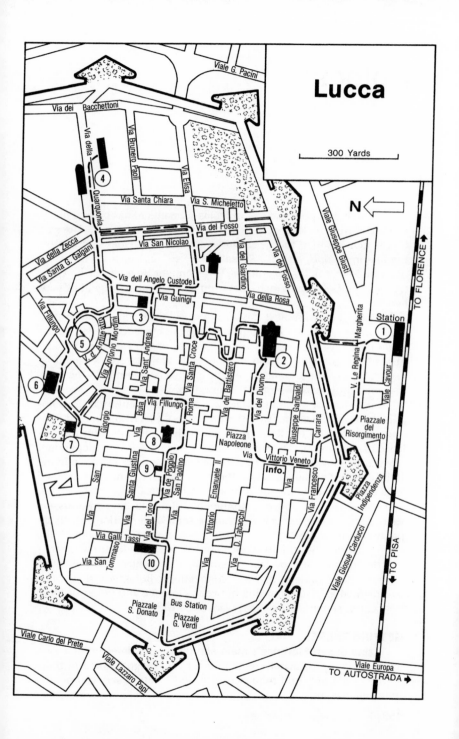

Bologna

Bologna, the principal city of Emilia-Romangna, has earned many epithets during its long centuries of existence. *"La Grassa"* (The Fat) for the richness of its food; *"La Dotta"* (The Learned) for its university, the first in Europe; and *"La Rossa"* (The Red), as much for the color of its buildings as for its politics. To this might be added "The Contented," for Bologna in many ways represents Italian living at its very best.

Surprisingly, with all it has to offer, Bologna gets relatively few foreign tourists. It has no singularly great sights, such as the Colosseum in Rome, the Leaning Tower in Pisa, or the canals of Venice. Instead, its attraction lies in its congenial atmosphere, its genuine hospitality, its fine art, and especially in what is regarded as the most delicious cooking in this nation of good cooks.

An Etruscan settlement as far back as the 6th century B.C., Bologna, then called *Felsina,* was overrun by the Gauls who named it *Bononia,* and then by the Romans. It fell to the Lombards after the collapse of the empire. During the Middle Ages it was an independent city-state, renowned throughout Europe as a center of learning. In the 16th century it became a part of the Papal States, to which it remained loyal almost up until the unification of Italy in 1860.

Despite its lack of great monuments, Bologna does have its full share of intriguing sights which can be seen while working up an appetite on the suggested walking tour, and later while burning off the excess calories. Be sure to allow plenty of time for a leisurely lunch.

This trip may also be taken from Milan or Venice, both of which have excellent rail and highway connections. Bologna makes a fine overnight stop when traveling between Florence and either of these base cities, something you may want to consider.

GETTING THERE:
Trains depart Florence's main station several times in the morning for the approximately 70-minute run to Bologna. Some of these are first class only and require reservations. Return service operates until late evening.

Trains depart Milan's Centrale Station fairly frequently for Bologna, the trip taking between 2 and 2½ hours. Again, some are first class only and need reservations. Return trains run until late evening.

Trains leave Venice's Santa Lucia Station several times in the morning for the 2-hour run to Bologna. At least one of these is first class only and needs reservations. There is return service until late evening.

By car from Florence, take the A-1 Autostrada all the way, a distance of 65 miles.

By car from Milan, it is 130 miles to Bologna via the A-1 Autostrada.

By car from Venice, take the A-4 Autostrada almost to Padua, then the A-13 south to Bologna, a total distance of 95 miles.

WHEN TO GO:

Bologna is a town for all seasons—even in the rain or summer sun you will be sheltered most of the way by many miles of arcades. The major museums are closed on Mondays and some holidays, others on Tuesdays. The local patron saint's day is October 4th, honoring St. Petronio.

FOOD AND DRINK:

You can get real bologna in Bologna, where it's called *mortadella*, but it would be a crime to settle for this in the city renowned as the gastronomic capital of all Italy. Any dish labeled *alla Bolognese* is bound to be rich and tasty, while the local *pasta* specialties are *Tortellini*, *Tagliatelle*, and *Lasagna*. The tradition of good cooking is so strong that you can hardly go wrong in selecting a restaurant, but here are a few of the better choices, more or less in the order of descending prices. Reservations are recommended for some of these.

Notai (Via dei Pignattari 1, next to St. Petronius) An elegant restaurant favored by a local clientele. For reservations call (051) 22-86-94. X: Sun. $$$

Taverna Tre Frecce (Strada Maggiore 19, a block southeast of the leaning towers) Elegant dining in a 13th-century mansion. Reservations (051) 23-12-00. X: Sun. eve., Mon. $$$

Grassilli (Via del Luzzo 3, near the leaning towers) Well-prepared traditional cuisine. For reservations call (051) 22-29-61. X: Wed. $$$

Rosteria Luciano (Via Nazario Sauro 19, between the station and the main square) An art-deco atmosphere. Reservations (051) 23-12-49. X: Tues. eve., Wed., Aug. $$ and $$$

Da Carlo (Via Marchesana 6, a block east of the Archaeological Museum) A popular trattoria with outdoor terrace dining in summer. X: Tues., Jan. $$

Rostaria Antico Brunetti (Via Caduti di Cefalonia 5, just north of the Governor's Palace) A good value in a very old restaurant. X: Wed. $$

Dal Duttour Balanzon (Via Fossalta 3, just north of the Governor's Palace) A large, busy, old-fashioned place with a loyal clientele. Eat in the main dining room. X: Sat. $$

Ruggero (Via degli Usberti 6, 4 blocks northwest of Palazzo Comunale) Traditional fare in an unspoiled trattoria. X: Sat. lunch, Sun., Aug. $$

Trattoria della Santa (Via Urbana 9, 5 blocks west of San Domenico church) Good home cooking. X: Sun., Aug. $

The best-known local wine is *Lambrusco di Sorbara,* a slightly sparkling, slightly sweet red beloved by nearly everyone except connoisseurs. There is also a velvety white, *Albana di Romagna.*

TOURIST INFORMATION:

The provincial tourist office, phone (051) 23-96-60, is at Piazza Maggiore 6. There is also a branch in the train station, phone (051) 24-65-41.

SUGGESTED TOUR:

From the **train station** (1) you can take a bus or cab to Piazza del Nettuno, the center of town and the real start of this tour. Walking there, however, is quite pleasant and takes less than 15 minutes. The route along Via dell' Indipendenza, a busy shopping street, is entirely under the **arcades** which have made Bologna's architecture so distinctive. There are about 22 miles of these sheltering roofs over the sidewalks in the city, making strolling enjoyable even in the rain or hot sun.

The **Piazza del Nettuno** is graced with the impressive 16th-century **Neptune Fountain**, the first major work by Giambologna, who is also known as Giovanni Bologna. Adjacent to this, and opening onto the larger Piazza Maggiore, is the **Palazzo Comunale** (2). Housing both the city hall and exhibition galleries, this massive complex was begun in the 13th century and greatly modified over the years. The left side of the façade has Gothic arches, a handsome clock tower and, under a small canopy above the third tier of windows, a lovely terracotta *Madonna* by Nicolò dell' Arca.

Enter under the statue of Bologna's own Gregory XIII, the 16th-century pope who invented the Gregorian calendar. Cutting across the interior courtyard at a diagonal, you will come to a grand, gently sloping equestrian staircase attributed to Bramante. Climb this all the way to the top, two flights up, and visit the elegant *Sala Farnese,* whose 17 rooms contain the **Communal Art Collection**. The beautifully fur-

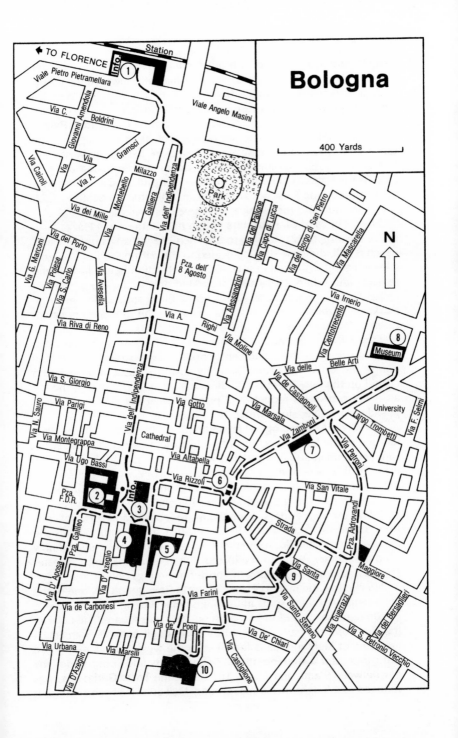

nished chambers are filled with outstanding Bolognese art, and offer magnificent views of the city from their high windows. Admission is free, and visits may be made from 9 a.m. to 2 p.m. (12:30 p.m. on Sundays) any day except Tuesdays and some holidays.

Directly across the square stands the imposing **Governor's Palace** *(Palazzo del Podestà)* (3), another complex of structures begun in the 13th century. The side facing Piazza Maggiore has a noteworthy Renaissance façade. Adjoining this, but opening onto Piazza del Nettuno, is the **Palazzo di Re Enzo**, built in 1246 and used as a prison for the captured King Enzo of Sardinia from 1249 until his death in 1272. Enter the courtyard for a look at its marvelous staircase.

The **Basilica of St. Petronius** (4), on the south side of Piazza Maggiore, was originally intended to be much larger than its present size, which is still immense. It is dedicated to the patron saint of Bologna, a local bishop who died in A.D. 450. Construction began in 1390 and remains unfinished. Its façade, decorated only to the top of the first arches, has some fine reliefs depicting Biblical stories. The most remarkable of these, over the central door, are the 15th-century **sculptures** by Jacopo della Quercia, his last major work.

Step into its enormous but somewhat austere interior, enlivened here and there with magnificent works of art—particularly the *Madonna and Child with Four Saints* by Lorenzo Costa in the seventh chapel on the left. There is a small **museum** at the far end of the left aisle which displays models and plans of what the church was supposed to look like, along with other treasures.

The **Civic Archaeological Museum** (5), to the east of the basilica, has one of the best collections of prehistoric, Egyptian, Greek, Etruscan, and Roman artifacts in Italy. Displayed in a rather old-fashioned manner, it is nevertheless fascinating to anyone with an interest in antiquities. Room 10 is particularly intriguing with its Umbrian and Etruscan finds from the area around Bologna. The museum is open Tuesdays through Fridays, from 9 a.m. to 2 p.m.; and on weekends from 9 a.m. to 1 p.m. and 3:30–7 p.m. Just south of this stands the **Palazzo Archiginnasio**, formerly occupied by the university and now used as a library. You can see its old 17th-century anatomical theater *(Teatro Anatomico)* by asking the porter (mornings only).

Now follow the map to **Piazza di Porta Ravegnana** (6), one of the most visually exciting spots in town. Pisa may have its Leaning Tower, but Bologna has two of them—both on the same square. The taller of the *Due Torri,* the early-12th-century **Torre degli Asinelli**, is an amazing 320 feet high and leans four feet to the west. What's more, you can climb it for a stupendous panorama of city and countryside, any day between 9 a.m. and 6 p.m. The other, the **Torre Garisenda**, was reduced to a height of 158 feet around 1360 after it began sinking. It

The Leaning Towers of Bologna

now tilts ten feet to the northeast. Bologna once had nearly 200 such towers, but most were demolished for safety reasons. Immediately south of these, in its own square, stands the **Palazzo della Mercanzia**, a handsome 14th-century chamber of commerce with a canopied balcony from which commercial decrees were announced.

Continue along Via Zamboni to the **Church of San Giacomo Maggiore** (7). Founded in the 13th century and later altered, the church is unusually rich in splendid art treasures. Don't miss the **Bentivoglio Chapel** at the end of the north aisle with its famous altarpiece, the *Virgin and Child with Four Saints* by Francesco Francia. The same chapel also has some excellent frescoes by Lorenzo Costa. Just opposite this, against the wall of the apse, is the interesting **tomb of Antonio Bentivoglio**, a late work by Jacopo della Quercia.

If time permits, you may want to visit the **National Picture Gallery** *(Pinacoteca Nazionale)* (8) by continuing up the street past the university buildings. The problem here is that it is only open from 9 a.m. to 2 p.m. (until 1 p.m. on Sundays and holidays), every day except Mondays and a few holidays. Perhaps you could come back on another day if you are staying overnight in Bologna. This is one of the best art museums in Italy and requires several hours to explore. Although the focus is on Bolognese works, many other schools—some foreign—are represented, and all are arranged chronologically and stylistically for easy comprehension.

The route now leads through some interesting streets to the **Basilica of Santo Stefano** (9), a fantastic complex of ancient churches, parts of which date from the Dark Ages. Be sure to explore all of its hidden nooks and crannies, especially the **Court of Pilate** with its obscure 8th-century basin. A layout map is available at the entrance. The church is closed between noon and 3:30 p.m.

From here find your way, following the map, to the **Church of San Domenico** (10). Begun in the 13th century, it houses the masterful **Tomb of St. Dominic**, the founder of the Dominican order. One of the most spectacular religious sculptures in Italy, it is the joint work of several famous artists over two centuries of time, including Nicola Pisano, Nicolò dell' Arca, and the young Michelangelo. While there, be sure to see the *Mystic Marriage of St. Catherine* by Filippo Lippi, in the chapel to the right of the choir. The church is closed between noon and 3:30 p.m.

Return to the station via the route on the map. If you have a little time before the next train, you might want to spend it relaxing in the delightful Montagnola park, just across Piazza Galliera.

Section IV
Daytrips from Milan
North West Italy

No other section of Italy offers quite as broad a range of daytrip possibilities as the North West. From its sophisticated modern cities to a secluded seaside village, from lovely alpine lakes to unspoiled medieval towns, there is truly something here for everyone.

Centering on Lombardy, but also touching the regions of Liguria, Piedmont, and Venetia, this section covers some of the most enjoyable destinations in the entire country. It is a cosmopolitan area strongly influenced by foreign domination in the past, when it was at times ruled by the French, the Germans, and the Austrians. Still a favorite playground for the people of northern Europe, its growing trade with the rest of the world has made it the most internationally minded corner of Italy.

The hub of all this is Milan, Italy's most dynamic metropolis and one of its two major gateways. A vast network of rail lines and highways converges here, making it the natural base city for one-day excursions throughout the area. Milan is also a fascinating tourist attraction in its own right, as the "get acquainted" walking tour outlined in the next few pages demonstrates. Although Milan has an enviable supply of hotels in all possible price ranges, some travelers may prefer to stay outside the city itself. A good choice for this is Como, which is well served by commuter trains and highways.

Two of the daytrips described in other sections of this book can also be made from Milan. These are Bologna and Vicenza. Verona, actually in Venetia, is easily visited from Venice as well as from Milan.

Milan

(Milano)

Tourists often consider bustling, sprawling Milan to be only a waystop in their Italian adventures, a place to change trains or catch a plane. This is a mistake, for Milan is more than an excellent base for daytrips in North West Italy—it is a surprisingly engrossing destination in itself.

Milan probably began as a Celtic settlement around the 5th century B.C. Later conquered by the Romans, it took the name *Mediolanum* and grew to become an important center of the empire. The Edict of Milan, promulgated by Constantine in A.D. 313, gave official recognition to the Christian faith for the first time. During the Dark Ages the town was frequently sacked by the invading Barbarians, but always rebuilt and eventually became the center of the Lombard League which defeated Frederick Barbarossa's army in 1176.

Power now fell into the hands of the Visconti family, whose sometimes despotic rule brought about a golden age of expansion. The line died out in the mid-15th century and, after a short republican period, Milan came under the brilliant control of the Sforza family. Foreign invasions, beginning around 1494, led to alternating rule by France and Spain, and later by Austria. Napoleon made Milan the capital of his new Cisalpine Republic in 1797, and of his Kingdom of Italy in 1805. When he fell from power the city reverted to Austrian domination, under whose cruel yoke it remained until the beginnings of Italian unification in 1859. Heavily bombed during World War II, Milan is today the most modern city in Italy.

With over one and a half million inhabitants, Milan spreads across a vast area. Fortunately, nearly all of its attractions are in a small downtown historic core within easy walking distance of each other. The suggested tour goes past more museums than anyone would want to see in a day, so you should read the descriptions of each first and visit only those that really strike your fancy. Stopping at a good *Gelateria* for some of that delicious Italian ice cream or a café for a refreshing drink can be every bit as enjoyable as seeing an art gallery.

GETTING THERE:

Trains from all over Italy and Europe call at Milan's mammoth Centrale Station. Some typical running times are: Rome—5 hours; Florence—3 hours; and Venice—3 hours.

By car, it is 355 miles to Rome, 185 to Florence, and 166 to Venice—all by Autostrada routes which radiate in every direction from Milan.

By air, Milan is served with direct flights from other major cities in Italy, throughout Europe, and around the world. The city has two main airports—Linate, 4 miles to the east; and Malpensa, for intercontinental service, 31 miles to the northwest.

GETTING AROUND:

You will probably want to use public transportation to get downtown from your hotel or the Centrale train station. The system consists of subways, buses, and streetcars, all operated by the ATM authority. The **subway** *(Metropolitana Milanese* or *MM)* is the fastest and easiest way to get around, and stops at all of the major train stations. It functions between about 6:30 a.m. and midnight. Tickets are valid for 75 minutes of continuous travel on the surface or underground, or a combination of both, and may be purchased from vending machines, newsstands, or ticket offices in subway stations. At present there are three connecting subway lines, the M1 (red), the M2 (green), and the M3 (yellow). Special bargain one-day transit passes are available at the *"Ufficio Abbonamenti"* office in the Duomo subway station or at tourist information offices, who can also supply you with a system map. Taxis are plentiful but fairly expensive.

WHEN TO GO:

Any time is a good time to visit Milan, but note that the *Milanese* desert their city in droves during August, leaving behind little but the tourists. Some attractions are closed on Mondays, and the local patron saint's day is December 7th, celebrated in honor of Saint Ambrose. Good weather is not really necessary to enjoy this walking tour as much of it is spent indoors. Save the sunshine for daytrips to the lakes or seaside.

FOOD AND DRINK:

Milan's most famous dish is *Costoletta alla Milanese,* a breaded veal cutlet strongly resembling the *Wiener Schnitzel* of its one-time Austrian rulers. Other local specialties include *Risotto alla Milanese* (rice in broth with saffron), *Osso Buco* (veal shank), and *Minestrone* (thick vegetable soup). *Panettone* is a Milanese coffeecake with raisins and candied fruit.

As a major international business center, Milan abounds in expensive restaurants featuring all of the world's cuisines. At a more reasonable price level you will find a good choice of regional Italian cooking, and in the inexpensive category quite a few pizzerias, self-service cafeterias, and a growing number of fast-food outlets. The list below is limited to a few choice establishments located on or near the suggested walking tour, and is given in tour sequence. It should not be regarded as a guide for the entire city.

Savini (Galleria Vittorio Emanuele II) A traditional grand luxury restaurant with local cuisine. Reservations preferred, phone (02) 80-58-343. X: Sun., mid-Aug. $$$

Al Cantinone (Via Agnello 19, 3 blocks southeast of the Opera) An old-time trattoria. X: Sat. lunch, Sun., Aug. $$

Biffi Scala (Piazza della Scala, near the Opera) Elegant and fashionable. X: Sun., mid-Aug. $$$

Antico Boeucc (Piazza Belgioioso 2, near the Poldi Pazzoli Museum) In an old palace. Reservations preferred, phone (02) 79-02-24. X: Sat., Sun. lunch, Aug. $$$

Franco il Contadino (Via Fiori Chiari 20, near Brera Palace) A typically local establishment. X: Tues., July. $$$

Rigolo (Largo Treves at Via Solferino, north of Brera Palace) A favorite with the locals. X: Mon., Tues. lunch, Aug. $$

Pizzeria Le Briciole (Via Camperio 17, 2 blocks south of Sforza Castle) Traditional Italian meals as well as pizza. X: Sat., Mon. $ and $$

La Bruschetta (Piazza Beccaria 12, 2 blocks east of the Duomo) Pizza as well as full meals. X: Mon., Aug. $ and $$

Peck (Via Victor Hugo 4, 2 blocks west of the Cathedral) This famous delicatessen also has a restaurant and a self-service cafeteria. X: Sun., July. Restaurant $$$, cafeteria $$

Al Mercante (Piazza Mercanti 17) Outdoor tables in summer. X: Sun., Aug. $$

Ciao (Piazza del Duomo) Self-service cafeteria. $

TOURIST INFORMATION:

The provincial tourist office, phone (02) 80-96-62, is located on Piazza del Duomo, opposite the south side of the Cathedral. There is also a busy branch, phone (02) 669-05-32, in the Centrale train station and another at Linate Airport. Ask for their free fact-filled booklet "Tutta Milano." You might also try the municipal office in the Galleria Vittorio Emanuele II for current "what's on" information.

Milan Cathedral

SUGGESTED TOUR:

Since the main train station *(Stazione Centrale)* is quite a distance from the center of town, this walk begins at Piazza del Duomo—the very heart of historic Milan. You can easily get there by subway, taking line M1 to *Duomo*.

The **Cathedral** *(Duomo)* (1) is one of the largest religious structures on earth, and one of the very few truly Gothic buildings in Italy. This style originated in northern France and never really became popular in a land of long, hot summers (Gothic churches have large windows which transmit heat), different building materials, and a unique architectural inheritance. Even so, this is a highly modified form of Gothic.

Begun in 1386 by the ruler Gian Galeazzo Visconti on the site of an earlier church, the cathedral was finally completed in 1813 on orders from Napoleon. A stroll around it will reveal its intricate splendors, adorned with literally thousands of statues and pinnacles.

Enter through the modern bronze doors on the west façade. The vast interior with its 52 soaring columns is large enough to hold a congregation of 40,000 worshippers. Details tend to become lost in such a space, but there are a few which should be singled out. The

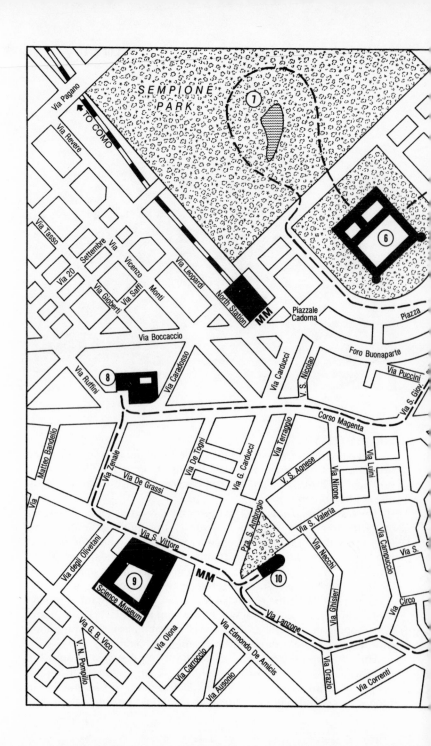

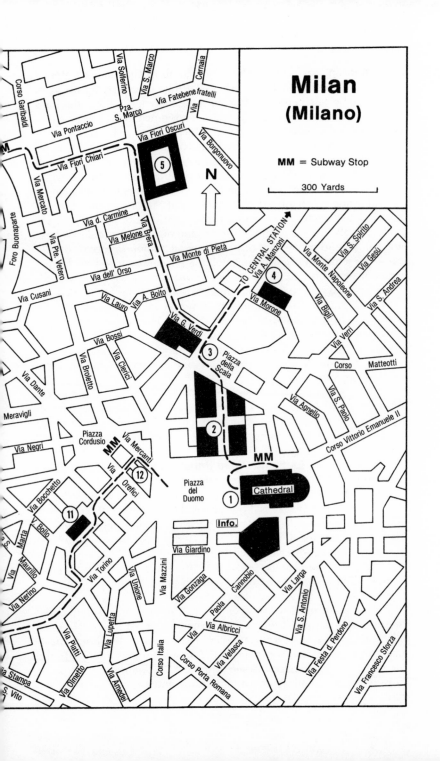

south transept has a fine 16th-century **tomb of Giacomo de Medici** and a grisly **statue** of the flayed St. Bartholomew carrying his skin, also from the 16th century. Close by is the entrance to the cathedral's treasury in the south sacristy. This also leads down to the **crypt**, where you can see the bones of St. Charles Borromeo, a 16th-century archbishop of Milan, displayed in a crystal sarcophagus. Back on the ground floor, the north transept is enlivened with a magnificent bronze **candalabrum** in the form of a tree with seven branches. Before leaving, you may want to visit the excavations of a 4th-century **baptistry** where St. Augustine was baptized in A.D. 387 by St. Ambrose. The entrance to this is just inside the cathedral's west front.

Now walk around to the outside of the north transept. From here you can ascend to the **roof** of the cathedral, either on foot or by elevator, for a marvelous stroll through the enchanted forest of statuary which makes this church so special—a visual treat not to be missed. There are also great panoramic **views** extending as far as the Alps.

The **Cathedral Museum**, in the former Royal Palace opposite the south side of the cathedral, has a splendid collection of religious art along with an interesting documentation of the cathedral's structural evolution. It is open Tuesdays through Sundays, from 9:30 a.m. to 12:30 p.m. and 3–6 p.m. You may want to return here after completing the walking tour.

One of Milan's best-known landmarks is the elegant **Galleria Vittorio Emanuele II** (2), a 19th-century shopping arcade lined with quality shops, restaurants, and "outdoor" cafés where you can sit down for an expensive drink and watch the world go by. Pass through it and continue on to Piazza della Scala.

The renowned **La Scala Opera House** *(Teatro alla Scala)* (3) was opened in 1778 and has seen the grand premières of works by Verdi, Rossini, Donizetti, Puccini, and others. Devastated by bombs during World War II, the theater was quickly rebuilt as a matter of the highest priority—where would the Italians be without their beloved opera? The best way to see it, of course, is to attend a performance. Operas are staged from early December through late May, with a concert season from then until late June and again from September through November. You just might be lucky enough to get tickets on short notice.

There is, fortunately, another way to glimpse La Scala's dazzling interior. This is to visit the adjacent **Scala Museum** *(Museo Teatrale alla Scala)*, which displays a large and fascinating collection of theatrical memorabilia and is especially rich in mementoes relating to the life of Verdi. You can look down into the auditorium from here. The museum is open daily from 9 a.m. to noon and 2–6 p.m., closing at 4 p.m. on Sundays and during the winter.

Art lovers might want to make a little side trip to the **Poldi-Pezzoli Museum** (4), gorgeously housed in a charming small mansion once occupied by the noted 19th-century collector, Gian Giacomo Poldi-Pezzoli. Among the varied treasures filling the sumptuously decorated rooms are the famed *Portrait of a Young Woman* by Antonio Pollaivolo, *St. Nicholas of Tolentino* by Piero della Francesca, a touching *Madonna del Libro* by Botticelli, and the rather impressionistic *Grey Lagoon* by the Venetian master Guardi. There is also a wonderful Persian carpet from the 16th century and many intriguing *objets d'art*. Visits may be made from Tuesdays through Sundays, 9:30 a.m. to 12:30 p.m. and 2:30–5:30 p.m. The museum is closed on Mondays, some holidays, and on Sunday afternoons in summer.

Via Giuseppe Verdi and Via Brera lead to the **Brera Gallery** *(Pinacoteca di Brera)* (5). Housed in a 17th-century palace built for the Jesuits, this is Milan's most formidable art museum and one of the very best in all Italy. Since at least an hour is required even to sample its vast holdings, and since it closes early, you may want to return here on another day. At least step into the splendid courtyard for a look at the famous statue of a naked Napoleon with a toga over his shoulder. The collections are mainly of northern Italian religious art seized after the suppression of the orders at the end of the 18th century, although they have since been extended to include other European schools along with 20th-century Italian works. Some of the treasures include Piero della Francesca's *Madonna with Saints and Angels,* Caravaggio's *Supper at Emmaus,* Bellini's *Pietà,* Mantegna's *Dead Christ,* Raphael's *Betrothal of the Virgin,* and Tintoretto's *Finding of the Body of St. Mark.* The museum is open every day except Mondays, from 9 a.m. to 7 p.m.

Now follow the map through some charming small streets to the massive **Sforza Castle** *(Castello Sforzesco)* (6), a 15th-century stronghold built to protect the ruling Sforza family. A previous fortress on the same site, erected by the Viscontis in the 14th century, was demolished in 1447 during the brief republican period between the two great dynasties. Greatly altered over the years, the present structure was used as a ducal palace and later as an army barracks. It was restored after severe World War II bombings and now houses the **Museum of Ancient and Applied Arts** *(Museo d' Arte Antica e Arte Applicata),* which you may want to see at another time. The most famous items in this immense collection include Michelangelo's last work, the *Rondanini Pietà,* Filippo Lippi's *Madonna and Saints,* Mantegna's *Madonna in Glory,* some decorations by Leonardo da Vinci, costumes, tapestries, armor, musical instruments, and Egyptian mummies. The castle is open Tuesdays through Sundays, from 9:30 a.m. to noon and 2:30–5:30 p.m., but closed on Mondays and some holidays.

The lovely **Sempione Park** (7), behind the castle, provides a welcome rest stop where you can buy an ice cream or drink to enjoy while taking in the view.

The route now leads through a succession of interesting streets to one of Milan's greatest tourist attractions. The **Church of Santa Maria delle Grazie** (8), while interesting in itself, is world famous for a wall painting in its adjoining refectory. Often referred to as a fresco, the **Last Supper** *(Il Cenacolo)* by Leonardo da Vinci was actually done in tempera, which is at the root of its problems. Within 50 years of its painting the colors already began to flake off, and mildew from the damp wall caused further damage. Numerous restorations have been attempted, with the one currently underway being the most success- ful. While you have doubtlessly seen many highly retouched repro- ductions of its late-15th-century masterpiece, the original has an un- matched power due both to its immense size and to its extension of the natural perspective and lighting of the former dining room in which it is located. The *Last Supper* depicts the dramatic moment when Je- sus, flanked by the apostles, utters the terrible words "One of you will betray me." Despite its poor—but hopefully improving—condi- tion, this is a sight that should not be missed by any visitor to Milan. It may be seen on any day from 9 a.m. to 1:15 p.m.

While there, be sure to stop in to the **church** itself, whose beauti- ful dome and choir were done by Bramante at the end of the 15th century. He also designed the exquisite **cloister**, reached via the north transept.

Having seen one of Leonardo's most celebrated works, you should now move on to experience quite another aspect of this Renaissance genius. The **Leonardo da Vinci Museum of Science and Technology** (9), just a few blocks away, is among the greatest institutions of its type in the world. One large hall is filled with models of his fascinating inventions, while the rest of the enormous museum is devoted to sci- ence and industry. Don't miss the separate railway building with its large collection of locomotives and rolling stock, or the sea and air transport building. There is also a splendid display of automobiles, along with just about everything else you can think of. To the scientif- ically minded, this museum alone is worth a trip to Milan, and cer- tainly deserves a full day in itself. You may want to return here after making a quick probe. It is open Tuesdays through Sundays, from 9 a.m. to 5 p.m., but closed on Mondays and some holidays.

Continue down Via San Vittore to the **Basilica of Sant' Ambrogio** (10), one of the most intriguing churches in Italy. Founded as far back as A.D. 379 and consecrated by St. Ambrose in 387, it was enlarged during the 11th and 12th centuries and restored after suffering heavy World War II damage. Among its riches are a gold-and-silver **high al- tar** from A.D. 835, a Romanesque **pulpit** from around 1200, and some

Galleria Vittorio Emanuele II

fine 10th-century **mosaics** in the apse. The bones of St. Ambrose, along with those of two other saints, rest in a **crypt** beneath the high altar. At the east end of the south aisle is the tiny **Chapel of St. Vittore** with its 5th-century mosaics. From the north aisle you can step outside to see the famous *Portico della Canonica,* an unfinished structure by Bramante.

Now follow the map to the **Pinacoteca Ambrosiana** (11), a remarkable art gallery in the noted 17th-century Ambrosiana Library. Specializing in paintings from the 14th to the early 19th centuries, its collection includes works by Botticelli, Raphael, Titian, Caravaggio, Breughel, Leonardo, and many other greats. They can be seen Sundays through Fridays, from 9:30 a.m. to 5 p.m.

From here it is only two blocks to the **Piazza Mercanti** (12), a quietly charming old square lined with impressive buildings from the Middle Ages to the 17th century. Just steps from the Piazza del Duomo, this is the perfect place to end your walking tour. There are many attractive cafés nearby where you can rest your weary feet.

Genoa
(Genova)

Although teeming Genoa is Italy's major seaport, its fifth-largest city, and sits at the junction of major transportation routes, it remains curiously overlooked by tourists. Not exactly a very elegant place in the conventional sense, the hometown of Christopher Columbus is a city of hidden surprises just waiting to be discovered as you probe the narrow alleyways of its Old Town.

Genoa began as a Ligurian trading post as far back as the 6th century B.C., and joined the Roman Empire in the 3rd century B.C. Hemmed in by mountains, it was in little danger of attack by the Barbarians but had to fight constant sea battles to maintain its independence. The Crusades brought profitable trade and prosperity. Internal strife among its great merchant families led to foreign domination until the 16th century, when a forceful leader named Andrea Doria established a mighty republic. This later fell to the French, who ruled it until the beginnings of Italian reunification in the 19th century.

Walking alone in some of the more deserted passages of the Old Town near the harbor can be dangerous, especially at night. For this reason the suggested tour route sticks to populated alleyways in that part of the city, although you should still remain alert. As in other Mediterranean ports such as Naples and Marseille, the threat is more imagined than real.

GETTING THERE:

Trains depart Milan's Centrale station several times in the morning for the 90-minute run to Genoa's Principe station. Note that Genoa *(Genova)* has another main station, Brignole. Get off at Principe, which comes first. A few trains require a supplementary fare, but not to holders of most railpasses. Return service operates until late evening.

By car, Genoa is 88 miles from Milan via the A-7 Autostrada. Parking is available near the Principe train station.

WHEN TO GO:

Avoid coming on a Monday, when several of the sights are closed. The colorful streets in the Old Town are less active on Sundays, and the museums close early then. June 14th is the local patron saint's day, celebrated in honor of St. John the Baptist.

FOOD AND DRINK:

Genoa has its own variations on Italian cooking, some of which are as familiar as *Ravioli*. Other local pasta dishes include *Gnocchi* and *Trenette*, usually served with *Pesto*, a sauce made from olive oil, basil leaves, garlic, pine nuts, and cheese. *Cima* is an unusual stuffed veal specialty, while *Burrida* is a fish stew similar to the Bouillabaisse of Marseille. Liguria is not a really great wine region, but you might enjoy the slightly sweet white *Cinqueterre* or the red *Dolceacqua*, both adequate table wines.

The choice restaurants listed below are all within the small historical area of Genoa covered by the walking tour, and are more or less in trip sequence. Other parts of the city are blessed with excellent establishments not mentioned here.

Saint Cyr (Piazza Marsala 8, just east of Villetta di Negro) Regional cuisine in an elegant setting. X: Sat., Sun. $$$

Pansön (Piazza delle Erbe 5, 2 blocks southeast of San Lorenzo Cathedral) Authentic Genovese cuisine, outdoor tables in summer. X: Sun., Mon., Aug. $$

Sâ Pesta (Via dei Giustiniani 16, 2 blocks south of San Lorenzo Cathedral) A local favorite for local home cooking. X: Sun. $

Mario (Via Conservatori del Mare 33, just east of Via S. Luca) Local dishes in an unpretentious setting. X: Sat. $$

Walter (Via Colalanza 2, at Via San Luca near Palazzo Spinola) Genovese cooking at bargain prices. X: Sun., Aug. $

TOURIST INFORMATION:

The main provincial tourist office, phone (010) 58-14-07, is at Via Roma 11, near Piazza Corvetto. There are also branches at both Principe and Brignole train stations.

SUGGESTED TOUR:

The walk begins at **Principe train station** (1), where you can ask at the tourist office about boat tours (11) of the harbor. In a small square in front of the station stands a statue of Christopher Columbus who, along with the musician Nicolò Paganini and the revolutionary hero Giuseppe Mazzini, is one of Genoa's most famous sons.

Cross via the underground passage and follow Via Balbi to the **Royal Palace** (*Pallazzo Reale*) (2). Originally built around 1650 and heavily remodeled in 1705, it is one of several surviving palaces that testify eloquently to Genoa's former magnificence. In the mid-19th century it became a seat of the royal House of Savoy and was decorated accordingly. The walls are hung with several fine works of art, including paintings by Van Dyck. Don't miss the splendid **Gallery of Mirrors** or the ballroom, and be sure to take a stroll in the garden overlooking

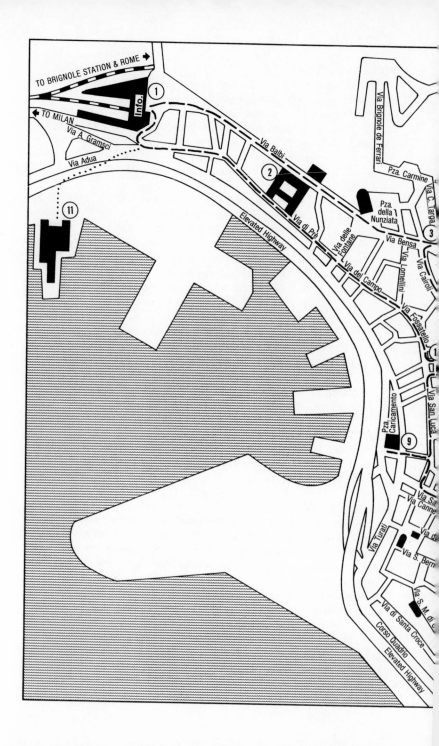

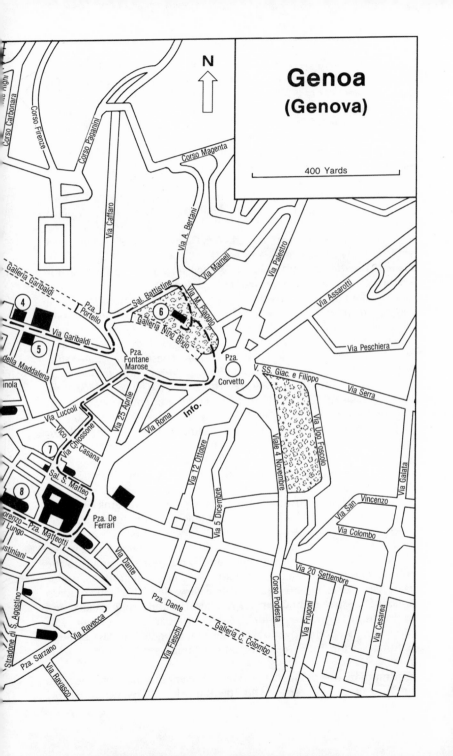

Genoa
(Genova)

N

400 Yards

Corso Carbonara

Corso Firenze

Corso Paganini

Corso Magenta

Via Caffaro

Via A. Bertani

Via Mameli

Via Palestro

Via Assarotti

Galleria Garibaldi

Pza. Portello

Sal. Battistine

Via M. Piaggio

Via Peschiera

④

⑤

Via Garibaldi

⑥

Galleria Nino Bixio

Pza. Fontane Marose

Pza. Corvetto

V. SS. Giac. e Filippo

Via Serra

della Maddalena

inola

Via Luccoli

Via 25 Aprile

Via Roma

Info.

Viale 4 Novembre

Via Ugo Foscolo

Via Galata

Vico Chiossone

Via Casana

⑦

Sal. S. Matteo

Via San Vincenzo

⑧

Via Colombo

orenzo – Pza. Matteotti
l Lungo

Pza. De Ferrari

Via Dante

Via 12 Ottobre

Via 5 Dicembre

Via 20 Settembre

Corso Podesta

Via Frugoni

Via Cesarea

stiniani

Stradone di S. Agostino

Pza. Dante

Via Ravecca

Pza. Sarzano

Via Ravasco

Via Fieschi

Galleria C. Colombo

the sea. Visits may be made on any day from 9 a.m. to 1:30 p.m. The 17th-century **University Palace**, across the street, has a wonderful courtyard and staircase. Step inside for a look.

Having glimpsed the sea, you may want to get a good birds-eye view of the entire city and its harbor. Continue along to the lower station of the **Monte Righi Funicular** (3) at Largo della Zecca. Buy a ticket from the machine and board the car for a quick ride to the summit. The viewing platform atop the upper station (off the map) offers a superb panorama, but you may prefer to walk uphill to the left following remnants of the ancient northern city walls. At the fork in the road turn right to the ruins of a fortress and another excellent view.

Return on the funicular and take Via Cairoli to Via Garibaldi, lined with wall-to-wall mansions and easily the most impressive street in Genoa. The 16th-century **Palazzo Bianco** (4) was originally built for the powerful Grimaldi family and enlarged in 1711. It now houses the city's best art museum, which—rare for Italy—is happily arranged in a modern manner. The focus is on Genoese paintings from the 14th through the 17th centuries, along with the Dutch and Flemish masters to which local painters had such a strange affinity. Other Italian schools are also represented. The museum is open Tuesdays through Saturdays, from 9 a.m. to 7 p.m., and on Sundays from 9 a.m. to noon.

Across the street is the **Palazzo Rosso** (5), a well-preserved 17th-century mansion filled with art treasures in gorgeous surroundings. Don't miss the Van Dyck portraits or the paintings by Dürer and Rubens. The hours of admission are the same as those for the Palazzo Bianco, above. Just opposite this is the **Palazzo Municipale**, a 16th-century palace now used as the City Hall. Visitors, on request, are shown Paganini's Guarnerius violin, some letters from Columbus, and other interesting items. All of the other mansions on the street are private, but you can usually enter the courtyards for a look. Some of these now occupied by banks have splendid decorations and won't mind if you step inside during regular business hours.

Now follow the map to Piazza Portello, a strange intersection where some of the streets enter tunnels, and wind your way uphill to the **Villetta di Negro** (6), an unusual park with delightful grottoes, waterfalls, dark passages, and gardens with a view. Amid this is the modern **Chiossone Museum of Oriental Art**, featuring prehistoric artifacts and armor from Japan along with all kinds of art from the Orient. This fascinating and often overlooked museum is open Tuesdays through Saturdays, from 9 a.m. to 7 p.m., and on Sundays from 9 a.m. to 12:30 p.m.

Return by way of Piazza Corvetto and Piazza Fontane Marose. You are now ready to enter the **Old Town**, a colorful area where narrow

In the Old Town

alleyways thread their way down to the harbor. The route follows the animated Via Luccoli and Via Chiossone to **Piazza San Matteo** (7), a picturesque square lined with the medieval homes of the Doria family. The **Church of San Matteo**, facing the piazza, was built in 1278 and contains in its crypt the tomb of Andrea Doria, the 16th-century ruler of Genoa.

A block away is the **Piazza de Ferrari**, a large, busy open square with a fountain and the remnants of a huge opera house destroyed in World War II. Continue on to Piazza Matteotti, bordered by the enormous **Palazzo Ducale**, once the residence of the rulers and now a courthouse. On the east side stands the **Church of the Gesù**, a 16th-century structure whose sumptuous baroque interior contains two major paintings by Rubens.

Adventurous souls may want to wander down Salita Pollaiuoli toward the harbor, perhaps stopping at the fine 12th-century **Church of San Donato** and at the **Church of Santa Maria di Castello**, which preserves some Roman columns. Try not to get lost in the labyrinth of passages, then return to Via San Lorenzo.

The **Cathedral of San Lorenzo** (8), consecrated in 1118, has a rather gloomy interior enlivened by the **Chapel of Saint John the Baptist** along the north aisle. This allegedly contains the ashes of the saint. Along the south aisle there is an unexploded shell which landed there during a World War II naval bombardment. Be sure to see the **Treasury**, at the end of the north aisle, whose displays include a 1st-century Roman glass cup traditionally associated with the Last Supper. Some believe it to be the true Holy Grail, although it must be remembered that the Crusaders were sold a lot of very questionable items in the Holy Land.

Stroll down Via San Lorenzo and turn right into a tiny passage leading to Via San Luca. At Piazza Banchi make a left to the 13th-century **Palazzo di San Giorgio** (9), located on an interesting square opening onto the harbor. Return and follow Via San Luca, the main street of Genoa during the Middle Ages and still a very animated place.

The **Palazzo Spinola** (10), hidden away to the east of Via San Luca, is a 16th-century mansion housing the nucleus of the **National Gallery of Liguria**. Parts of it are open and display a small but rich collection of art in splendidly decorated room settings. Visits may be made Tuesdays through Saturdays, from 9 a.m. to 5 p.m., and on Sundays and Mondays from 9 a.m. to 1 p.m.

From here the map leads back through some colorful streets to the train station. You may want to make a little detour to the **Maritime Station** (11), where one-hour boat trips in the harbor are offered at variable times. Check with the tourist office for current schedules before going out of your way.

Portofino

Portofino is quite possibly the most enchanting spot on the entire Riviera. What's more, you can enjoy its sublime beauty on a daytrip from Milan without too much effort. This is a marvelous escape from the usual tourist diet of museums, cathedrals, and palaces, and a wonderful place to unwind during your probably hectic European adventures.

Once a simple fishing village on the loveliest of harbors, Portofino has long since been taken over by wealthy escapists. Fortunately, its outward appearance remains much the same as it did when it was first discovered by 19th-century artists. Its tiny waterfront abounds in lively outdoor cafés, and there are short scenic walks to take and boat rides to make. This is really a day reserved for sun and fun.

GETTING THERE:

Trains depart Milan's Centrale station several times in the morning for **Genoa** *(Genova)*, where you change for another train to either Santa Margherita Ligure or Rapallo. Santa Margherita is slightly preferable. There is a better selection of trains from Genoa's Brignole station, so if the train you are taking from Milan only stops at Genoa's Principe station you can change to any eastbound train going to Brignole. From there take a train to Santa Margherita Ligure or Rapallo. The total trip from Milan takes about 2½ hours, with return service operating until mid-evening. There are also direct boats from Portofino to Genoa in the late afternoon. This is a nice way to return since you can easily get a train from Genoa to Milan at just about any hour. Inquire locally about the boat schedules.

During the summer season there is a daily train direct from Milan to Santa Margherita Ligure and Rapallo, leaving before 7 a.m. On Saturdays and holidays in summer there is another train leaving Milan at a more reasonable hour, but it is second-class only and may be crowded. Be sure to check the current schedules carefully at the train information office in Milan's Centrale station.

Once in either Santa Margherita Ligure or Rapallo it is very easy to get to Portofino by **bus** or **boat**. Buses depart every 20 minutes or so. Those from Rapallo may require a change at Santa Margherita. Buy your ticket before boarding. Boats are the best way to get to Portofino, and are not at all expensive. They leave every 30 minutes from Rapallo and stop at Santa Margherita en route.

By car, it is 106 miles from Milan to Portofino. Take the A-7 Autostrada to Genoa, then head east on the A-12 Autostrada in the direction of La Spezia. Get off at the Rapallo exit and follow the narrow coastal road south through Santa Margherita to Portofino.

The map should make the local transport options clear. Getting to Portofino sounds more complicated than it actually is, as you will discover.

WHEN TO GO:

Portofino is at its liveliest in the warm season, when the outdoor cafés are open and the harbor is full of yachts. Good weather is essential to enjoy this trip.

FOOD AND DRINK:

Dining well in Portofino can be very expensive, although reasonably priced meals are available at several trattorias and pizzerias just a short stroll from the harbor. Then, too, you can always get by with a sandwich at one of the many cafés. Among the better restaurants in the village are:

Splendido (Salita Baratta 10, on the hill north of the harbor) One of the most luxurious hotels on the Riviera, with a noted restaurant overlooking everything. Local Ligurian cuisine. Reserve ahead by phoning (0185) 26-95-51. X: winter. $$$

Il Pitosforo (Molo Umberto I, 9, on the harbor) Very popular with yachtsmen, this pricey establishment features seafood specialties. X: Tues., Jan., Feb. $$$

Delfino (Piazza Martiri dell' Olivetta 40, on the square facing the harbor) Noted for both seafood and meat dishes. X: Thurs., Nov., Dec. $$$

Da Puny (on the square facing the harbor) Fine meals in a contemporary setting. X: Thurs., Jan., Feb. $$$

Eden (Vico Dritto 21, in the village) A budget choice in a small hotel, with outdoor dining in a garden. X: winter $$

TOURIST INFORMATION:

The tourist office, phone (0185) 26-90-24, is at Via Roma 35, on the main street leaving the harbor.

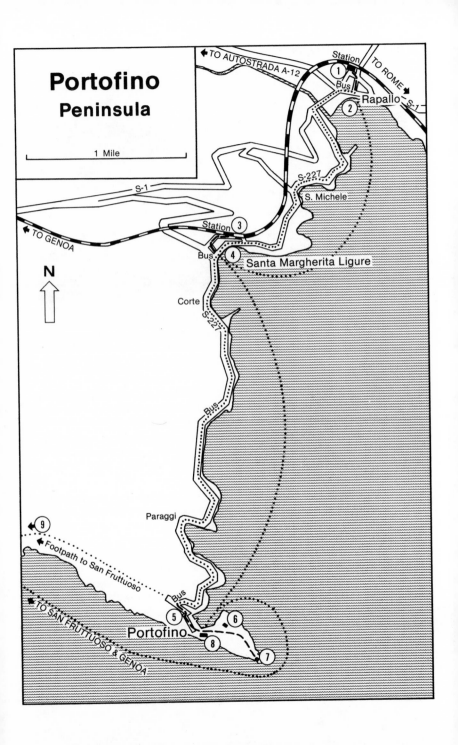

Portofino Harbor

SUGGESTED TOUR:

Those arriving by train at **Rapallo** (an express stop) should leave the **station** (1) and walk straight down to the **harbor** (2), where you can get a boat for Portofino. These depart every 30 minutes or so, and stop at Santa Margherita en route. Alternatively, you can take a bus, which probably requires a change at Santa Margherita. The total distance to Portofino is five miles.

If you took a local train from Genoa, get off instead at **Santa Margherita Ligure** (3) and walk down to **Piazza Martiri Libertà** (4), on the waterfront. From here you can take either a boat or a bus direct to Portofino Mare, only three miles away.

The village of Portofino (5) opens onto a small natural harbor, known to the Romans as *Portus Delphini* and today a favorite with the international boating crowd. Many of its quaint old houses are now restaurants and cafés, with tables spilling over onto the sidewalk in summer. Heading inland, there are a few short blocks of boutiques, galleries, and more restaurants before coming to the densely wooded hills which extend clear across the peninsula.

Just above everyone who comes to Portofino makes the lovely short walk to the **Castle** (6), high atop a promontory overlooking the harbor. Just follow the trail marked "*Al Faro*" from the port. The views from here are spectacular, and there are botanical gardens leading

View from the Castle

into the castle itself, which is now a small museum. The castle is open from 9 a.m. to noon and 3-6 p.m., daily except on Mondays and all of January. Continue along the path to the **lighthouse** *(Faro)* (7) at the very end of the peninsula for another great panorama.

On the way back, be sure to stop at the delightful little **Church of San Giorgio** (8), which has wonderful views in both directions. It is reputed to be the final resting place for the bones of St. George, obtained by the Crusaders in the Holy Land.

Another popular short excursion is to take a 20-minute boat ride to the tiny settlement of **San Fruttuoso** (9) off the map. Not connected by any road, this isolated hamlet can only be reached on foot or by boat. It has a noted former abbey founded around the 10th century, as well as a few restaurants.

A particularly enjoyable way to return to Milan is to take a boat to Genoa (check the schedules at the port), where you can walk just a few blocks to Principe station and catch an evening express train.

Turin
(Torino)

You probably know Turin as a mighty industrial giant, the home of Fiat and Lancia, the Detroit of Italy. What you may not be aware of is that it is also an exceptionally elegant place with first-rate attractions, strongly influenced by the nearby French who frequently occupied it. The fourth-largest city in the nation, Turin was the first capital of a united Italy from 1861 to 1865 and is now the capital of the Piedmont region.

Turin began as a Ligurian or Celtic settlement which was destroyed by Hannibal and rebuilt by the Romans, who called it *Augusta Taurinorum*. Although little remains of its ancient past, the indelible imprint of Roman rule lives on in the grid-like pattern of its streets. After the fall of the empire, the region was dominated by a succession of foreign invaders. The real history of Turin, however, starts with the rise of the House of Savoy in the 11th century, a remarkable dynasty which retained its power on and off right into our own times. Italian unity had its origins here in the 19th century, and it was the Savoys who gave the new nation its first—and only—kings.

GETTING THERE:

Trains leave Milan's Centrale station several times in the morning for the Porta Nuova station in Turin *(Torino)*, a ride of about 90 minutes. These stop first at Turin's Porta Susa station, but you should stay on to Porta Nuova—at the end of the line. Return service operates until mid-evening.

By car, Turin is 87 miles from Milan via the A-4 Autostrada. Parking is available near the Porta Nuova station.

WHEN TO GO:

Avoid coming on a Monday or holiday, when nearly all of the attractions are closed. Good weather is important as the walk can be fairly long if you visit the car museum. The local patron saint's day is June 24th, celebrated in honor of St. John the Baptist.

FOOD AND DRINK:

The cuisine of Turin and the surrounding Piedmont district has strong French overtones, and is usually less delicate than traditional Italian cooking. This is an excellent wine region, producing such sturdy reds as *Barolo, Barbera,* and *Barbaresco.* It is also the home of the rather sweet *Asti Spumante* sparkling wines and a major center of the Vermouth trade.

The restaurants listed below represent some of the better choices along or near the suggested walking tour, which covers only a small part of the city. They are given in approximate trip sequence.

Vecchia Lanterna (Corso Re Umberto 21, 2 blocks west of the station) Opulent dining in a 19th-century ambiance. Reservations suggested, phone (011) 53-70-47. X: Sat. lunch, Sun., Aug. $$$

Buca di San Francesco (Via San Francesco da Paola 27, 3 blocks east of the station) A popular trattoria. X: Mon., mid-July to mid-Aug. $$

Del Cambio (Piazza Carignano 2, opposite the Science Academy) Turin's oldest restaurant, founded in 1757. Very elegant, reservations needed, phone (011) 54-66-90. X: Sun., Aug. $$$

Da Mauro (Via Maria Vittoria 21, 2 blocks southeast of the Science Academy) Very popular with the local crowd. X: Mon., July $

Spada Reale (Via Principe Amedeo 53, near Piazza Vittorio Veneto) Tuscan and Piedmontese cooking in a modern atmosphere. Reservations suggested, phone (011) 83-28-35. X: Sun., mid-July to mid-Aug. $$

TOURIST INFORMATION:

The provincial tourist office, phone (011) 53-59-01, is at Via Roma 222 in Piazza San Carlo. There is also a branch, phone (011) 53-13-27, in the Porta Nuova train station.

SUGGESTED TOUR:

The Porta Nuova **train station** (1) is a splendid introduction to Turin. Built in the 1860s, when the Savoys sat on the throne of a rapidly developing Italy, it is almost cathedral-like in conception. Leave this and stroll into **Piazza Carlo Felice**, a small park of manicured beauty.

Follow Via Roma, the main street of Turin, past the twin 17th-century baroque churches of San Carlo and Santa Cristina into the impressively arcaded **Piazza San Carlo**. The equestrian statue in its center is of Duke Emmanuel Philibert, shown sheathing his sword after regaining the land for the Savoys in 1557.

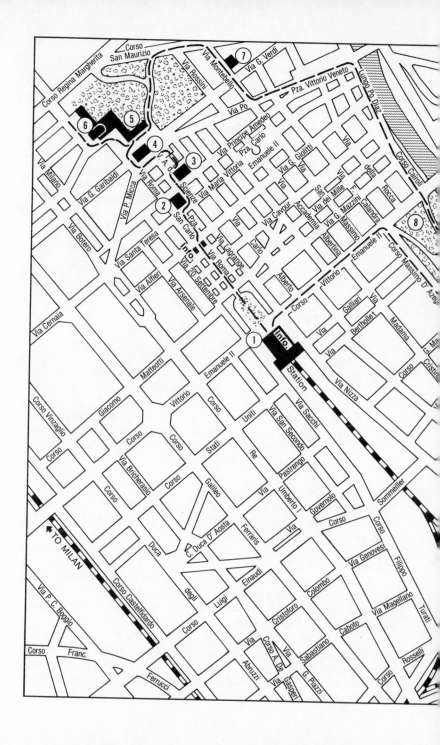

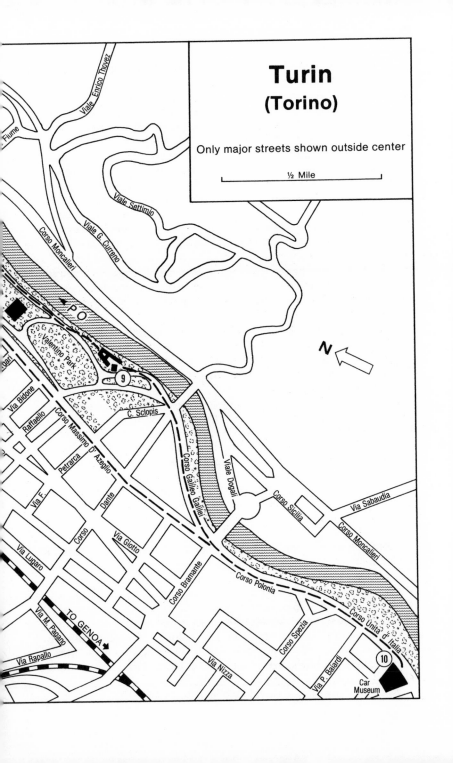

To the north of the square is the **Academy of Science** *(Palazzo del' Accademia delle Scienze)* (2), whose entrance is around the corner. Originally built as a Jesuit college in the 17th century, this rather somber building houses two of Turin's greatest museums. On the first two floors is the **Egyptian Museum** *(Museo Egizio)*, whose collection of antiquities is perhaps second only to that of the Cairo Museum. Unfortunately, its treasures are displayed in a very old-fashioned manner, but their richness overcomes this handicap and certainly merits a visit. Don't miss the reconstructed tomb of Khaiè and Meriè, dating from the 14th Century B.C., or the several copies of the famed *Book of the Dead* exhibited among the mummies, preserved food, jewelry, furniture, clothing, and the like. The museum is open Tuesdays through Sundays, from 9 a.m. to 2 p.m., but closed on Mondays and some holidays.

The floor above this is home to the remarkable **Galleria Sabauda**, an art museum famous for its extensive holdings of Dutch and Flemish paintings as well as works by Piedmontese and other Italian masters. Among the well-displayed items are Rembrandt's *Old Man Asleep*, Memling's *Passion*, Van Eyck's *St. Francis Receiving the Stigmata*, Van Dyck's *Children of Charles I of England*, and Botticelli's *Venus*. Visits may be made Tuesdays through Saturdays, from 9 a.m. to 2 p.m. and on Sundays from 9 a.m. to 1 p.m. Buy your ticket before making the long climb.

Just beyond this, in Piazza Carignano, stands the 17th-century **Palazzo Carignano** (3). This was the birthplace, in 1820, of King Vittorio Emmanuel II, the first ruler of a united Italy. It was here, also, that the first Italian parliament met from 1861 to 1865. Fittingly, the upper floor now houses the **Museum of the Risorgimento**, a fascinating place to visit if you have an interest in the 19th-century struggle for unification and can read at least a little Italian. There is also a section devoted to the World War II Resistance movement. It is open Tuesdays through Saturdays, from 9 a.m. to 6:30 p.m., and on Sundays from 9 a.m. to 12:30 p.m.

Continue on through the small Galleria Subalpina to the **Palazzo Madama** (4) in Piazza Castello. This imposing 15th-century castle, incorporating parts of earlier structures including the east gate of the Roman city, was named after the two royal ladies who resided there. Between 1861 and 1865 it was the seat of the Italian senate, and now houses the **Museum of Ancient Art**. Step inside to see the splendid collection of Romanesque and Gothic art along with the beautifully decorated rooms and various *objets d'art*. Visits may be made Mondays through Saturdays, from 9 a.m. to 7 p.m., and on Sundays from 10 a.m. to 1 p.m. and 2–7 p.m.

Now stroll over to the **Royal Palace** *(Palazzo Reale)* (5), a large but

The Borgo Medioevale

simple 17th-century building which was home to the princes of Savoy until 1865. You can take a one-hour guided tour (in Italian) of its luxurious interior, from 9 a.m. to 1:30 p.m., any day except Mondays and certain holidays.

The adjacent **Cathedral of St. John the Baptist** (6) is a late 15th-century structure of slight distinction. It does, however, contain the world-famous **Chapel of the Holy Shroud** *(Capella della Santa Sindone)*, designed in the late 17th century by Guarino Guarini, the architect who contributed so much to the understated elegance of Turin. Inside several protective containers on the altar is the enigmatic Holy Shroud of Turin, very rarely shown to the public. This 14-foot-long handwoven strip of linen poses questions that modern science has never been able to explain, despite all the tests that bits of it have been subjected to in recent years. It is imprinted with the unmistakable negative image of a crucified man. Was this actually the shroud in which the body of Christ was wrapped after the Crucifixion? Tradition says yes, but scientists consider it a 14th-century fake. Since you almost surely cannot see the shroud itself, you will have to be content with an exact reproduction, displayed along with the scientific evidence, on the north side of the nave. The chapel is open Tuesdays through Saturdays, from 9 a.m. to noon and 3–6 p.m., and on Sundays in the morning only.

Next to the cathedral are some interesting Roman ruins, including a town gate from the 1st century B.C. and the remnants of a theater from the same era. Now follow the map to the **Mole Antonelliana** (7), a very weird structure which has become the symbol of Turin. Begun in 1863 as a synagogue, it was acquired by the city and completed around 1890. Reaching the then-incredible height of 550 feet, it is an architectural monstrosity of sublime fascination, topped by a Greek temple and an intricate spire. You can ascend by elevator to the observatory level on any day except Mondays, from 9 a.m. to 7 p.m.

The route leads through Piazza Vittorio Veneto and follows the left bank of the Po, a river which completely bisects northern Italy and runs into the Adriatic south of Venice. **Valentino Park** (8), fronting on the river, is a delightful place for a rest stop. Nearly a mile long, it contains a botanical garden and a 17th-century castle currently used by the university. Near its southern end is the **Borgo Medioevale** (9), a fake medieval village built in the Piedmontese style in 1884 as part of an international exhibition. Its rather interesting buildings house various crafts shops, and there is a picturesque **castle** which may be toured from 9:30 a.m. to noon and 3–6 p.m., any day except Mondays and certain holidays.

From here it is a walk of slightly over a mile to the **Automobile Museum** (*Museo dell' Automobile Carlo Biscaretti di Ruffia*) (10), one of the best of its type in the world. If you have a passion for cars you will certainly enjoy the vast and thoroughly documented collection, ranging from the earliest wind and steam road vehicles to the latest motoring developments. If not, it is best to turn around and head back to the station. Housed in a gigantic, specially designed modern structure, the museum is open every day except Mondays and some holidays, from 9:30 a.m. to 12:30 p.m. and 3–7 p.m., closing at 5 p.m. in winter. It could be the highlight of your visit to Italy's motor city.

Bergamo

Another one of those marvelously well-preserved medieval hill towns that often get overlooked by tourists speeding by on the Autostrada, Bergamo makes an easy and highly satisfying daytrip from nearby Milan. Perhaps would-be visitors are put off by its spacious, pleasantly modern but rather unexciting Lower Town. Those who ascend to the ancient walled Upper Town, however, are in for a visual treat, an unspoiled holdover from the Middle Ages that never fails to work its special magic.

Originally a Gallic settlement, Bergamo fell to the Romans in 197 B.C. and was named *Bergomum*. It remained an unimportant place until the 12th century when it joined the Lombard League and soon came under the control of Milan. After years of internal fighting between the noble families, it finally threw in its lot with Venice, to whom it belonged from 1498 till 1797. Conquered by Napoleon and later under Austrian domination, it played a pivotal role in the Risorgimento which led to Italian unity in the mid-19th century.

GETTING THERE:

Trains leave Milan's Centrale station shortly before 9 a.m., and at other times from Milan's Garibaldi or Lambrate stations, for the 50-minute ride to Bergamo. Most of these are second class only but rarely crowded. Return service operates until mid-evening, with a few trains terminating at Garibaldi or Lambrate stations in Milan, both easily reached by subway.

By car, Bergamo is 30 miles from Milan via the A-4 Autostrada. Park near the station or Piazza della Libertà and avoid driving in the Upper Town.

WHEN TO GO:

Bergamo may be visited at any time, but note that the Art Museum is closed on Tuesdays and some holidays. Fine weather is necessary to enjoy the views from the Upper Town.

FOOD AND DRINK:

For a town of its size, Bergamo has an unusually good selection of fine restaurants—some of which serve the local specialty, *Polenta e Ucelli di Bergamo,* a dish of small roasted birds in cornmeal mush. A few choices in the **Upper Town** are:

> **Taverna del Colleoni** (Piazza Vecchia 7, on the main square) Dining in a 16th-century atmosphere, with outdoor tables in summer. X: Mon., Aug. $$$
>
> **Agnello d'Oro** (Via Gombito 22, between the Rocca and Piazza Vecchia) An old inn with a cozy ambiance. X: Mon., Jan. $$
>
> **Trattoria Barnabò** (Via Colleoni 31, west of Piazza Vecchia) Regional cooking at a good price. X: Thurs. $

And in the **Lower Town**:

> **Da Vittorio** (Viale Papa Giovanni XXIII, between the station and Piazza Matteotti) Locally popular, with a wide selection of dishes. X: Wed., Aug. $$$
>
> **Taverna Valtellinese** (Via Tiraboschi 57, just west of Piazza Matteotti) Well known to residents of Bergamo. X: Sun. eve., Mon., Aug. $$

TOURIST INFORMATION:

The local tourist office, phone (035) 23-27-30, is at Piazza Vecchia 9, in the Upper Town.

SUGGESTED TOUR:

From the **train station** (1) in the **Lower Town** *(Città Bassa),* you can either take a bus to the funicular (3) (one ticket covers both), or walk the pleasant distance of slightly less than one mile. On foot, follow Viale Papa Giovanni XXIII to **Piazza Matteotti** (2), a monumental open square beyond the 19th-century Porta Nuova gate which marks the 15th-century town boundaries. To the right is the Teatro Donizetti, an opera house named for the composer Gaetano Donizetti, born in Bergamo in 1797. All of the broad streets and elegant squares around you are the result of a highly successful urban plan developed at the beginning of this century, when the Lower Town still had relatively few buildings.

Continue straight ahead to the lower station of the **funicular** (3) which quickly lifts you to the ancient **Upper Town** *(Città Alta),* perched high above the plain. Follow the map uphill from the picturesque Piazza del Mercato delle Scarpe to the **Rocca Fortress** (4), built in 1331 and enlarged by both the Viscontis and the Venetians. In 1848 it was used by the Austrians as a platform from which to bomb the Lower Town. Just beyond this lies the lovely **Park of Remembrance** with its splendid closeup views of the Upper Town as well as a sweeping pan-

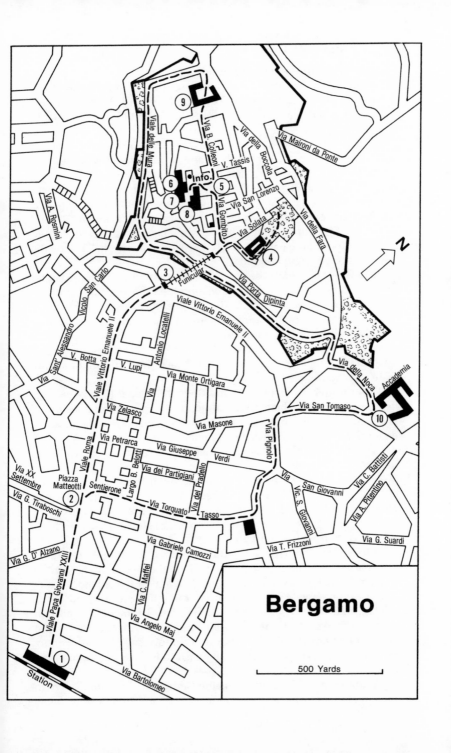

Bergamo

500 Yards

orama of the surrounding countryside.

Return to the square and continue up the narrow Via Gombito, passing on the left the **Gombito Tower**, erected in 1100 to an impressive height of 210 feet but later lowered to 170 feet for fear of instability.

A hundred yards or so beyond this the street opens into what has to be one of the most beautiful squares in Italy, the **Piazza Vecchia** (5), historically the center of Bergamo. The atmosphere of times long gone by is so intense here that you are literally transported into another era. At the far end, crowned with the winged lion of Venice, is the **Palazzo della Ragione**, built in 1198, destroyed by fire in 1513 and rebuilt in 1554. On its right, a 14th-century covered staircase leads to the main floor of the palace, which was used as a town hall during the times of the Venetian Republic.

An elegant little 18th-century fountain splashes away in the center of the square, while to the right, beyond the staircase, the **Torre Civica** rises to a height of 175 feet. This 12th-century tower was built by a Ghibelline family to lord it over their Guelph neighbors and later, in the 15th century, acquired a clock and a bell which still sounds the curfew every evening at 10 o'clock. In more recent times an elevator was installed, making it easy for you to reach the platform for an intimate view across the rooftops.

Pass through an archway to the **Colleoni Chapel** (6). Exceedingly flamboyant in its multicolored marble, it rises above the question of taste and becomes, instead, a gem of Lombardian Renaissance architecture. Built in 1476 to receive the remains of that great *condottiere,* the soldier-of-fortune Bartolomeo Colleoni who at various times served both Venice and Milan, it houses the exquisite tomb of his daughter Medea as well as, perhaps, himself, although this is not known for certain. Step inside to see the **frescoes** by Tiepolo, a delicate **sarcophagus** by Amadeo, and the leader's **equestrian statue** executed in gilt wood by the German master, Sisto Siry of Nuremberg. The chapel is open daily from 9 a.m. to noon and 3–6 p.m.

Adjacent to the chapel is the **Basilica of Santa Maria Maggiore** (7), a Romanesque structure begun in 1137 on the site of an 8th-century church. Its marvelous north porch gives a hint of the splendors to be found within its wildly baroque interior, lavishly redecorated during the late 16th century. Be sure to examine the elaborately carved 18th-century **confessional**, the Florentine and Flemish **tapestries**, the inlaid wooden **choir stalls** from the 16th century, and the 14th-century **frescoes** in the north transept. The basilica is closed between noon and 2 p.m.

At the far end of the square is the **Cathedral** *(Duomo)* (8), a 15th-century structure with an 18th-century interior and a 19th-century dome

Piazza Vecchia

and façade. Although richly decorated with some fine paintings by Tiepolo and others, it is of considerably less interest than the two previous buildings.

Stroll past the small **Baptistry**, a charming 14th-century octagonal structure adorned with statues, and return to Piazza Vecchia (5). From here follow Via Colleoni to Piazza Mascheroni. A small gateway opens into **Piazza Cittadella** (9), bordered by buildings which were once a residence of the Viscontis and their representatives and, later, the seat of the Austrian delegation. They now house the Archaeological and Natural History museums.

Continue on to Largo Colle Aperto and turn left on Viale delle Mura, built atop the imposing fortified walls erected by the Venetian Republic in the 16th century. Along here you will have glorious views of the pre-Alps, the Lower Town, the plains of Lombardy, and, if the weather is really clear, the spires of the Milan Cathedral. At Porta San Giacomo bear left and follow the map to the Porta Sant' Agostino at the foot of the Upper Town.

Just beyond this, turn left on Via della Noca, really a pedestrian way, and walk down to the **Accademia Carrara** (10), an outstanding art museum famous for the exceptionally high quality of its collections. The gallery is not large enough to intimidate or exhaust you,

View from the Park of Remembrance

but can certainly provide at least an hour's enjoyment of superb paint-ing, mostly of the northern Italian schools but including some good foreign works as well. Don't miss this special treat of Bergamo, open every day except Tuesdays, from 9:30 a.m. to 12:30 p.m. and 2:30–5:30 p.m.

Now bear right and stroll up Via San Tomaso, making a left onto Via Pignolo, two very picturesque streets lined with fine old buildings. A right turn at the interesting **Church of Santo Spirito** brings you onto Via Torquato Tasso, ending at the Sentierone, an elegant promenade with outdoor cafés on one side and the Donizetti Opera House on the other. This is a fine place to relax before heading back to the station.

The Borromean Islands

(Lake Maggiore)

The Italian Lake District in the foothills of the Alps north of Milan has long been a favorite vacation paradise for Europeans of various nationalities. These long, thin bodies of sparkling water combine mountain grandeur with the luxurious vegetation of a Mediterranean land, providing welcome relief from the summer heat of bustling northern cities. For the tourist they also offer a brief chance to escape those steady cultural treks through museums, cathedrals, and palaces.

Which of the lakes is best for an enjoyable daytrip is very much a matter of personal taste, and three of the most accessible are described in this book. Each has its own virtues, but only Lake Maggiore has the Borromean Islands—easily among the most memorable sights in Italy. Three of these can be visited, including the strange fantasy world of Isola Bella, the impossibly picturesque Isola dei Pescatori, and the lush gardens of Isola Madre. To finish the day, you may want to ride a cable car to the summit of Monte Mottarone for a glorious panoramic view of the lake and the nearby Swiss Alps.

The Borromean Islands are easily reached by frequent boats from Stresa, a fashionable lake resort on a major rail line. Lake Maggiore, barely three miles across at its widest point, is some 40 miles long, extending from the plains of Lombardy north to Locarno in Switzerland. It is the second-largest lake in Italy.

GETTING THERE:

Trains leave Milan's Centrale station several times in the morning for **Stresa**, a ride of about one hour. Some of these require a supplementary fare, but not to holders of most railpasses. There are also slower local trains to Stresa from Milan's Porta Garibaldi station, taking about 90 minutes. All trains to Stresa are marked for Domodossola and usually continue on to Geneva or Paris. Return service to Milan Centrale operates until mid-evening; to Milan Porta Garibaldi until late evening.

By car, Stresa is 50 miles northwest of Milan via the A-8 Autostrada and the S-33 road. Park near the pier.

WHEN TO GO:

The Borromean Islands may be visited any day between about late March and October. The exact dates vary from year to year, so if you're traveling in the early spring or in fall be sure to check first. Good weather is essential for this trip.

FOOD AND DRINK:

Lake Maggiore is a popular international resort, with a wide selection of restaurants and cafés in all price ranges. Some of the better choices in **Stresa** include:

Hôtel des Iles Borromées (Corso Umberto I, between the pier and the cable car) A grand resort hotel in the 19th-century tradition, with a renowned luxury restaurant. $$$

Emiliano (Corso Italia 48, near the pier) Considered to be the best restaurant in the area. Reservations needed, phone (0323) 31-396. X: Tues., Wed. Lunch, Feb. $$$

Ariston (Corso Italia 60, near the pier) Dining in a small hotel with a view of the lake. X: Dec. through Feb. $$

Luina (Via Garibaldi 21, 1 block inland from the pier) Excellent food in a convenient location. X: Dec. to mid-Mar. $$

Pappagallo (Via Principessa Margherita 46, just off Corso Umberto I) Pizza and other traditional Italian foods. X: Wed. $

On **Isola Bella** there are a number of simple restaurants and outdoor cafés. A good choice is:

Elvezia (across from the pier) A small inn with a restaurant. X: Nov. to Mar. $$

And on **Isola dei Pescatori** there are again several restaurants and outdoor cafés. For good local fish try:

Verbano (behind the church) Outdoor dining with a view. X: Wed., Nov. to Mar. $$

TOURIST INFORMATION:

The local tourist office in Stresa, phone (0323) 30-150, is at Via Principe Tomaso 70, midway between the train station and the pier.

SUGGESTED TOUR:

Leaving the **train station** (1) in Stresa, turn right on Via Carducci and left on Via Principle Tomaso, which will take you past the **tourist office** (2). Continue down to the large boat terminal on the **pier** (3). There are other small boat services operating from the lakefront around here, but these are much costlier than the regular scheduled boats. Buy a roundtrip ticket good for stops at Isola Bella, Isola Superiore (also called *dei Pescatori*), Isola Madre, and return. If you intend to extend your trip to include Villa Taranto (7) you should get the more

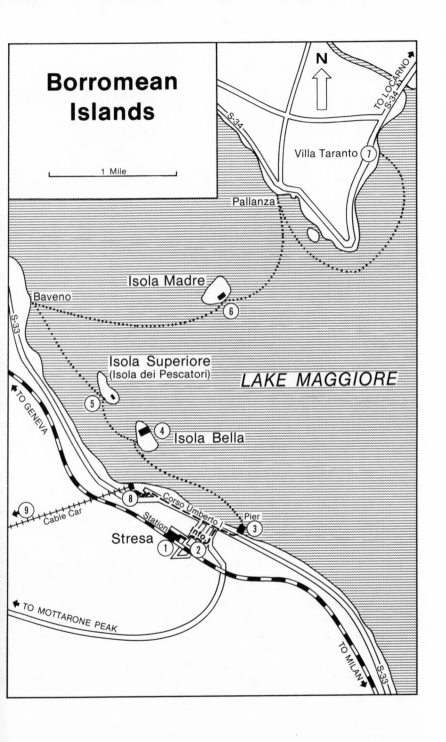

Borromean Islands

1 Mile

N

TO LOCARNO
S-34

S-34

Villa Taranto ⑦

Pallanza

Isola Madre

Baveno

S-33

⑥

Isola Superiore
(Isola dei Pescatori)

LAKE MAGGIORE

⑤

Isola Bella

④

TO GENEVA

⑨ Cable Car

⑧

Corso Umberto I

Pier

Station

Info.

③

Stresa

① ②

TO MOTTARONE PEAK

TO MILAN

S-33

expensive ticket which goes at least that far. Posted signs in English explain all of the options, but be sure to ask for a free schedule booklet *(Orario)* so you can plot your moves between the islands as the day progresses.

Board the first boat to Isola Bella, a quick hop of about five minutes. Always ask to make sure that you are on the right boat so you don't wind up somewhere else on this very large lake.

Isola Bella (4) is almost completely a creation of man. Originally just a rock inhabited by few people, it was transformed in the 17th century by Count Vitaliano Borromeo into its present dream-like fantasy of stepped gardens, incredible statuary, and a lavish palace. There is no other place on earth quite like this, and while all of it is grossly overdecorated, the island never fails to enchant—or at least amuse—its many visitors. The whole ensemble is still owned, along with Isola Madre, by the Borromeo family.

Buy a ticket and enter the **palace**. You can either join a guided tour or just stroll through on your own, which is easy as all of the rooms have explanatory signs in English. Some of the opulent chambers are of historic interest—Napoleon slept in one and Mussolini held a 1936 conference of European leaders in another. A descent to the **grottoes** takes you into a different world. Returning to the palace above, walk out into the spectacular **gardens**, where white peacocks stroll amid exotic vegetation and bizarre sculptures. Try to allow an hour for both the palace and gardens, which are open daily in season from 9 a.m. to noon and 1:30–5:30 p.m.

Return to the pier and take the next boat to **Isola Superiore** (5), more popularly known as **Isola dei Pescatori** for the fishermen who live there. Wander around the back alleyways of the tiny village, and go down to the water on the side opposite the pier, a spot not frequented by tourists, where local children play along the rocky beach. Be sure to visit the simple but inspiring **church** and the tiny graveyard behind it. From here, the narrow Via Ugo Ara squeezes its way between ancient houses to a little **park** at the island's northwestern end. There are those who complain that Isola dei Pescatori has been ruined by mass tourism, but they've probably never been beyond the commercialized pier area, to which you should now return for a boat ride to the next island.

Isola Madre (6) is the largest, the least-visited, and in some ways the most delightful of the Borromean Islands. It, too, has a villa, but compared to the outrageous palace on Isola Bella this is a simple affair, with interesting portraits and mementoes of the Borromeo family's history on display. The main attraction, though, is the setting itself—a semi-tropical world of luxuriant **gardens** and natural splendor with the Alps for a backdrop. Visits may be made any day in season,

In the Gardens on Isola Bella

from 9 a.m. to noon and 1:30–5:30 p.m.

At this point you will probably want to return to Stresa. Those with a particular interest in gardens might prefer to continue on to **Villa Taranto** (7), a botanical paradise reached by boat after first making a stop at Pallanza. An enormous variety of flora from all over the world is cultivated in a truly magnificent setting. The **gardens** are open daily in season from 8:30 a.m. until sunset.

Back in Stresa, it is possible to get an overall view of the lake and surrounding mountains by taking the cable car to the top of **Monte Mottarone**. The lower station (8) is a bit less than one mile from the pier. Follow Corso Umberto I along the water's edge to the point where it turns inland, then take Via Borromeo and Via Torino to the cable car at Lido. Check the schedules carefully as the cars only run until late afternoon or early evening. The **summit** (9), at 4,900 feet, offers a marvelous alpine panorama extending as far south as Milan.

Lake Como

(Lago di Como)

Probably the most famous lake in Italy, Como may also be the most romantic. Its limpid blue waters are surrounded by steep mountain walls, increasing in height to 8,500 feet as you head north. Elegant holiday resorts dot its narrow shores, along with terraced subtropical gardens and isolated villas. These incursions by man, however, become miniscule when viewed against the natural splendor of the setting.

Shaped like an inverted "Y," Lake Como is 31 miles long and 2½ miles wide at one point, but narrows to less than a mile across in its southern section. At 1,345 feet, it is the deepest lake in Europe. Its eastern arm is known as Lake Lecco.

Lake Como has been a popular retreat since the days of the Romans, who called it Lacus Larius; hence its alternative name of Lago Lario. Both Pliny the Elder and his nephew the Younger had villas on its shores, and Virgil sang its praises. Today it is a playground for Italians as well as other Europeans, especially the many British vacationers who come back year after year. You can join them on this exceptionally easy and pleasurable daytrip, which takes you on a delightful cruise to Bellagio, the most enchanting spot on the lake.

GETTING THERE:

Trains depart Milan's Centrale station several times in the morning for the half-hour ride to Como's San Giovanni station. Some of these require a supplementary fare, but not to holders of most railpasses. All trains are marked for Chiasso. There is also local service out of Milan's Porta Garibaldi station, taking about 55 minutes. In addition, the independent Nord-Milano Railway has fairly frequent service from Milan's Nord station, taking about 50 minutes, but these go to Como's Lago station (closer to the pier) and do not accept railpasses. Return service on the State Railway *(FS)* operates until late evening, while the Nord-Milano Railway has returns until mid-evening.

By car, Como is 30 miles north of Milan on the A-9 Autostrada. Park as close to the pier as possible.

WHEN TO GO:
An excursion on Lake Como can be enjoyed between mid-spring and mid-fall. Fine weather is absolutely essential as the entire trip is out of doors.

FOOD AND DRINK:
Being a popular vacation spot for Italians and foreigners alike, Lake Como offers an abundance of restaurants and cafés in every possible price bracket. Some good choices in **Bellagio** include:

> **Grand Hotel Villa Serbelloni** (in a garden just north of the pier) A very famous dining room with Old World elegance. X: Oct. to Mar. $$$
>
> **Du Lac** (near the pier) Dining outdoors or indoors, facing the lake. X: Oct. to Mar. $$
>
> **Florence** (near the pier) An old favorite with vacationers. X: Oct. to Apr. $$
>
> **Bilacus** (Salita Serbelloni 9, near the top) With outdoor garden tables. X: Nov. to mid-Mar. $$

The town of **Como** has several good restaurants, including:

> **Imbarcadero** (Piazza Cavour 20, near the pier) Considered the best in town. X: early Jan. $$$
>
> **Da Angela** (Via Ugo Foscolo 16, off Pza. Matteotti behind Lago Station) An intimate place for local cuisine. Reservations (031) 30-46-56. X: Sun., Aug. $$$
>
> **Da Pizzi** (Viale Gene 12, just beyond the funicular) Outdoor dining in a garden. X: Thurs., Jan. $$

TOURIST INFORMATION:
The provincial tourist office in Como, phone (031) 26-20-91, is located at Piazza Cavour 16, close to the pier. In Bellagio there is a local tourist office, phone (031) 95-02-04, at Piazza della Chiesa, by the parish church.

SUGGESTED TOUR:
Arriving at Como's **San Giovanni station** (1) *(State Railways)* or **Lago station** (2) *(Nord-Milano Railway)*, follow the map to the pier (3) and check the schedule of boats to Bellagio. There are two types of these, the regular ferries which take about 1½ hours and the more expensive, faster hydrofoils *(Aliscafi)*. A leisurely cruise on the regular ferry is more enjoyable and certainly more comfortable. Be sure to ask for a free schedule *(Orario)* brochure so you can plot your return trip.

If there is a considerable wait before your chosen cruise, you may want to explore a bit of the town itself. Largely a rather attractive industrial city engaged in the making of textiles, Como has an interest-

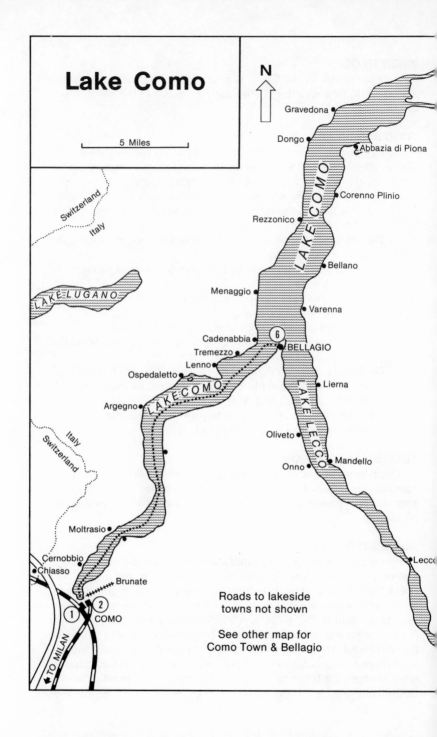

Lake Como

N

5 Miles

Switzerland
Italy

LAKE LUGANO

Italy
Switzerland

Gravedona
Dongo
Abbazia di Piona
Corenno Plinio
Rezzonico
Bellano
Menaggio
Varenna
Cadenabbia
Tremezzo
Lenno
Ospedaletto
Argegno
Moltrasio
Cernobbio
Chiasso
Brunate
COMO

LAKE COMO

LAKE COMO

⑥ BELLAGIO
LAKE LECCO
Lierna
Oliveto
Mandello
Onno

Lecco

① ②

TO MILAN

Roads to lakeside
towns not shown

See other map for
Como Town & Bellagio

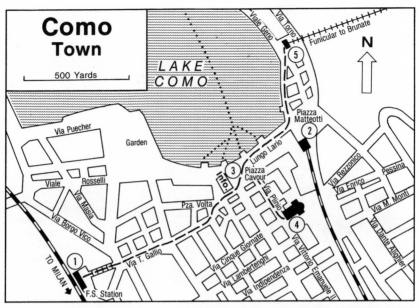

Como
Town

500 Yards

LAKE COMO

N

Viale Geno
Via Torno
Funicular to Brunate
Piazza Matteotti
Via Puecher
Garden
Lungo Lario
Via Rezzonico
Pessina
Via Enrico
Via M. Monti
Viale
Rosselli
Info.
Piazza Cavour
Pza. Volta
Via Plinio
Via Masia
Via Borgo Vico
Via Dante Alighieri
Via T. Gallio
Via Cinque Giornate
Via Lambertenghi
Via Indipendenza
Via Vittorio Emanuele II
TO MILAN
F.S. Station

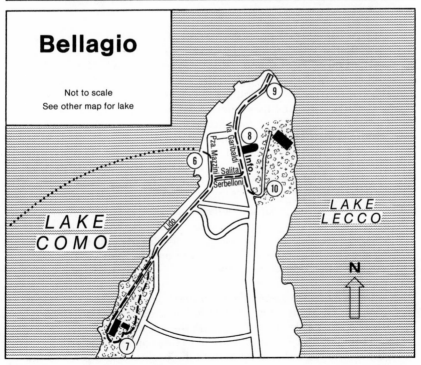

Bellagio

Not to scale
See other map for lake

LAKE COMO

LAKE LECCO

N

Via Garibaldi
Pza. Mazzini
Info.
Salita Serbelloni
Lido

The Salida Serbelloni in Bellagio

Return to the village and climb the steep **Salita Serbelloni**, a stepped alleyway lined with restaurants and tourist shops. At the top turn left on Via Garibaldi to the **Parish Church of San Giacomo** (8), which you might want to visit. Begun in the 12th century and much modified over the years, it has an interesting Romanesque apse. The tourist office is next door.

A further stroll along the same street brings you to the end of the peninsula, from which there is a fabulous **panoramic view** (9) of the lake at its widest point, where the two arms divide.

Bellagio's most famous attraction, the gardens of the **Villa Serbelloni** (10), are not generally open to the public. The villa is owned by the Rockefeller Foundation of New York and used as a study center. To see its lush **gardens** you will have to take a guided tour, usually conducted at 11 a.m. and 4 p.m. daily in season, except on Mondays. Arrangements for this can be made at the tourist office by the parish church. Try not to miss this treat.

Lake Garda
(Lago di Garda)

Of all the northern Italian lakes, Garda is the most distant from Milan and in many ways the most interesting, offering a combination of extraordinary sights along with its natural beauty. It is also the largest lake in Italy, being some 32 miles long, and 11 miles wide at its southern end.

Although well known to the Romans as *Lacus Benacus,* it now seems to be most popular with sun-seeking German tourists, who have easy access via the Autostrada to Innsbruck. Actually, the lake has long been a favorite retreat for northern Europeans, including such luminaries as Goethe, Nietzsche, and Mann. Their successors carry on the tradition, with German being a common language in these parts.

What makes Lake Garda so special is the intriguing variety of experiences it presents. This daytrip takes you by boat to the weird fantasy world of Il Vittoriale at Gardone Riviera, the perfectly preserved medieval castle at Sirmione, and the monumental Roman ruins just beyond. Along the way you will be able to soak up some sun and enjoy strolling through two delightful lakeside resorts.

GETTING THERE:
Trains leave Milan's Centrale station several times before 8:30 a.m. for the 70-minute ride to Desenzano del Garda. These are marked for either Verona or Venice *(Venezia).* It is also possible to get to Desenzano by taking one of the more frequent trains to Brescia and a bus from there. Return trains run until late evening.

By car, Desenzano is 73 miles from Milan via the A-4 Autostrada. Park as close to the pier as possible.

WHEN TO GO:
This trip can be made on a warm, clear day between about April and late September, but avoid coming on a Monday or major holiday when some of the best sights are closed.

FOOD AND DRINK:
Three of Italy's most delicious table wines come from this area. Nothing could be more local than the light red *Bardolino,* whose grapes

FOOD AND DRINK:
Three of Italy's most delicious table wines come from this area. Nothing could be more local than the light red *Bardolino,* whose grapes are grown right on the southeastern shores of the lake. Other local wines of note are the white *Lugana* and the rosé *Chiaretto.* You may also want to try the white *Soave* or the red *Valpolicella,* both from the neighboring Verona region.

Both Gardone Riviera and Sirmione have a wide variety of restaurants and pizzerias in all price ranges. Some good choices in **Gardone Riviera** are:

La Stalla (Via al Vittoriale, on the way to Il Vittoriale) Excellent food in a rustic setting, with outdoor tables in summer. X: Tues. in low season, Jan. $$

Sporting (Via Carere 4, near Il Vittoriale) A popular spot with a good location. $

Emiliano (Via Repubblica, near the tourist office) A pizzeria which also serves full meals. $

And in **Sirmione** try:

Risorgimento dal Rösa (Pza. Carducci 5, in town) Outdoor dining in season. X: Winter. $$

Osteria al Pescatore (Via Piana 20, in town, on way to grotto) A simple place for seafood. X: Wed. off-season, Jan. $$

Grifone da Luciano (Via delle Bisse 5, near the castle) Terrace dining with a view. X: Wed., Nov. to Mar. $$

TOURIST INFORMATION:
The tourist office in Gardone Riviera, phone (0365) 20-347, is at Corso Repubblica 35, a block inland from the pier. In Sirmione there is an office, phone (030) 91-62-45, near the pier.

SUGGESTED TOUR:
Leaving the **train station** (1), at Desenzano del Garda, you can either take a bus or walk straight ahead downhill to the **pier** *(Imbarcadero)* (2), a distance of less than a mile. Once there, ask for a free schedule booklet *(Orario)* so you can plan ahead, then board the next boat to Gardone Riviera. The cruise takes about 1 to 1½ hours, with both regular ferries and the faster, more expensive hydrofoils *(Aliscafi)* being used.

Arriving at the **Gardone Riviera pier** (3), follow the many signs to its major attraction, Il Vittoriale, a slightly uphill walk of about 10 to 15 minutes. Along the way you will pass the lovely **Hruska Botanical Garden** (4), which may be visited between March and October, daily from 8 a.m. to 7 p.m., closing at 6 p.m. in March, April, and October. Just outside Il Vittoriale there is a fine parish church with a view, as

Entrance to Il Vittoriale

well as a number of restaurants and cafés. Since Il Vittoriale is closed between 12:30 and 2 p.m., you may want to have lunch at one of these.

Il Vittoriale (5), also known as *Vittoriale degli Italiani* (Victory of the Italians) is one of the strangest sights in the country. It was the villa of the nihilistic poet and war hero Gabriele D'Annunzio, who died here in 1938 and is buried in the grounds along with his fighting comrades. Born in 1863, D'Annunzio anticipated the rise of Fascism in his writings and was greatly admired by Mussolini, who gave him this property. The estate is managed virtually as a shrine to a faded imperialistic dream, and consists of the villa, a museum, a mausoleum, an auditorium with a World War I airplane hanging from the ceiling, and, incredibly enough, the prow of the warship *Puglia* sticking out of the hillside.

Be sure to take a guided tour of the **house**, which is conducted in several languages. The gloomy rooms are very small, dark, and stuffed to overflowing with bizarre objects, all symbols of his weird life style. Among the clutter you will find a machine gun and a coffin. Emerging from this decadence and back in the sunlight, you can take a stroll through the beautiful **gardens** before returning to the pier. Il Vittoriale is open Tuesdays through Sundays, from 9 a.m. to 12:30 p.m. and 2–6 p.m.

Now board the boat to **Sirmione** (6), a ride of about one hour.

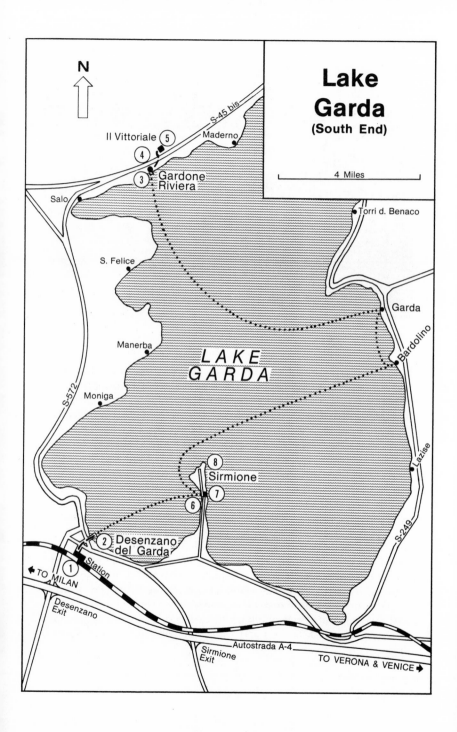

Lake Garda
(South End)

N

4 Miles

S-45 bis

Il Vittoriale ⑤
④
③ Gardone Riviera
Maderno
Salo
Torri d. Benaco
S. Felice
Garda
Bardolino
LAKE GARDA
Manerba
Moniga
Lazise
S-572
⑧ Sirmione
⑦
⑥
② Desenzano del Garda
S-249
① Station
← TO MILAN
Desenzano Exit
Sirmione Exit
Autostrada A-4
TO VERONA & VENICE →

In the Grotte di Catullo

Verona at the time, and was visited by Dante. You can climb its massive tower for a magnificent view, and walk around its formidable battlements. The castle is open Tuesdays through Sundays, from 9 a.m.
to 1 p.m. and 2:30–6:30 p.m., with shorter hours in the winter season.

A stroll through the center of town brings you to a small hill at its
north end, where stands the **Church of San Pietro in Mavino**, founded
in the 8th century and rebuilt in the 14th. It has some fine early frescoes. From here the road continues for a short distance to the northern tip of the peninsula and Sirmione's most famous attraction.

The **Grotte di Catullo** (8) is a bit of a misnomer. Actually it is the
very romantic ruins of a gigantic Roman structure from about the 1st
century B.C. Tradition holds that this was the villa of the poet Catul-
lus, although there is no supporting evidence and the complex seems
much too large for that purpose. Start your visit at the little **museum**
by the entrance, which has an orientation map and some fragmented
frescoes. After that you can climb all over the remains and down to
the lake for some more marvelous views before returning to Sirmione
and the 20-minute boat ride back to Desenzano. The ruins are open
every day except Mondays and some holidays, from 9 a.m. to near
dusk.

Verona

The ancient, romantic city of Verona is best known as the setting for a story that never happened. Or did it? Fantasy mixes with reality here, and you can easily imagine Romeo and Juliet strolling through these timeless streets.

The very origins of Verona are as cloudy as the Shakespearean tragedy it gave life to. Two thousand years ago it was already an important city, and an old one even then, having been occupied since prehistoric times. For the Romans it was a vital strategic center, situated on the plains just south of a point at which the Alps could be crossed. Verona's greatest era was under the Scaligers, from 1260 to 1387, followed by a dark period at the hands of the Viscontis. From 1405 to 1796 it flourished under Venetian rule. Then came the French, succeeded by the Austrians in 1814. In 1866 Verona finally became part of a unified Italy.

Few cities in Europe have preserved their past quite as well. Several Roman structures remain in use today, including its Arena, the third-largest Roman amphitheater in the world. A lingering medieval atmosphere still fills the streets, and there are many splendid Renaissance buildings to enliven the scene.

This daytrip can also be taken from Venice, which has excellent rail and highway connections to Verona.

GETTING THERE:

Trains depart Milan's Centrale station for Verona's Porta Nuova station fairly frequently until about 9 a.m., the trip taking a bit less than 1½ hours. Some of these require a supplementary fare, but not to holders of most railpasses. Return service operates until late evening, although the last of these may go to Milan's Lambrate station instead.

Trains depart Venice's Santa Lucia station several times in the morning for the under-two-hour journey to Verona's Porta Nuova station. There is considerably better service out of Venice's Mestre station, on the mainland and easily reached by any train leaving Santa Lucia. Return trains run until late evening.

By car from Milan, take the A-4 Autostrada to the Verona-Sud exit, a distance of 98 miles. Park as close to Piazza Brà as possible.

By car from Venice, it is 75 miles to Verona via the A-4 Autostrada. Get off at the Verona-Est exit and follow the S-11 road into the city, turning left on Via Torbido to Piazza Brà.

WHEN TO GO:

Verona may be visited in any season, but avoid coming on a Monday or major holiday, when nearly everything is closed. An early start is recommended

FOOD AND DRINK:

The local cuisine of Verona is basically similar to that of its long-time ruler, Venice. One local specialty, however, is *Pandoro*, a delicate light cake. The best regional wines are the dry white *Soave*, the fragrant red *Valpolicella*, and the light red *Bardolino*.

Several good restaurant choices, in the approximate sequence in which you will pass or come close to them on the walking tour, are:

Ciopeta (Vicolo Teatro Filarmonico 2) An inn 1 block west of Piazza Brà. X: Fri. eve., Sat. (except July and Aug.) $$

Accademia (Via Scala 10) Conveniently located just east of Via Mazzini. X: Sun. eve., Wed. (except June–Aug.) $$

Greppia (Vicolo Samaritana 3) Only 1 block southwest of the House of Juliet. X: Mon., $$

12 Apostoli (Corticella San Marco 3, 1 block southwest of Piazza delle Erbe) Very old and world famous. X: Sun. eve., Mon., mid-June. $$$

Nuovo Marconi (Via Fogge 4, 1 block northwest of Piazza dei Signori) Great food in elegant surroundings. X: Sun. $$$

Arche (Via Arche Scaligere 6, next to the Scaligeri tombs) Specializes in seafood. Reservations, (045) 800-74-15 X: Sun., Mon. lunch, July. $$$

Re Teodorico (Piazzale Castel San Pietro) Overlooking the city from its perch by the Castel San Pietro, with a view. X: Wed., Nov. $$

Alla Pergola (Piazzetta Santa Maria in Solaro 10, 3 blocks southwest of the cathedral) Good value in a colorful neighborhood. X: Wed., late Aug. to mid-Sept. $

TOURIST INFORMATION:

The provincial tourist office, phone (045) 59-28-28-, is located at Via Dietro Anfiteatro 6, behind the Arena.

Juliet's Balcony

SUGGESTED TOUR:

From the **Porta Nuova train station** (1) you can either take a bus or walk the rather boring three-quarter-mile distance to Piazza Brà. Along the way you will pass through the Porta Nuova gate, a part of the massive 16th-century fortified town walls built by the noted Veronese architect Michele Sanmicheli. **Piazza Brà** is entered through the Portoni della Brà, erected in 1389 by the Visconti as part of their defenses. To the right is the bulky 17th-century Palazzo della Gran Guardia and, just beyond, the Neoclassical Palazzo Barbieri, now the city hall. On the opposite side of the park is the Liston, a fashionable promenade lined with elegant cafés and restaurants.

The main attraction in the Piazza Brà is the **Arena** (2), the third-largest amphitheater in the Roman world. Built in the 1st century A.D., it is still in excellent condition. Only four arches of the outermost wall survived the earthquake of 1183, however the inner section is virtually complete. You can climb all over the interior, which seats some 20,000 spectators who in the past may have enjoyed gladiatorial contests during the Roman era, executions in the Middle Ages, tournaments during the Renaissance, and plays in the 19th century. It is now used for operas during July and August, of which the most spectacular is that perennial favorite by Verdi, Aïda. The Arena is open every day except Mondays and a few holidays, from 8:45 a.m. to 6:45 p.m., closing earlier in winter and at 1:30 p.m. on performance days.

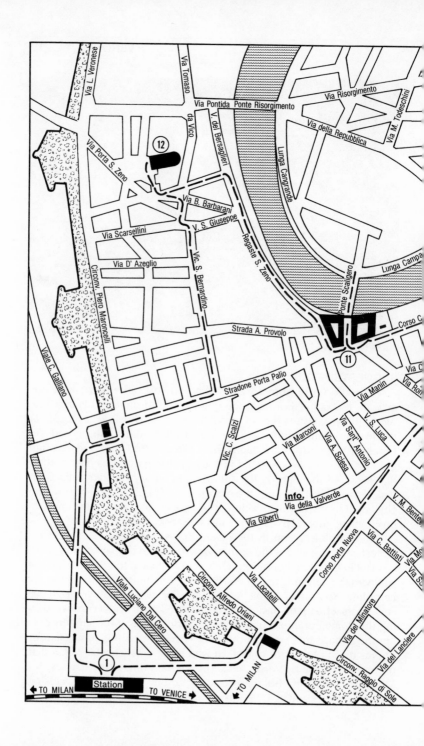

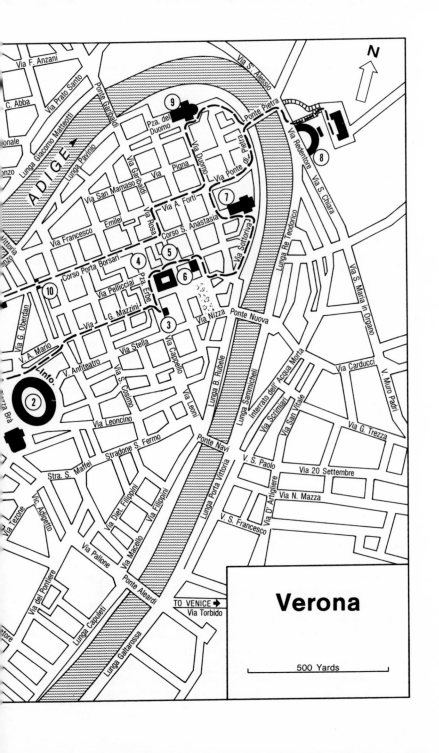

Verona

500 Yards

Now follow the elegant Via Mazzini, a pedestrians-only street lined with quality shops, to the **House of Juliet** *(Casa di Giullietta)* (3) at Via Cappello 23. Step into the courtyard to see the famous **balcony** from which Shakespeare's characters exchanged their declarations of love. The building dates from the 13th century, but no evidence of any real Romeo and Juliet exists. It's a nice illusion, however, and you can go out on the balcony to complete it. The house is open Tuesdays through Sundays, from 8 a.m. to 6:45 p.m.

Stroll over to the **Piazza delle Erbe** (4), a market place on the site of the Roman forum. Amid the colorful bustle of the market stands the Madonna of Verona fountain, erected in 1368 and now the symbol of the city. All around you are various houses, palaces, and towers, some dating as far back as the 12th century.

Pass under the Arco della Costa, which has a whalebone hanging from it, and into **Piazza dei Signori** (5), a surprisingly quiet and dignified square in the midst of so much commotion. An opening on the right leads into the courtyard of the Mercato Vecchio from which you may ascend all 270 feet of the 12th-century **Lamberti Tower** by elevator for a marvelous view. Stroll back into Piazza dei Signori, where a statue of Dante recalls the poet's stay here after being exiled from his native Florence. Behind him is the Loggia del Consiglio, the finest Renaissance structure in Verona.

Among the more unusual sights in town are the **Tombs of the Scaligers** *(Arche Scaligere)* (6), reached through an archway at the far end of the Piazza dei Signori. These outdoor canopied Gothic structures are the most elaborate medieval tombs in Italy, a fitting memorial for the Scaliger dynasty. Note in particular the one over the doorway of the adjacent **Church of Santa Maria Antica**, surmounted by an equestrian figure. The tombs can be seen from the street, or visited close up, any day except Mondays or holidays, from 9 a.m. to noon and 2:30–6:30 p.m.

Now make a right onto Via Arche Scaligere past the so-called Romeo's House at Number 4, a medieval building in poor condition presently housing a seedy bar. Its age may be authentic, but that's all. Continue down Via Ponte Nuova and turn left into Via Sottoriva, a picturesque street with porticoed houses in the Venetian Gothic style.

The **Church of Sant' Anastasia** (7), although huge, doesn't look like much from the outside. Its interior, however, is quite another story. Begun in 1290 by the Dominicans, it was completed in the 15th century. Step inside to see the famous holy-water **stoups** supported by hunchback human figures. The fresco of *St. George and the Princess*, in the Giusti Chapel at the end of the left transept, is a major 15th-century work by Pisanello. Note also the terracotta reliefs by Michele da Firenze depicting the life of Christ, in the Pellegrini Chapel

On the Scaliger Bridge

to the right of the chancel.

The route now leads across the Adige river to the **Roman Theater** (8), an outdoor structure dating from the late 1st century B.C. Performances of Shakespeare's plays are given here in July and August. From the theater you can take an elevator to the **Archaeological Museum** in the former convent building above, which also offers a fine view. The theater complex is open every day except Mondays and some holidays, from 8 a.m. to 6:45 p.m. It is not actually necessary to go in, however, as you can see a great deal from the steps to the left of its entrance. Continue climbing those same steps all the way to the **Castel San Pietro** at the top of the hill for a sweeping panoramic view of Verona, truly worth the effort.

Return to the river and follow the map to the **Cathedral** *(Duomo)* (9), begun in the 12th century on the site of an earlier church. It was greatly altered in later years, acquiring a splendid campanile designed by Sanmicheli in the 16th century. Inside, the major art works include a fabulous 16th-century *Assumption* by Titian, over the first altar on the left. Another interesting work, this by Liberale da Verona, is the *Epiphany* above the second altar on the right. The polished marble enclosure around the chancel, dating from 1534, is by Sanmicheli.

Continue on, following the route on the map, through the **Porta Borsari** (10), a well-preserved Roman gateway from the 1st century A.D. Beyond this is the Corso Cavour, a remarkable street lined with Gothic, Renaissance, and baroque structures, foremost of which is Sanmicheli's **Palazzo Bevilacqua** at number 19. In the little park next to the castle stands the **Arco dei Gavi**, a reconstructed 1st-century Roman triumphal arch.

The **Castlevecchio** (11) is a massive medieval stronghold built in the 14th century by the ruling Cangrande II Scaliger as a refuge from his unruly subjects. It was later put to various uses by the Venetians, the French, and the Austrians, finally becoming a museum in 1925. There are two distinct parts, the fortress and the palace, linked by a keep which also forms the head of the Ponte Scaligero, a bridge across the river. Badly damaged during World War II, the complex has been thoroughly restored and is once again used as an **art museum**. Enter through the courtyard to see the superb collection of medieval sculptures as well as the many fine paintings from the 16th through the 18th centuries, including works by Veronese, Tintoretto, Bellini, Tiepolo, Guardi, and others. As you cross into the last section of the museum you can get a good look at the famous equestrian statue of Cangrande I, magnificently displayed on a plinth over the courtyard. The Castelvecchio is open Tuesdays through Sundays, from 8 a.m. to 6:45 p.m.

Be sure to stroll across the heavily fortified and utterly delightful **Scaliger Bridge** (Ponte Scaligero) to the far side of the river for a wonderful view. At this point you could easily return by way of Via Roma to Piazza Brà, where there are many cafés and where you can get a bus to the train station. To do this, however, is to miss one of the best sights in Verona, reached by following the route on the map.

The 12th-century **Church of San Zeno Maggiore** (12) is among the best examples of Romanesque architecture in Italy. Its celebrated primitive **bronze doors** depict scenes from the Old and New Testaments as well as events in the life of St. Zeno. Enter through the cloister to the left. The spacious interior is quite unusual and contains, above the high altar, one of the most important early Renaissance paintings in Italy, the noted San Zeno Triptych by Mantegna. The balustrade near this is decorated with fine statues of Christ and the Apostles. Below, in the crypt, is the tomb of St. Zeno himself. The church is usually open daily, from 7 a.m. to 12:30 p.m. and 3:30–6 p.m. Leaving it, the best route back to the train station is shown on the map, or you could take a bus.

Section V

Daytrips from Venice

North East Italy

With Venice being the undisputed tourist mecca of northeastern Italy, the region's other attractions often tend to get overlooked. Yet they have a great deal to offer, and can easily be included along with a visit to the magic city on the lagoon. Like many of life's most intense pleasures, a little bit of Venice can go a long way, and after a few days there you may feel the urge to restore your sense of reality by making brief forays back to the mainland. The daytrips featured in this section cover the four most enjoyable destinations on *terra firma* within easy reach of Venice.

But first you will most certainly want to explore the marvels of Venice itself. While the city cannot possibly be seen in one day, or even a week, the "get-acquainted" walking tour described in the following pages offers a brief but quite comprehensive introduction to one of the great wonders of the world. After taking it you will have a good idea of which sights interest you enough to merit deeper probes.

Venice can be extremely crowded in season, making decent accommodations difficult to find without advance reservations. A very workable solution to this is to stay on the mainland instead. The city of Mestre, actually a part of Venice, has an excellent selection of hotels and *pensioni*, mostly near the train station. Although Mestre is no beauty spot, it is only ten minutes from the Grand Canal by train, with virtually continuous service. All trains in and out of Venice stop at Mestre and there are, in fact, many international expresses which stop *only* at Mestre, so that your choice of trains for the daytrip destinations is actually greater than it would be from Venice itself. Parking a car is quite easy, and the town is right on the A-4 Autostrada. Another alternative base, farther away but nicer and still practical, is to stay in Padua, only 30 minutes from the Grand Canal by one of the very frequent trains, or a bit longer by bus.

Two of the daytrips described in other sections of this book can also be made from Venice. These are Bologna and Verona. Vicenza, covered in this section, is easily visited from Milan as well, as is Ferrara from Florence.

Venice
(Venezia)

Unique is defined by dictionaries as meaning the only one of its kind or without equal—certainly an apt description of Venice. Where else on the face of this earth is there a city without real streets or wheeled traffic? How many other cities, for that matter, seem to be slowly sinking into the sea? And how many are regarded as an almost foreign state even by citizens of its own country? The language is subtly different here, as is the architecture, food, and just about everything else you will encounter. On top of that, there is probably no other major city in the world whose economy is quite as dependent on tourists.

Venice may also be unique among Italian cities in that it has no Roman past. Indeed, it was the fall of the empire which led the inhabitants of the surrounding mainland to seek refuge on these islands in the lagoon. Safely protected from the invading Barbarians, they became a semi-independent province of Byzantium in the early 9th century. Growing trade between Europe and the East brought great prosperity to the tiny republic, which expanded onto the mainland as far west as Bergamo and across the Adriatic to what is now Yugoslavia.

A decline began in the mid-15th century with the capture of Constantinople by the Turks, the discovery of America which shifted trade to the West, and the development of new sea routes to India. Wars with Austria, Spain, and France brought about the final blow in 1797, when the "Most Serene Republic"—La Serenissima—fell at last to Napoleon. It remained primarily under Austrian rule until becoming a part of a newly united Italy in 1866. In recent decades a large number of its citizens have moved to the mainland industrial district of Mestre, which belongs to the city.

Venice occupies about 117 small islands separated by over 100 canals spanned by roughly 400 bridges. It is divided into two parts by the reverse-S-shaped Grand Canal, one of the most magnificent waterways on earth. All structures in Venice rest on pilings driven into a solid bed of clay. This has been undermined by the pumping of water from the subsoil and the rising level of the Adriatic. Enormous engineering works are now underway to stop the sinking and, with luck, save the city for posterity.

The suggested walking tour is only a beginning, a way to orient yourself and discover whether you are among those who love Venice or are one of those who loathe its moody personality. The route was designed to cover not only the popular tourist attractions but some quiet, less frequented neighborhoods as well. You can easily complete it in a day provided you make an early start and are selective about which museums, churches, and palaces you actually visit this time around. After that you may want to study a good guidebook devoted solely to Venice and probe its many additional splendors. If the city gets to be too much, you can always escape for a while by taking one of the daytrips described later in this section.

GETTING THERE:

Trains connect Santa Lucia station, on the Grand Canal in Venice proper, with other towns in northeastern Italy at frequent intervals. Typical running times are: Padua—30 minutes, Ferrara—1½ hours, Vicenza—1 hour, Trieste—2 hours, Verona—under 2 hours, and Bologna—2 hours. For more details see the chapters for those specific destinations. There are also convenient schedules from Rome (6 or so hours), Florence (3 hours), and Milan (3 hours). Direct service is provided north to Vienna and east to Belgrade. All trains stop at Mestre on the mainland, actually a part of Venice and only ten minutes away, where easy connections can be made to those through trains which call only at Mestre.

Buses are practical for such short trips as Mestre and Padua. They leave from Piazzale Roma, on the Grand Canal not far from Santa Lucia station.

By car, Venice is 328 miles from Rome, 158 miles from Florence, and 166 miles from Milan—all by Autostrada. Distances to the daytrip destinations are: Padua—23 miles, Ferrara—69 miles, Vicenza—43 miles, Trieste—98 miles, Verona—75 miles, and Bologna—95 miles. The most convenient, and expensive, parking is at Piazzale Roma. Otherwise, you will have to leave the car on Isola del Tronchetto or on the mainland.

By air, Venice is served with flights throughout Italy and to major cities in Europe. Its Marco Polo airport is reached by bus from Piazzale Roma, or by a more expensive boat ride.

GETTING AROUND:

Other than walking, the only way to get around Venice is by boat. Your options are:

Waterbuses, called *Vaporetti,* are the sole form of public transportation available in town. Virtually all large folding maps of Venice show their routes and landing stages. Service is quite frequent, and fares reasonable. Day passes can be purchased and may be a bargain if you make more than five trips in one day. The #1 *"Accelerato"* line makes all the stops along the Grand Canal and continues on to the Lido, the #2 "*Diretto*" is a slightly more expensive express, and the #4 "*Turistico*" is a special summer service of interest to visitors. There are several other lines as well.

Motorboat taxis can take you directly to where you're going, but are costly unless at least four of you split the fare.

Gondolas are the ultimate Venetian experience. They don't come cheap and there are extras for such frills as music. Still, you might want to try it once. Be sure to agree on the price before climbing aboard. A gondolier's hour, by the way, is reckoned as 50 minutes.

Gondola Ferries (*Traghetti*) are an inexpensive way to take a short ride on a gondola across the Grand Canal. They leave from many well-marked points along the way.

WHEN TO GO:

The late spring and early fall, say May or October, are the best times to visit Venice. Summers are often hot and always crowded, although the mobs thin out greatly once you get beyond the Piazza San Marco. Winter is becoming an increasingly popular season for those whose primary interest is in art and culture. The walking tour can be made on any day, but note that a few attractions are closed on Mondays and a few others on Tuesdays. An early start, before 9 a.m. if possible, is recommended since there is a lot of ground to cover. The local patron saint's day is April 25, celebrated in honor of Saint Mark.

FOOD AND DRINK:

Dining well in Venice tends to be rather expensive until you get beyond the tourist areas. There are, of course, pizzerias, self-service cafeterias, sandwiches (*Panini*) in bars, and even some fast-food outlets, which can provide adequate meals at low cost if you choose carefully. Avoid the obvious tourist traps, of which there are many.

Being surrounded by water, the restaurants of Venice excel in seafood dishes. Some items to look for include *Brodetto di Pesce*, a fish soup, and *Grigliata Misto di Pesce*, a mixed fish grill. The most famous local meat dish is *Fegato alla Veneziana*, a fried calf's liver with onions. In place of *pasta*, you may want to try *Risi e Bisi,* a classic Venetian dish of garnished rice and peas, or *Polenta,* a tasty cornmeal mush.

The mainland area near Venice is a great wine-producing region. Among the best-known types are the dry white *Soave*, the light red *Bardolino,* and the more fragrant red *Valpolicella*.

Some of the better restaurants are listed below in the sequence that you will pass or come close to them along the walking route. You may have to ask locally for their exact location as some are hidden in that you will pass or come close to them along the walking route. You may have to ask locally for their exact location as some are hidden in little alleyways, particularly those which cater primarily to a local clientele.

Harry's Bar (Calle Vallaresso 1323, by the San Marco landing stage) Renowned all over the world, a Venetian experience. X: Mon., Jan., Feb. $$$

Do Forni (Calle dei Specchieri 468, 2 blocks north of the Basilica) Big, brassy, and always crowded. X: Thurs. off-season $$$

Noemi (Calle dei Fabbri 909, 1 block north of San Marco) Gracious dining in a refined atmosphere. X: Sun., Mon. lunch, Jan. $$$

La Colomba (Piscina di Frezzeria 1665, 3 blocks northwest of San Marco) A *Trattoria* decorated with excellent modern art. X: Wed. in winter. $$$

Antico Martini (Campo San Fantin 1983, by the Fenice opera west of San Marco) Traditionally elegant, and often regarded as the best in town. X: Tues., Wed. lunch, Dec. through Mar. $$$

Da Raffaele (Fondamenta delle Ostreghe, between San Marco and the Accademia) Very popular with the local clientele, has outdoor tables on a canal. X: Thurs., Jan. $$$

Montin (Fondamenta di Borgo 1147, 5 blocks west of the Accademia) A neighborhood *Trattoria* in a romantic setting. X: Wed. $$

Trattoria San Tomà (Campo San Tomà 2864, 2 blocks southeast of the Frari) A pizzeria with a regular menu as well. X: Tues. $ and $$

Madonna (Calle della Madonna 594, 2 blocks east of the Frari) Specializes in seafood. X: Wed., Jan., early Aug. $$

Poste Vecie (Pescheria 1608, between the Frari and the Pesaro) A typical Venetian fish restaurant. X: Tues. $$

Fiaschetteria Toscana (San Giovanni Crisostomo 5719, 3 blocks north of the Rialto bridge) A simple and unpretentious place specializing in seafood. X: Tues., early July. $$

Antica Carbonera (Calle Bembo 4648, 3 blocks south of the Rialto bridge) A typical old *Trattoria*. X: Tues., late July to mid-Aug. $$

TOURIST INFORMATION:

The provincial tourist office, phone (041) 522-63-56, is at the southwest corner of Piazza San Marco. There is also a branch, phone (041) 71-50-16, in the Santa Lucia train station, and another, phone (041) 522-7402, at the Piazza Roma bus station and parking lot.

SUGGESTED TOUR:

Before starting this walk you should buy a large folding map *(Pianta),* as it is impossible to show the maze of tiny alleyways on anything smaller. A scale of 1:6,000 is preferable. Suitable maps published by Studio F.M.B., L.A.C., Tobacco, and other firms are available at news-stands and shops all over town. Those given away by the tourist office are usable in a pinch, but do not show nearly all of the passages. The map in this book is for general route guidance only. Even with the best of maps you may occasionally get lost, but that's part of the fun. All along the route you will find yellow signs pointing the way to main destinations such as *Ferrovia* (train station), *San Marco, Rialto,* and *Accademia.* These can be relied on if you become momentarily dis-oriented.

Begin your tour right in the living room of Venice, **St. Mark's Square** *(Piazza San Marco),* easily reached by waterbus from anywhere in town. One of the most beautiful squares in the world and for centuries the center of Venetian life, it is populated by countless tourists and pi-geons. At the entrance from the water, in what is actually the *Piazzetta* San Marco, stand two enormous columns brought from the Middle East and erected here in the late 12th century. One is surmounted by the winged Lion of St. Mark, the symbol of Venice, the other by a statue of St. Theodore, the first patron saint of the republic.

The **Doges' Palace** *(Palazzo Ducale)* (1) was the seat of the Vene-tian government and the official residence of the doge, an elected chief executive with limited powers, from the 9th century until the end of the republic in 1797. The present structure dates mainly from the 14th and 15th centuries, and replaces several earlier palaces. Its exotic appearance is almost Oriental in style, reflecting Venice's Byz-antine connections. Note in particular the fine sculptures at its three corners representing, to the northwest, the *Judgement of Solomon;* to the southwest, *Adam and Eve;* and to the southeast, the *Drunken-ness of Noah;* as well as the elaborate ceremonial balconies on the west and south façades.

Enter the palace through the **Porta della Carta**, next to the Basilica. Over the doorway is a carving of Doge Francesco Foscari kneeling in front of the winged Lion of St. Mark, symbolizing the submission of the individual to the State. Above this is a bust of St. Mark and, higher still, a statue of *Venice as Justice.* The inner courtyard is in the Renais-sance style, and is graced with a grand ceremonial staircase called the *Scala dei Giganti* after the two colossal statues of *Mars* and *Neptune* at its head, symbols of Venice's power on land and sea. These are the work of the noted 16th-century Venetian sculptor Jacopo Sansovino. The wide landing at the top is where the doges were crowned, and where one of them who became too powerful in the 14th century was beheaded.

In the Villa Melzi Gardens

ing past dating from pre-Roman times. There are two major attractions, both within easy strolling distance of the pier.

The **Cathedral of Como** *(Duomo)* (4) is unusual in that it is built completely of marble. Begun in the late 14th century, it is a remarkably effective mixture of Gothic and Renaissance styles. The elaborate west portal is flanked by statues of the two Plinys, both native sons from the 1st century A.D. Step inside to admire the outstanding 16th-century **tapestries** and other fine works of art.

Another nice way to spend some time before setting out on the lake is to ride the **funicular** (5) up to the village of **Brunate** for magnificent views of the surrounding countryside. Allow about 1½ hours for this.

Now board the boat for **Bellagio**, which makes several stops at attractive resort villages along the way. All of these are very lovely, but Bellagio is truly worthy of its nickname, the "Pearl of the Lario." Arriving at its **pier** (6), you will have plenty of time to enjoy its spectacular setting while taking in the sights, whose locations are shown on the map insert.

Begin by walking along the main street past several outdoor cafés. Continue on to the utterly delightful grounds of the **Villa Melzi** (7). The lakeside **gardens** here are worth the journey in themselves, and you can also visit the small museum in the orangery as well as the chapel. The grounds are open from the beginning of April until the end of October, from 9 a.m. to 6 p.m.

View of St. Mark's Square from the Basilica

Step inside and follow the route, which varies according to restoration works in progress, through the many rooms of the palace. Along the way you will see the marvelous **Golden Staircase** by Sansovino; the **private apartments** of the doges, the *Anticollegio*, with its lovely painting by Veronese of the *Rape of Europe*; the *Sala del Collegio* or cabinet room, partially decorated by Veronese and Tintoretto; and the richly adorned *Sala del Senato,* where the senate met amid pictures by Tintoretto. Beyond this is the *Sala del Consiglio dei Dieci,* used as a meeting place by the dreaded Council of Ten, who ran the secret state security apparatus. Other outstanding rooms include the armories and the **Grand Council Chamber** *(Sala del Maggior Consiglio),* an enormous hall with what is reputed to be the largest oil painting in the world, *Paradise* by Tintoretto. Portraits of the first 76 doges form a frieze. Note the blacked-out one of the unfortunate 14th-century doge who lost his head. Pass through the Ballot Room *(Salo dello Scrutinio)* and take the steps down to the **Bridge of Sighs** *(Ponte dei Sospiri),* which leads across a canal to the prison and dungeons. Prisoners were said to have gotten their last glimpse of freedom from its windows before being locked up. You can do the same before touring the cells, but you'll be returning in a few minutes to end your visit. The Doges' Palace is open daily from 8:30 a.m. to 6 p.m., with shorter hours in winter.

Leave the palace and stroll around to its south side to see the ex-

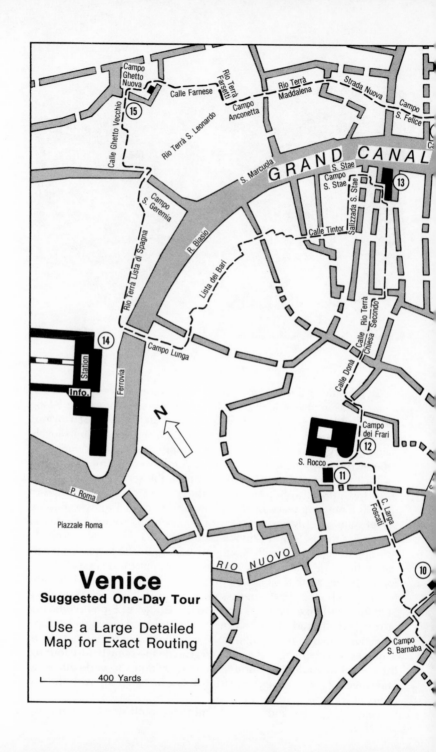

Campo Ghetto Nuova

Calle Farnese

Rio Terrà Farsetti

Rio Terrà Maddalena

Strada Nuova

Campo S. Felice

(15)

Calle Ghetto Vecchio

Rio Terra S. Leonardo

Campo Anconetta

GRAND CANAL

S. Marcuola

S. Stae

Campo S. Stae

Salizzada S. Stae

(13)

Campo S. Geremia

R. Biasio

Calle Tintor

Rio Terrà Lista di Spagna

Lista dei Bari

Calle Rio Terrà Secondo

(14)

Station

Info.

Ferrovia

Campo Lunga

Calle Donà

Calle Chiesa

N

Campo dei Frari

(12)

S. Rocco

(11)

P. Roma

C. Larga Foscati

Piazzale Roma

RIO NUOVO

(10)

Venice
Suggested One-Day Tour

Use a Large Detailed
Map for Exact Routing

Campo S. Barnaba

400 Yards

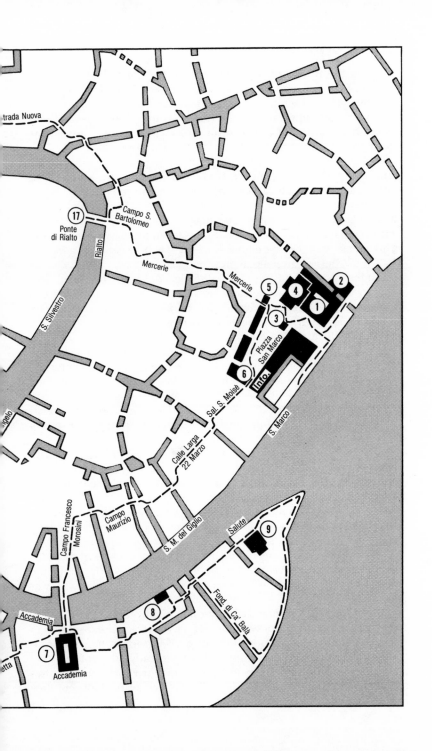

trada Nuova

Campo S. Bartolomeo

(17) Ponte di Rialto

Rialto

S. Silvestro

Mercerie

Mercerie

(5)

(4)

(2)

(1)

(3)

Piazza San Marco

(6) Info.

Sal. S. Moisè

S. Marco

Calle Larga 22 Marzo

Campo Francesco Morosini

Campo Maurizio

S. M. del Giglio

Salute

(9)

Fond. di Ca' Balà

Accademia

(8)

(7)

Accademia

etta

terior of the **Bridge of Sighs** (2), one of the great classic sights of Venice. Now return to Piazza San Marco and its **Campanile** (3), at 324 feet the tallest structure in Venice. Begun in the 9th century, it took on its present appearance in 1514 and has long served several purposes besides that of a bell tower. For mariners it was a welcome navigational landmark, for Galileo a platform from which to test his telescope. In July of 1902, after a thousand years of use, bits of it began falling, the people moved back, and suddenly the whole thing collapsed, killing one cat and three pigeons. Reconstruction began almost immediately and was completed by 1912. The present tower, an exact replica, has the great advantage of an elevator which you may ride to the top for one of the most spectacular urban vistas anywhere. This special treat can be enjoyed on any day between 9:30 a.m. and 7:30 p.m., but not after 4 p.m. in winter.

At the base of the Campanile is the elegant **Loggetta**, a small 16th-century structure by Jacopo Sansovino built to shelter the nobility who gathered here before entering the palace. Later used as a guard room, it now houses tourists waiting to ascend the tower.

The **Basilica of San Marco** (4) is a dazzling vision right out of a Byzantine fairy tale, shamelessly flaunting the loot of Venice's 13th-century sack of Constantinople. It was begun in the 9th century to house another bit of stolen booty, the relics of Saint Mark, snatched from Alexandria in 828. The Venetians were anxious to have a more impressive patron saint than their first, Saint Theodore, and apparently sent a secret team to Egypt for the express purpose of seizing those all-important bones.

The present structure dates mainly from the late 11th century, with a few segments of the 9th-century church remaining. Embellishments added over the years have greatly altered its appearance which, despite the total lack of anything resembling architectural unity, is today one of the most beautiful structures on earth. Originally built to glorify the Venetian State, it was the doge's chapel until finally acquiring cathedral status in 1807.

The west façade is pierced by five arches. Take a look at the 13th-century **mosaic** above the northernmost doorway, depicting the *Translation of the Body of St. Mark* and showing the basilica as it was in 1210.

Enter through the central arch, surmounted by recent copies of the famous **Four Bronze Horses**, the originals of which are displayed in the museum inside. Although their origin is uncertain, they are probably Hellenistic Roman sculptures from the early 4th century A.D., and were stolen from Constantinople during the Fourth Crusade. Napoleon carted them off to Paris in 1797 as part of his loot, but they were thankfully returned in 1815.

Inside, you can take a guided tour or just wander around on your own. There are enough riches here to satisfy several return visits, for which you should really purchase an illustrated comprehensive guide book with a floor plan. In any case, be sure to see San Marco's greatest treasure, the **Pala d'Oro**, an unbelievably elaborate gold altarpiece begun in Constantinople in the 10th century and enlarged in the 14th. It is located in the raised chancel behind the lovely marble rood screen facing the nave. A small admission is charged for this, and the ticket is also valid for the treasury. Here, too, you will find the **High Altar**, surmounted by a beautiful stone canopy. Beneath the altar is the sarcophagus of Saint Mark himself.

The **treasury**, reached through the right transept, contains a fabulous wealth of gold and relics, many of which were plundered during the sack of Constantinople. It is open, along with the chancel, from 9:30 a.m. to 4:30 p.m., Mondays through Saturdays, and 2–4:30 p.m. on Sundays. The same ticket is valid.

Among the other sights on the main floor are the Baptistry, entered from the right aisle, and the adjoining Zen Chapel, opening onto the front portico. Before leaving the basilica, be sure to climb the steep steps from the portico to the open galleries for a wonderful view of the church interior. The **Marciano Museum** is up there too, and it houses, among other treasures, the original bronze horses stolen from Constantinople. From here you can walk out on the open **loggia** above the west façade for a marvelous panorama of the entire Piazza San Marco.

Another popular attraction on the piazza is the **Clock Tower** (*Torre dell' Orologio*) (5), atop which two bronze figures incorrectly known as "Moors" strike the hours. A more elaborate show is put on during Ascension Week and at Epiphany, when figures of the Magi are led by an angel to bow before the statue of the Madonna every hour. Both the tower and its intricate clock mechanism date from the late 15th century. Note the winged Lion of St. Mark against a mosaic of gold stars on a blue background, added in 1755. The magnificent clock face tells not only the time but the phases of the moon and the signs of the zodiac as well. You can admire it all from ground level or climb up to the top for a close-up inspection. The tower is open Tuesdays through Saturdays, from 9 a.m. to noon and 3–5 p.m., and on Sundays from 9 a.m. to noon. The entrance is under the archway.

Stroll west through the piazza past two world-famous cafés. The **Florian**, on the south side, was established in 1720 and has long been a favorite of the Venetians, who in the past shunned the **Quadri** on the north side as it was patronized by the occupying Austrians. Both feature live music, and either makes a wonderful place to end your walking tour later in the afternoon.

At the west end of the square is the entrance to the **Correr Museum** (6), located in the Procuratie Nuove, a 16th- to 17th-century structure which was once a royal residence used by Napoleon, among others. Along with the many works of art there is a vast collection of items relating to the history of Venice, including documents, manuscripts, coins, costumes, arms and armor, and the like. Some of the artists represented are the various Bellinis, Carpaccio, Alvise Vivarini, Cosè Tura, as well as several Flemish masters such as Brueghel, Rogier van der Weiden, Dirk Bouts, and Hugo van der Goes. A visit here will take at least an hour, so you may want to save this for another day and get on with the walking tour. The museum is open from 10 a.m. to 4 p.m. on Mondays and Wednesdays through Saturdays; and from 9 a.m. to 12:30 p.m. on Sundays.

The route now leaves St. Mark's Square for an introduction to the rest of Venice. Follow the map along some narrow but busy streets and cross the Grand Canal to the **Academy of Fine Arts** *(Gallerie dell' Accademia)* (7), generally just called the **Accademia**. Specializing in Venetian painting from the 14th through the 18th centuries, this is by far the most important art museum in town, and one of the finest on earth. If you have time—or energy—for only one museum, it should be this. The rooms are arranged in a more-or-less chronological sequence, beginning with 14th-century paintings. There is no need to point out individual works as they are all superb and very well labeled; but you may want to keep your eyes open for the *Coronation of the Virgin* by Veneziano, the *Madonna and Saints* by Giovanni Bellini, the *Tempèsta* by Giorgione, the *Supper in the House of Levi* by Veronese, the *Miracle of St. Mark* by Tintoretto, the *Fortune Teller* by Piazzetta, the *View of Venice* by Gentile Bellini, the *Legend of St. Ursula* cycle by Carpaccio, and the *Presentation of the Virgin at the Temple* by Titian. The museum is open Mondays through Saturdays, from 9 a.m. to 2 p.m., and on Sundays and holidays from 9 a.m. to 1 p.m.

From here it is only a short stroll to one of the most charming and unusual sights in Venice. The **Palazzo Venier dei Leoni** (8) was the home of the late Peggy Guggenheim, a leading collector of modern art who died in 1979. Operated by the Guggenheim Museum of New York, the small unfinished *palazzo* with its lovely gardens contains a magnificent personal collection *(Raccolta Peggy Guggenheim)* of modern painting and sculpture from the period roughly between 1910 and 1960. Just about every famous name is represented here, including Picasso, Giacometti, Kandinsky, Chagall, Braque, Klee, Brancusi, Léger, and many others. Of particular interest are works by her former husband, Max Ernst, and by her great discovery, Jackson Pollock. All of this is set in the atmosphere of a home rather than that of a museum, making a visit here a wonderfully refreshing interlude between the other art treasures of Venice. It is open from April through October, daily except on Tuesdays, from 11 a.m. to 6 p.m., staying open on Saturdays until 9 p.m. Don't miss it.

Continue on to the nearby **Church of Santa Maria della Salute** (9), built in thanksgiving for deliverance from the plague of 1630 and today one of the major landmarks of Venice. Dominating the entrance to the Grand Canal, this monumental structure was not conceived of as a church in the normal sense but rather as the focus of a votive procession across a bridge of boats from San Marco, still held annually on November 21st. It is the masterpiece of the great baroque architect Baldassare Longhena, who spent the last fifty years of his life building it. The rather austere but still impressive interior contains some excellent works of art, especially those by Titian and Tintoretto. The best of these are in the sacristy to the left of the high altar, for which an admission is charged. The church is open daily from 8 a.m. to noon and 3–6 p.m.

The route now threads its way back past the Accademia and continues on via a series of narrow passages to the next attraction. You may get temporarily lost in the maze, but reference to a good map will clarify matters. In any case, follow the yellow signs in the direction of *Ferrovia*.

The **Ca' Rezzonico** (10) is a marvelous 17th- and 18th-century *palazzo* fronting on the Grand Canal. It was begun in 1667 by Longhena, the same architect who designed the previous church, and completed in 1752 by Massari. Once the home of the poet Robert Browning, who died there in 1889, it now houses the splendid Museum of the Venetian Eighteenth Century *(Museo del Settecento Veneziano)*, where art and furnishings from that era are displayed in palatial surroundings. If you make a stop here be sure to see the allegorical **ceiling fresco** depicting the *Marriage of Ludovico Rezzonico* in room 2, among the finest works by G. B. Tiepolo. Other noted treasures include a series of *Scenes from Venetian Life* by Pietro Longhi. The palace is open daily from 9 a.m. to 7 p.m.

Now follow the map to the **Scuola Grande di San Rocco** (11), built in the 16th century as one of Venice's many charitable religious fraternities *(scuole)*. This particular one is world-famous for its unequaled series of paintings by Tintoretto, 56 in all, which the artist spent 23 years of his life creating. One of the most important **painting cycles** in all of Italian art, this should not be missed by anyone interested in the subject. The *Scuola* is open daily from 9 a.m. to 1 p.m. and 3:30–6:30 p.m., with shorter hours in winter.

The massive complex of buildings opposite contains, among other institutions, the **Church of Santa Maria Gloriosa dei Frari** (12)—known simply as the **Frari**. Considered to be one of the major treasures of the city and crowned with a bell tower second in height only to that of San Marco, this enormous Franciscan church was built in the Gothic style during the 14th and 15th centuries. Walk around to its entrance on Campo dei Frari and step inside for a look at some of the most magnificent religious art anywhere. Titian's *Assumption of the Virgin*, over the high altar, is particularly outstanding, as is his *Pesaro Madonna* along the left aisle of the nave. Titian, by the way, is buried here in a grandiose monument on the right aisle. Be sure to see also the *Madonna and Child with Saints* by Giovanni Bellini, over the altar in the sacristy. The Frari is open daily from 9:30 a.m. to noon and 2:30–6 p.m., closed Sunday mornings. There is a small admission charge.

Referring to the detailed map which you had the foresight to bring along, pick your way through the labyrinth of tiny passageways to the next attraction. Located on the Grand Canal, the **Ca' Pesaro** (13) is one of the greatest baroque palaces in Venice, and was designed by Baldassare Longhena—the same architect who did the Ca' Rezzonico and the Church of Santa Maria della Salute previously visited. It houses the Gallery of Modern Art and is open on Tuesdays through Saturdays from 10 a.m. to 4 p.m., Sundays 9:30 a.m. to 12:30 p.m. There is also an Oriental Museum. Even if you are not interested in the art, the interior is so stupendous that it should not be missed.

From here follow the yellow signs to *Ferrovia*—the **Santa Lucia Train Station** (14), a modern structure built in 1955. The route now takes you well off the beaten path and into the ancient **Ghetto** (15). Between 1516 and 1797 the entire Jewish population of Venice, about 5,000 strong, was required to live in this formerly walled-off district. The term *ghetto* probably derives from the Venetian word for an iron foundry, which had previously occupied the site. Although Jews often held high positions in Venice, they were forced to wear distinctive garments and were locked in this crowded area between dusk and dawn. Five of their synagogues still survive, three of which may be seen by inquiring at the **Museum of the Jewish Community***(Museo Ebraico)* on Campo del Ghetto Nuova. The museum itself, although small, is quite interesting and well worth a visit. It is usually open Sundays through Fridays, from 10 a.m. to 12:30 p.m. and 3–5:30 p.m.

Continue on to one of the main shopping streets of Venice, known variously as Rio Terrà San Leonardo, Rio Terrà della Maddalena, and Strada Nuova. This is among the very few thoroughfares in town that resemble a real street, although it carries no traffic. The **Ca' d'Oro** (16), on the Grand Canal, dates from the mid-15th century and is probably the most ornate palace in Venice. Once covered with gold leaf—hence the name—it now houses the **Franchetti Gallery**, another important art museum. Among the masterpieces on display are *St. Se-*

The Ponte di Rialto

bastian by Mantegna and a marvelous *Venus* by Titian. The museum is open only from 9 a.m. till 1:30 p.m., Mondays through Saturdays, and from 9 a.m. to 12:30 p.m. on Sundays and holidays, so you may want to return here on another day.

Now follow the yellow signs to *Rialto,* the original commercial center of medieval Venice. The name derives from the Latin *rivo alto,* meaning high bank. From the earliest times there has been a bridge across the Grand Canal at this spot—until 1864 it remained the only way pedestrians could cross the water. The present span, the famous **Ponte di Rialto** (17), was built in the late 16th century by an architect named, appropriately enough, Antonio da Ponte. Its three walkways are divided by two rows of small shops. A stroll halfway across it will reward you with wonderful views of the Grand Canal.

From here the route back to Piazza San Marco follows a series of intriguing, narrow shopping streets known collectively as the **Mercerie**—each of the street names begins with *Merceria.* Just follow the yellow signs to San Marco and you won't get lost. When you return to your starting point you can at last sit down at either the Florian or the Quadri café for some well-earned refreshment.

Padua
(Padova)

According to an ancient myth related by the Roman historian Livy, Padua was founded around 1184 B.C. by Antenore, who fled to Italy after the destruction of Troy by the Greeks. Be that as it may, the city is certainly among the oldest in the land. It also makes a fine destination for the easiest worthwhile daytrip from Venice.

Legend aside, ancient *Patavium*, as it was then called, was an important city in the early Roman Empire. Frequently invaded by barbaric hordes from the north, it regained its prosperity by the 12th century. From 1405 to 1797 Padua belonged to Venice and shared in its fortunes. In 1222 its university—the second oldest in Italy—was founded and attracted great talents including Petrarch, Dante, and Galileo.

The name most closely associated with Padua is, of course, that of Saint Anthony. Born in Lisbon in 1195, he set out on a mission to Africa but was driven by a storm at sea to Italy instead. There he met St. Francis of Assisi, who sent him north to Padua. His charismatic preaching converted many to the faith, and soon after he died in 1231 a basilica was erected to house his tomb. This still remains one of the major places of pilgrimage in all Christendom.

By getting off to an early start and rushing a bit, a visit to Padua could be combined in the same day with one to either Ferrara or Vicenza, described in the next two chapters. Because of its excellent transportation facilities, Padua makes a fine alternative to nearby Venice as a base for daytrips in the region.

GETTING THERE:

Trains depart Venice's Santa Lucia station at least hourly for Padua *(Padova)*, the trip taking about 30 minutes. There is even better service from Venice's Mestre station on the mainland. Very few of the trains require reservations, and a few are second-class only. Return service operates until late evening.

Buses leave Piazzale Roma in Venice at frequent intervals for Padua, where they stop at the terminal on Via Trieste, a short walk from the train station. The trip takes about 40 minutes.

By car, Padua is 23 miles west of Venice via the A-4 Autostrada. Parking is available near the bus and train stations.

240

WHEN TO GO:
Padua may be visited at any time, but most of the sights are closed on Mondays. Many of the local inhabitants escape the summer heat by deserting their city between late July and the end of August.

FOOD AND DRINK:
Located in the heart of an important agricultural region, Padua has a bountiful supply of fresh ingredients for its cooking, which strongly resembles that of Venice with a few influences from Bologna thrown in. Some favorite local dishes include *Pasta e Fasoi*, a pasta-and-beans combination; *Risi e Bisi,* the Venetian rice-and-peas dish which Padua claims to have invented; and *Poenta e Osei,* a mixture of polenta and roulade. There is little interest in meats, but plenty of fish and poultry. Padua is noted for its bread and polenta. The local wines are not well known, but you may want to try the red or white *Colli Euganei.*

Some good restaurant choices are:

El Toulà (Via Belle Parti 11, 2 blocks north of Palazzo della Ra- gione) Reservations, (049) 875-1822, are essential for this modern, sophisticated Venetian-style restaurant. X: Sun., Mon. lunch, Aug. $$$

Da Placido (Via Santa Lucia 59, north of Palazzo della Ragione) A simple but friendly place with traditional Italian dishes. X: Sat. eve., Sun., Aug. $$

Cavalca (Via Manin 8, west of Palazzo della Ragione) A long- time favorite with the locals. X: Tues. eve., Wed. $$

Al Fagiano (Via Locatelli 45, a block southwest of the Basilica) A small inn with traditional fare. X: Mon., July. $

Al Pero (Via Santa Lucia 72, just north of Palazzo della Ragione) Busy with local students who love the low prices. X: Sun., Aug. $

Vecchia Padova (Via Zabarella 61, south of the Scrovegni Chapel) Self-service with low prices at lunch. X: Mon., Aug. $

No visit to Padua is complete without a stop at the **Caffè Pedroc- chi**, an elegant 19th-century coffeehouse which has long been a land- mark of the city. It is centrally located on the Piazza Cavour, near the end of the walking tour.

TOURIST INFORMATION:
The local tourist office, phone (049) 875-20-77, is in the train sta- tion. There is also a branch at the Civic Museum, phone (049) 875-11- 53.

SUGGESTED TOUR:
Leave the **train station** (1) and stroll down Corso del Popolo to the

public gardens on the left. Beyond the scant remains of a town wall and a Roman amphitheater from the 1st century A.D. is the tiny **Scrovegni Chapel** *(Cappella degli Scrovegni)* (2), an unpretentious structure housing one of the world's most important art treasures. Once part of a private estate—now demolished—the chapel was built in the early 14th century by the very wealthy Enrico Scrovegni as an atonement for his father's ill-gotten gains from usury.

Purchase tickets at the nearby Civic Museum (3) and step inside to view the fabulous **cycle of frescoes** by Giotto, probably painted between 1303 and 1305 and generally considered to be the turning point in the evolution of art from the Byzantine tradition to the modern portrayal of the human figure in depth. The paintings deal with the theme of Christian redemption, beginning with the *Expulsion of Joachim* and ending with the *Last Judgement*. Perhaps the most remarkable panels are those depicting the *Kiss of Judas* and the *Lamentation*. Be sure to pick up a plan at the entrance so you can identify the scenes. The Scrovegni Chapel, also known as the Arena Chapel, is open daily from 9 a.m. to 7 p.m., with shorter hours in winter. It is closed on winter Mondays and a few major holidays. Don't miss this.

The nearby **Civic Museum** (3) has an interesting, although rather eclectic, collection of art curiosities—mostly minor works by famous painters. It is open on Tuesdays through Sundays, from 9 a.m. to 7 p.m., closing at 6 p.m. in winter.

Now follow the map to Padua's most famous attraction, the **Basilica of St. Anthony** *(Basilica di Sant' Antonio)* (4), commonly known as **Il Santo**. Built between 1232 and 1307 to house the tomb of the saint, this massive and ornate structure is a fascinating mixture of the Byzantine, Romanesque, and Gothic styles. It has always been, and still remains, an important center of pilgrimage—as you will quickly discover when you step inside. Before doing that, though, take a look at the magnificent **equestrian statue** of Gattemelata, a noted 15th-century soldier-of-fortune. Prominently located in the square in front of the basilica, this work by Donatello was the first significant bronze casting of its type since classical times.

Enter the basilica, easily among the most ornately decorated churches in Italy, and pick up a printed floor plan. The **Tomb of St. Anthony**, in the left transept, is the center of attraction for countless pilgrims for all over the world. It is embellished with recent ex-votos which touchingly attest to miracles performed on behalf of the faithful, with tiny metal plaques representing parts of the body healed.

The **High Altar** is adorned with marvelous 15th-century bronze sculptures by Donatello and his assistants. At the rear of the apse is the **Treasury Chapel**, where the incorrupt tongue and jaw of St. Anthony are displayed in elaborate reliquaries, along with other relics.

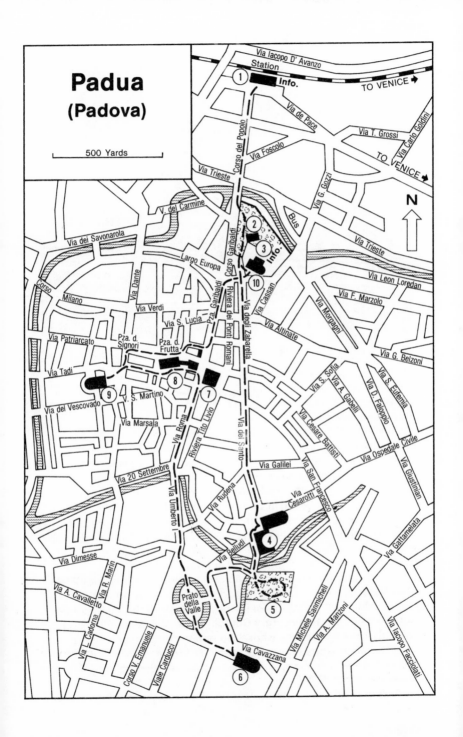

The Basilica of St. Anthony

There are enough additional items of interest to keep you busy for a while, for which you may want to purchase an illustrated guide booklet. The basilica is open daily from 6:30 a.m. to 7:45 p.m., closing at 7 p.m. in winter.

Adjoining Il Santo are the **Oratorio di San Giorgio** and the **Scuola di Sant' Antonio**, both renowned for their splendid frescoes, including the three earliest documented works by Titian in the latter.

After all this art, a stroll through the nearby **Botanical Gardens** *(Orto Botanico)* (5) will provide welcome relief. Operated by the university, they were founded in 1545 and are the oldest in Europe. Through the windows of a hothouse you can see the ancient palm tree which inspired Goethe in his theory on the metamorphosis of plants. The gates to the garden are open daily from 9 a.m. to 1 p.m. and 3–6 p.m., closing on afternoons, Sundays and holidays during winter.

A few steps along Via Donatello brings you to the spacious **Prato della Valle**, an 18th-century oval park surrounded by a moat flanked on both sides with 78 statues of famous Paduans. At the southeast end of this stands the 16th-century **Church of Santa Giustina** (6), a huge but rather plain structure whose interior is exceptionally well-decorated. Don't miss the enormous painting of the *Martyrdom of St. Justina* by Veronese, in the apse just beyond the wonderfully carved choir stalls.

Continue up Via Umberto I and Via Roma to the headquarters of the **University of Padua** (7), locally known as the Palazzo Bò. The actual schools are scattered all over the town, but this building—named after an inn which once occupied the site—contains the most interesting sights. In it are the 16th-century **Anatomical Theatre**, the oldest in Europe, where William Harvey studied in 1602, and the Room of Forty, with Galileo's chair. The university, founded in 1222, is second only to Bologna as the oldest in Italy. Guided tours will again be conducted once restorations are completed. Use the southern entrance and follow the signs.

You are now in the medieval heart of Padua, where bustling market squares are linked by narrow passageways. Amble over to the **Piazza delle Erbe**, a spot where vegetable sellers huddle up close to the **Palazzo della Ragione** (8). Known locally as *Il Salone,* this enormous 13th-century structure once housed the courts of law. From the Town Hall, a flight of stairs leads to the entrance to its vast main hall, decorated with fine 15th-century frescoes and containing a huge, very curious, **wooden horse** from 1466. There is also the stone "chair of shame," on which debtors were made to sit before being expelled from the city. The hall is open Tuesdays through Sundays, from 9 a.m. to 7 p.m., closing at 1 p.m. in winter and closed on some holidays.

The nearby **Cathedral** *(Duomo)* (9) is no match for the previously visited Basilica of St. Anthony, but it does have a marvelously frescoed baptistry on its north side, parts of which date from the 12th century and certainly merit a stop.

The route now leads through the attractive Piazza dei Signori with its Palazzo del Capitanio, once home to the Venetian governors. Continue through the colorful fruit market at Piazza della Frutta to the landmark **Caffè Pedrocchi**, an early-19th-century neoclassical building facing Piazza Cavour, where you can sit down for a well-earned drink in style. Possibly the most elegant café in Europe, it has long been the favorite hangout of university intellectuals. Recently restored, it is now owned by the city.

On the way back to the train station you will pass the late-13th-century **Church of the Eremitani** (10), famous for what it was and sadly is no more. Almost totally destroyed by bombs during World War II, it has been carefully rebuilt, but nothing can ever replace the masterful 15th-century **frescoes** by Mantegna, only fragments of which remain. Still, even these are worth seeing, particularly what is left of the *Assumption,* in the chapel to the right of the high altar, and the *Martyrdom of St. Christopher* to its right.

Ferrara

Relatively unknown to foreign tourists, the strangely haunting city of Ferrara makes an unusual but highly rewarding destination for a daytrip from either Venice or Florence. During the Renaissance it was one of the most brilliant centers of art and culture in all Italy, and its mercantile wealth culminated in a program of urban development rarely seen before. Although economic decline started as early as the 17th century, its elegant streets and many sumptuous palaces remain to delight us today.

The history of Ferrara really begins with the ancient Etruscan port of Spina, which slowly sank into the marshes as the Po river changed course early in the Christian era. Looking for more solid ground, its inhabitants migrated 25 miles inland and presumably founded Ferrara, whose existence was not documented until the 8th century. It remained a rather unimportant place until the 13th century, when it was turned over to the House of Este. Seldom is the story of a town so completely tied to one family as that of Ferrara is to the Estes. For well over three centuries they provided a continuous line of sometimes despotic but usually brilliant rulers who, through their wealth and love of art, attracted great talent to the city. The line ran out in 1598, when the last Este failed to produce a legitimate male heir. After that Ferrara became a part of the Papal States, beginning a long decline which was not reversed until recent decades.

By getting off to an early start, cutting the walking tour short, and rushing a bit, a trip to Ferrara could be combined in the same day with one to Padua.

GETTING THERE:
Trains depart Venice's Santa Lucia station several times in the morning for the approximately 90-minute run to Ferrara. These are usually marked for Bologna. Return service operates until late evening.

Trains depart Florence's main station several times in the morning for Ferrara. Some require a change at Bologna. The average travel time is about two hours. Return trains run until late evening.

By car from Venice, take the A-4 Autostrada almost to Padua, then the A-13 south to the Ferrara Nord exit. The total distance is 69 miles. Park as close to the Este Castle (2) as possible.

By car from Florence, take the A-1 Autostrada north to Bologna, then continue on the A-13 north to the Ferrara Sud exit. The total distance is 93 miles.

WHEN TO GO:

Avoid coming to Ferrara on Monday, when many of its best sights are closed. Although the terrain is flat, the walking tour is fairly long—making decent weather important.

FOOD AND DRINK:

The cooking of Ferrara tends to be rather hearty. Located on the edge of the fertile Po delta, the city enjoys an abundant supply of fresh fish, meats, vegetables, fruits, and grains. It is especially noted for the quality of its semolina flour, which arguably makes the best bread in Italy. To complement this, the local butter is also renowned. Two of its most famous specialties are salami and a hat-shaped pasta known as *Cappelletti*. Unfortunately, there are no local wines of any particular merit.

The best selection of restaurants will be found in the area around the Este Castle and the cathedral. Some good choices are:

Ripagrande (Via Ripagrande 21, 3 blocks south of the cathedral) Located in an old mansion now used as a hotel. This popular restaurant serves traditional Italian dishes. X: Mon., mid-July to mid-Aug. $$

Grotto Azzurra (Piazza Sacrati 43, 2 blocks west of the castle) Inventive northern Italian cooking. X: Wed., late July. $$

Al Giglio (Corso Isonzo 1, halfway between the station and the castle) Outdoor dining in season. X: Mon. $$

Le Grazie (Via Vignatagliata 61, 3 blocks south of the cathedral) Local specialties, atmospheric setting. X: Tues. $$

Da Giacomo (Via Garibaldi 135, a few blocks west of the cathedral) A trattoria with good-value meals. X: Sat., Aug. $

TOURIST INFORMATION:

The provincial tourist office, phone (0532) 209-370, is at Piazza Municipale 19, directly opposite the cathedral.

SUGGESTED TOUR:

From the **train station** (1) it is a pleasant but not very exciting walk of about three-quarters of a mile down Viale Cavour to the first attraction. You can also go by bus or take a taxi.

The massive, brooding **Este Castle** (*Castello Estense*) (2), surrounded by moats and drawbridges, was built in the 14th century to protect the ruling family from popular revolts among the overtaxed citizens. It was later transformed into a luxurious ducal residence and eventually became a seat of provincial government, which it remains today. You can visit some of the richly decorated apartments and the **Chapel of Princess Renée of France** which, strangely enough, is Protestant, as was the princess. Also shown are the sinister **dungeons** beneath the northeast tower. Here, in 1425, the second wife of Nicolò III and his natural son Ugo were both beheaded for their adulterous relationship. The castle is open Tuesdays through Sundays, from 9 a.m. to 1 p.m. and 2:30–6:30 p.m.

From here you may want to make a short side trip into the newer part of town, a grandiose civic project of broad streets and palaces begun in the late 15th century by Duke Ercole I and known as the *"Addizione Erculea."* With this near-doubling of size, Ferrara became Europe's first truly modern city. A stroll up Corso Ercole I d'Este leads to the **Diamond Palace** (*Palazzo dei Diamanti*) (3), a sumptuous Renaissance structure faced with some 12,600 diamond-faceted blocks of marble. It now houses the **National Picture Gallery** (*Pinacoteca*), noted for its outstanding collection of paintings of the Ferrarese school. Among the artists represented are Cosimo Tura, Garofalo, Dosso Dossi, and Ercole Roberti. The museum is open Tuesdays through Saturdays, from 9 a.m. to 2 p.m., and on Sundays from 9 a.m. to 1 p.m. A separate gallery on the ground floor has changing exhibitions of contemporary modern art and is usually open for longer hours. Another group of highly specialized art museums you may want to check out are housed in the nearby **Palazzo Massari** at Number 5 Corso Porta Mare. Ask at the tourist office for current information.

Return to the castle and continue into the medieval part of town. In the square next to the castle stands a statue of Girolama Savonarola, the 15th-century religious zealot who met his fiery end at the stake in Florence. He was a native of Ferrara. By now you may have noticed the amazing number of bicycles in the streets, a logical form of transportation on so level a terrain.

The **Cathedral** (*Duomo*) (4) was begun in 1135 and shows a particularly engaging variety of styles. Its broad west façade is beautifully detailed with fine carvings, worthy of careful examination. Take a look at the interesting arcade of shops along the south side, which have

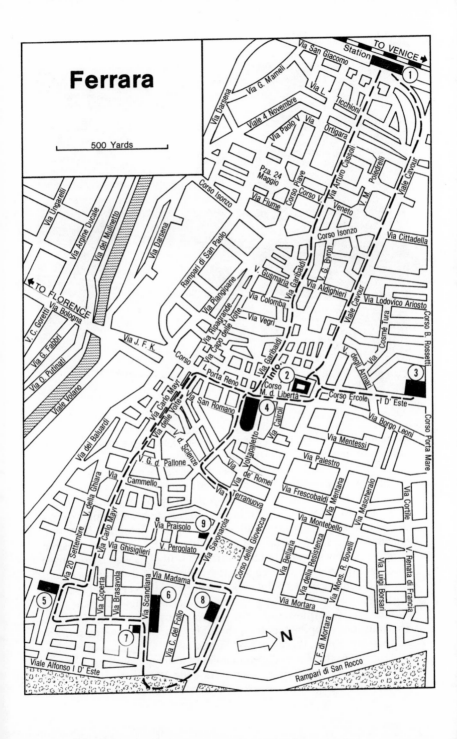

The Cathedral

been there since 1473 and are still in use. The majestic Renaissance bell tower, to the rear, is especially attractive.

The interior of the cathedral was drastically remodeled in the 18th century and, although richly decorated, contains few masterpieces. Two items to look for are the *Last Judgement* by Bastianino, in the apse, and the finely inlaid walnut stalls in the choir depicting exploits of the Este family. The real treasures are in the **Cathedral Museum**, reached via a staircase on the north side of the vestibule. Cosimo Tura, the first major artist of the Ferrarese school, is well represented with his splendid *St. George and the Dragon* and the *Annunciation*, two 15th-century works painted on the doors of the cathedral's former organ. Also notable are the 12th-century marble reliefs of the *Months* and the lovely marble statue of the *Madonna* by Jacopo della Quercia. The museum is open Mondays through Saturdays, from 10 a.m. to noon and 4–6 p.m. It is closed on Sundays.

From here the suggested tour follows a complicated route down the evocative, highly atmospheric **Via delle Volte** with its medieval arches, and along other streets to the **Palace of Ludovico the Moor**

(5) on Via 20 Settembre. According to an old legend this was built in the late 15th century for Ludovico Sforza, the ruler of Milan who was married to Beatrice d'Este, as a place of refuge in case his own city was invaded. There is no documented evidence to support this story, but the *palazzo* is really a masterpiece of the Ferrarese architect Biagio Rossetti. It now houses the **National Archaeological Museum of Spina**, a fascinating exhibition of objects found in the excavations of the ancient Etruscan city of Spina—the forerunner of Ferrara which disappeared into the Po marshes early in the Christian era and was rediscovered only in recent decades. The museum is open Tuesdays through Sundays, from 9 a.m. to 2 p.m.

Continue on to the nearby **Schifanoia Palace** (6), a 14th- and 15th-century pleasure house in which the Estes could escape the rigors of court life. What is perhaps Ferrara's most outstanding museum, the **Museo Civico**, now occupies the building. Step inside to admire the fabulous **frescoes** of secular 15th-century life in the *Sala dei Mesi* which, though badly damaged, are a treat for the eyes. There is also a magnificent collection of coins and various objects of art. Visits may be made daily between 9 a.m. and 7 p.m., except on a few major holidays. The same ticket also admits you to the small **Lapidary Museum** (7), across the street in a 15th-century church, where Roman carvings and sarcophagi are on display.

Now follow the map along remnants of the old city ramparts and turn up Corso della Giovecca to the delightful **Palazzina di Marfisa d'Este** (8), a miniature palace of great charm built in the late 16th century, just before the decline of Este power in Ferrara. It is noted for its unusual painted ceilings and period furniture as well as for its gardens. You can see these on any day, from 9 a.m. to 12:30 p.m.

Heading back through the medieval quarter, you may want to make a stop at the **Romei House** *(Casa Romei)* (9). This 15th-century residence of a wealthy merchant family is exceptionally well preserved and has two graceful courtyards. Visits may be made Tuesdays through Sundays, from 8:30 a.m. to 2 p.m., but you may have to ring the doorbell for admission.

From here return to the cathedral via the route on the map and continue on to the train station. If you decide to walk there you will find the Via Garibaldi a more pleasant route to follow, as it passes a number of small squares with outdoor cafés.

Vicenza

Few places are as stamped by the genius of a single person as is Vicenza, that delightful small city between Venice and Verona. Andrea di Pietro della Gondola, known to the world as Palladio, was the greatest architect of the Renaissance. Born of humble parentage in Padua in 1508, he came to Vicenza in 1524, just around the time the city was recovering from the devastation of a long war. The local aristocracy wanted splendid new buildings to reflect their recent prosperity—what they got was an entirely new style which was quickly seized upon by other architects and spread first throughout the region and eventually was widely adopted in both England and America. If some of the structures seem vaguely familiar, it is because they were the original inspiration for the classical style we all know so well.

Although its site was inhabited by prehistoric tribes, the history of Vicenza really begins with the Roman *municipium* of *Vicetia* in the 2nd century B.C. Later destroyed by barbarian invasions, it rose from the ashes to become a free commune, coming eventually under the protection of the Scaligers of Verona. In 1404 it joined Venice and shared the fortunes of that republic until the 19th century, when it suffered under Austrian domination and finally became part of the newly united Italy.

Travelers with a special interest in architecture may want to get additional information on other buildings by Palladio and his followers, both in Vicenza and the surrounding area. The friendly tourist office will be pleased to help with this.

With an early start and just a little bit of rushing, it is possible to combine a daytrip to Vicenza from Venice with one to Padua, which is better seen first. This trip can also be taken from Milan, although in that case it is difficult to add Padua.

GETTING THERE:

Trains leave Venice's Santa Lucia station several times in the morning for Vicenza, with slightly better service out of Venice's Mestre station on the mainland. The trip takes roughly one hour, and most trains are marked for either Verona or Milan. Return service operates until late evening.

Trains depart Milan's Centrale station several times in the morning for the two-hour run to Vicenza. These are all marked for Venice and some require a supplementary fare, but not to holders of most railpasses. Return trains run until late evening, but the last service may go to Milan's Lambrate station instead.

By car from Venice, take the A-4 Autostrada west to the Vicenza Est exit and follow signs into town. The total distance is 42 miles. Park as close to the train station as possible.

By car from Milan, Vicenza is 127 miles to the east on the A-4 Autostrada. Use the Vicenza Ovest exit and park near the train station.

WHEN TO GO:

Most of the sights in Vicenza are closed all day on Mondays, and also on Sunday afternoons. Although the walk is rather short, much of the time will be spent out of doors, so you will appreciate good weather.

FOOD AND DRINK:

The cooking of Vicenza strongly resembles that of Venice, which dominated it for centuries. There are no local wines of note but, moving slightly farther afield you can choose from the excellent white *Soave,* the light red *Bardolino,* or the more fragrant red *Valpolicella.*

Most of the good restaurants of Vicenza are within a few blocks of its main square, Piazza dei Signori. Some choices are:

Scudo di Francia (Contrà Piancoli 4, 2 blocks southeast of Pza. dei Signori) Elegant dining in a *palazzo.* X: Sun. eve., Mon., Aug. $$

Tre Visi (Contrà Porti 6, 2 blocks north of Pza. dei Signori) Another restaurant in a *palazzo,* this has a warm tavern-like atmosphere. X: Sun. eve., Mon. $$

Gran Caffè Garibaldi (Piazza dei Signori 5) A traditional old-fashioned café with drinks and sandwiches on the ground floor, full restaurant upstairs. X: Tues. eve., Wed. $$ and $.

Al Pozzo (Via Sant' Antonio 1, 2 blocks southeast of the cathedral) A turn-of-the-century ambiance. X: Tues. $$$

Al Grottino (Piazza delle Erbe 2, behind the Basilica) A wine bar with light lunches. X: Sun. $

TOURIST INFORMATION:

The provincial tourist office, phone (0444) 32-08-54, is at Piazza Matteotti 12, right next to the Olympic Theatre (8). Ask them about outlying Palladian villas.

SUGGESTED TOUR:

Leave the **train station** (1) and walk up Viale Roma to the **Porta Castello** (2), an 11th-century bastion which was once part of the Scaligers' fortifications. From here the Corso Andrea Palladio, lined with several structures by Palladio and his followers, leads into the heart of the town. Follow it as far as Stradella Loschi and turn right into Piazza del Duomo.

The **Cathedral** *(Duomo)* (3), mostly dating from the 14th through the 16th centuries, was badly damaged by bombs during World War II and has since been restored. Compared to other buildings in Vicenza, it is of little architectural interest but does have a fine Gothic façade. Step inside to see its major treasure, a luminous 14th-century polyptych by Lorenzo Veneziano which shows a strong Byzantine influence. You'll find it in the fifth chapel on the right. There is also an exceptionally attractive high altar.

Return to Corso Andrea Palladio and follow the map to the town's spacious main square, the **Piazza dei Signori**. Totally dominating its south side is the majestic **Basilica** (4), Palladio's first major civic work and perhaps his ultimate masterpiece. The word "basilica" is here used in its Roman sense to describe a hall of justice; it has nothing to do with religion. The core of the building dates from the mid-15th century and began to collapse in 1496. In an attempt to save it, the local government held a competition among architects. This was won by Palladio in 1546, who supervised the construction for the rest of his life. It was not completed until 1614, 34 years after his death. The use of alternating pillars and arches cleverly conceals the irregularities of the original structure, which could not be changed. Today, the basilica is used for special exhibitions and may usually be visited Tuesdays through Saturdays, from 9:30 a.m. to noon and 2:30–5 p.m., and on Sundays from 10 a.m. to noon. Admission is free.

The **Torre di Piazza**, a slender 267-foot-high belfry attached to the basilica, predates the rest of the structure and was begun in the 12th century by a wealthy family for their own defense. Just beyond this are two elegant columns, one bearing the winged Lion of St. Mark— the emblem of Venice—and the other a statue of the Redeemer. Along the north side of the *piazza* is the 16th-century Monte di Pietà, a long building split in the middle by the 17th-century Church of San Vincenzo.

The unfinished **Loggia del Capitanio** (5) was begun in 1571 by Palladio as the residence of the Venetian commander. Now a part of the town hall, only three of its seven planned arches were ever completed. One of its side walls is decorated with a scene depicting the victory at Lepanto, while the missing section is occupied by a delightful outdoor café.

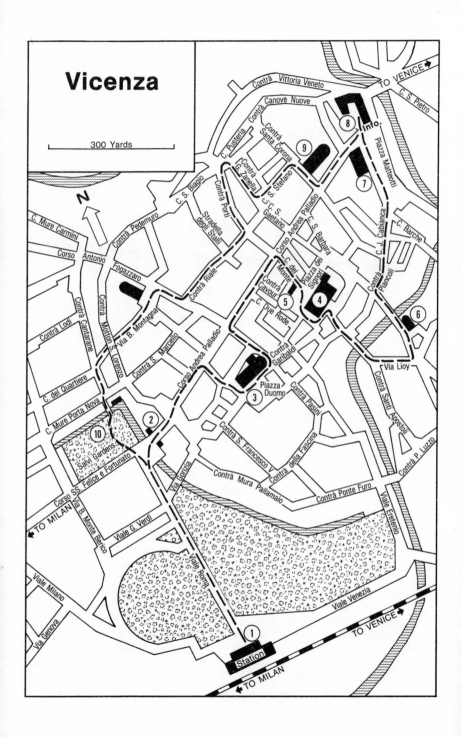

The Palazzo Chiericati

In the little square beyond the southwest corner of the *piazza* is a statue of Palladio. Beyond this make a left through a tiny alleyway into Piazza della Erbe, a quaint vegetable market with a medieval prison tower. Continue on, following the map, and cross the narrow Retrone stream, from which there are nice views. Before recrossing the water on the next bridge, stop at the **Oratory of San Nicola da Tolentino** (6), a richly decorated 17th-century baroque gem with wall paintings by Francesco Maffei.

The route now leads to Piazza Matteotti and two of Palladio's greatest achievements. The **Palazzo Chiericati** (7), in many ways the most interesting private residence designed by him, was begun in 1550 and not completed until well into the 17th century, although his original plans were faithfully followed. It now houses the **Civic Museum**, a superb collection of Vicenzan art as well as works by Venetian and Flemish masters, mostly of the Renaissance. There are also archaeological displays. Visits may be made between Tuesdays and Saturdays, from 9:30 a.m. to noon and 2:30–5 p.m., and on Sundays from 10 a.m. to noon.

Nearby, next to the tourist office, is Palladio's final work, the **Olympic Theatre** *(Teatro Olimpico)* (8). Often regarded as his most brilliant project, it was begun in 1580—the year of his death—and opened in 1585 with a production of Sophocles' "*Oedipus.*" The permanent stage setting representing a street scene in Thebes, a triumph of perspective, and the perfect acoustics make this a jewel of a theater in which to experience classical drama. Although the work was completed by his protogé Scamozzi, it retains the full impact of Palladio's ideas. Still used for productions, it is open to visitors Mondays through Saturdays, from 9:30 a.m. to 12:20 p.m. and 3–5:20 p.m., and on Sundays from 9:30 a.m. to 12:15 p.m. The hours are slightly shorter in winter. Don't miss this treat.

A short stroll up Corso Andrea Palladio brings you to the **Church of Santa Corona** (9), an early Gothic structure begun in 1261. Considered to be the most beautiful church in Vicenza, it contains two fabulous paintings, the *Baptism of Christ* by Giovanni Bellini on the fifth altar along the left aisle, and the *Adoration of the Magi* by Paolo Veronese in the third chapel on the right aisle. There are also some fine 15th-century inlaid choir stalls.

Now follow the map through some interesting streets to the **Salvi Gardens** (10), a wonderful place to relax before returning to the train station. The charming Loggetta Valmarana, spanning the water, was built in 1592 in a pure adaptation of Palladio's style.

NEARBY SIGHTS:

The area around Vicenza is rich in Renaissance villas and other architectural gems. Three of these are within a two-mile walking range southeast of the station, and can also be reached by bus numbers 8 and 13 from the station. They are the **Villa Rotonda**, which was designed by Palladio and which looks remarkably like Jefferson's Monticello, the **Villa Valmarana "dei Nani,"** and the **Basilica of Monte Bèrico**, a baroque structure with a great view over Vicenza. Ask at the tourist office for specific directions and a map to these and other nearby attractions.

Trieste

From an Italian point of view, Trieste might seem like the end of the world. Practically surrounded by Yugoslavia, it has changed nationality so many times that it almost seems more an outpost of the old Austro-Hungarian Empire than anything else. Its faded elegance is haunted with memories of a splendid past and questions about the future. Little-known to overseas tourists, it certainly makes an unusual and highly fascinating daytrip destination for those who favor atmosphere over cultural assets.

Possessing one of the best natural harbors on the Adriatic, Trieste has been a major port since ancient times. By the 2nd century B.C., under the name *Tergeste*, it became a part of the growing Roman Empire. Rivalry with Venice led to an alliance with Austria in 1382, which lasted on and off for many centuries. The growing cause of Italian unity, however, took hold in the late 19th century, and after World War I the city was ceded to Italy. In 1945 it was annexed to Yugoslavia, becoming a free territory under United Nations control in 1947. It was not until 1954 that it again joined Italy. Even so, it still looks primarily to Austria for its port traffic.

This is an easy trip with no major tourist sights, to be taken more for its ambiance than for any specific attractions. The ride there, especially by train, offers some spectacular views as you near Trieste.

GETTING THERE:

Trains depart Venice's Santa Lucia or Mestre stations several times in the morning for Trieste, a ride of about two hours. Return service operates until late evening.

By car, Trieste is 98 miles northeast of Venice via the A-4 Autostrada. Park as close to the Canale Grande as possible. You may want to use the car to avoid the steep climb to the castle.

WHEN TO GO:

Trieste is much more interesting on a workday, when the streets throb with activity. The local patron saint's day is November 3, celebrated in honor of Saint Giusto.

FOOD AND DRINK:

The cuisine of Trieste, although basically Italian, combines many elements of Middle European cooking, with strong Austrian and Hungarian overtones. For the most part it is a robust peasant fare. Buffet-style service is very common.

The local *Friuli* wines are quite good but little-known outside the region. They often have varietal names such as the red *Refosco, Terrano, Cabernet,* or *Merlot;* or the white *Tocai, Riesling,* or *Pinot.* The local beers are also very popular.

Some good restaurant choices are:

Harry's Grill (Via dell' Orologio 2, near the south side of Pza. Unità d' Italia) Elegant and favored by businessmen. X: Sun. $$$

Al Granzo (Piazza Venezia 7, 6 blocks south of Pza. Unità d' Italia) Famous for its seafood. X: Sun. eve., Wed., Nov. $$

La Bottega del Vino (in the castle of San Giusto) Traditional Italian dishes in a romantic setting. X: Tues. $$

Buffet Benedetto (Via 30 Ottobre 19, just north of San Spiridione) Your choice of buffet or waiter service, price varies accordingly. X: Mon., Aug. $$ and $

Da Pepi (Via Cassa di Risparmio 3, just south of the Canale Grande) Buffet service with local cooking. $$ to $

Ai Due Triestini (Via Cadorna 10, just south of Pza. Unità d' Italia) Hearty food in an unpretentious atmosphere. $

Barattolo (Piazza San Antonio Nuova 2, at the end of the Canale Grande) A pizzeria with other dishes available. X: Mon. $

TOURIST INFORMATION:

The local tourist office, phone (040) 42-01-82, is in the train station. There is also an office by the Castle of San Giusto, phone (040) 30-92-98.

SUGGESTED TOUR:

Leave the **train station** (1) and follow the map to the **Canale Grande**, an inlet from the harbor built in 1756 to allow boats to sail into the business center. It is now used as a marina for small craft. At the end of the canal, to the right, is the gorgeous **Serbian Orthodox Church of San Spiridione** (2), erected in the mid-19th century on the foundations of an Orthodox church dating from the 8th century. Its splendid Byzantine interior is decorated with many valuable icons, some quite ancient, and may be visited daily from 9 a.m. to noon and 4–7 p.m. As you explore Trieste you will notice churches and temples representing quite a variety of faiths, a reflection of the city's mixed ethnic past.

A few steps from here is the busy outdoor market around **Piazza Ponterosso** (3), where all sorts of food and merchandise are sold on weekdays. This spot is favored by visiting Yugoslavs looking for goods they cannot find at home.

Continue on to the **Roman Theatre** (4), built in the 2nd century A.D. and not excavated until 1938. Now partially restored, it is once again used for theatrical productions. Return to Corso Italia, a main shopping street, follow it to Piazza Goldoni, and turn right. Facing you is a long set of steep steps, the Scala dei Giganti, which ascends to the top of the historic Capitoline hill. If the climb looks too formidable, you may want to take a taxi via a more roundabout route—just ask for the *Castello San Giusto.*

Arriving at the top, your first visit should be to the monumental **Fortress of San Giusto** *(Castello)* (5). There has been a defensive bastion here ever since Roman times. The present structure was begun in 1368 by the Venetians and completed in 1630 by the Austrians, for whom it served as a governors' residence until the 18th century. The panoramic view from its ramparts extends over the city, across the bay, and all the way to Yugoslavia. Inside, there is an interesting **museum** of arms, armor, period furnishings, and the like. This is open every day except Mondays, from 9 a.m. to 12:45 p.m. Other parts of the castle, especially the dungeons, are used for temporary exhibitions, some of which can be fascinating. There is also a noted wine restaurant on the premises.

The adjacent **Cathedral of San Giusto** (6), a most unusual structure, is really two early churches joined together in the 14th century. Built between the 5th and the 11th centuries, they were dedicated to Saint Giusto *(Justus)*—a 4th-century martyr thrown into the sea during the reign of Diocletian—and Saint Maria Assunta. The baptistry, to the left, was a third Romanesque church. The whole complex stands on the site of a Roman temple. Note the magnificent rose window on the west façade, and the pillars of the main doorway, made from ancient tombstones.

Step inside to see the 13th-century **mosaics** in the chapels on either side of the high altar, the remains of a 5th-century mosaic floor, and the 9th-century font in the adjoining baptistry. The bell tower can be climbed for an even more spectacular view.

Slightly to the north of the cathedral are the remains of a **Roman basilica** from the 1st century A.D. and an enormous war memorial erected in 1935.

Close to the cathedral is the small **History Museum** and **Archaeological Garden** *(Museo di Storia e d'Arte* and *Orto Lapidario)* (7) which displays a wide variety of relics from the region. It is open Tuesdays through Sundays, from 9 a.m. to 1 p.m.

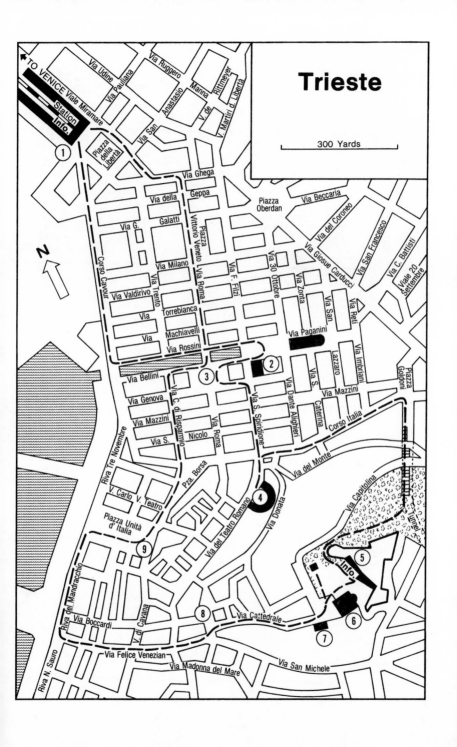

The Canale Grande

Continue downhill on the delightful Via della Cattedrale, passing the **Arco di Riccardo** (8), a Roman arch from the 1st century B.C. which was once believed to be part of a prison holding Richard the Lionhearted on his return from the Crusades. From here follow the map to the waterfront, where short boat trips in the harbor are usually offered.

The **Piazza dell' Unità d' Italia** (9) is an enormous open square lined with imposing buildings reflecting the one-time ambitions of the Austro-Hungarian Empire. Don't miss the ornate fountain near its southeast corner. Opening directly onto the sea, this is a pleasant area to stroll in, perhaps resting at one of its outdoor cafés. From here return, following the map, to the Canale Grande and continue on to the train station.

Section VI

Daytrips from Naples

Southern Italy

With its rugged seacoast, delightful islands, historic sites and, above all, sunny climate, the southern region of Campania is often regarded as the most romantically beautiful corner of Italy. Many of its attractions are admittedly isolated and do not lend themselves to daytrips, but those centering on the Bay of Naples and the Gulf of Salerno—certainly among the most enticing destinations in the entire country—are easily and quickly reached by train, bus, boat, or private car.

The natural base for exploring Campania is the bustling old port of Naples. Whether you will enjoy staying there is a matter of personal taste. The city itself is surely an exciting place, full of throbbing energy and an emotionally charged life style that sometimes rubs visitors the wrong way. There is a great deal of squalor, confusion, and noise along with the spectacular setting, magnificent art treasures, and great food. You can, however, avoid this if you wish by basing yourself in the resort town of Sorrento—long popular with British tourists and well equipped with hotels accustomed to English-speaking guests. All of the daytrips in this section can readily be made from there, and instructions for doing so are given in each case. If you don't mind the extra travel involved—a bit over two hours by train or 136 miles by car—it is even possible to do most of them from Rome.

Naples
(Napoli)

Everything you've ever heard about Naples is probably true. It is filthy dirty. *It's the most beautifully sited city on the Mediterranean.* It's riddled with crime and corruption. *It has some of the best cultural attractions in Italy.* Its drivers are color blind and cannot distinguish red from green, do not know the difference between a street and a sidewalk, nor recognize the shape of one-way arrows. *It has superb restaurants and wonderful cooking.* It is trapped in a cycle of poverty from which there seems to be no escape. *It is filled with an energetic lust for life.* Its cabbies are thieves. *Its citizens are profoundly religious.* Its citizens are superstitious beyond belief. *The cheerful Neapolitans are filled with kindness and compassion.* In short, Naples is a study in extreme contrasts, and for that reason one of the most fascinating cities anywhere.

Naples has a history as colorful as its streets. It probably began around the 9th century B.C. as *Parthenope,* a settlement of sailors from Rhodes. Several centuries later the Greeks founded their colony of *Neapolis* next to this, and both towns—now united—were conquered by the Romans in the 4th century B.C. Until the reign of Constantine in the 4th century A.D., Greek remained the official language, and much of the Hellenistic culture is alive today. Naples developed into a center of learning and a retreat for wealthy Romans. During the Dark Ages it was a duchy under Byzantine domination, yielding in the 12th century to Norman invaders. For a long time after that it was ruled by the Germans, the French, the Spaniards, and finally the Austrians. Naples became the capital of the Kingdom of the Two Sicilies in the 18th century and remained under Bourbon rule until the unification of Italy in 1860. This long history of foreign supremacy has left Neapolitans with a deeply ingrained distrust of authority, a trait that remains very much with them to this day. The city was severely damaged in World War II and has never really recovered, its economy still a shambles.

This "get acquainted" walking tour goes through a variety of Neapolitan neighborhoods and visits several of the most important historic sites. Many of the city's greatest treasures, however, are in museums that close at 2 p.m. It is not possible to see more than one or two of these in a day, so another time should be set aside for the remainder. To avoid unpleasant incidents, you should be careful not to call attention to yourself in any way. Keep your money safely hidden from pickpockets, wear simple clothes, and be cautious about taking photos in the Spacca district. You must also be aware that Neapolitan drivers pay absolutely no attention to any traffic regulations, and that speeding cars may show up anywhere, any time—even on the sidewalks.

GETTING THERE:

Trains from Rome and other Italian cities call at Naples' modern Centrale station. Some of these actually stop at the Piazza Garibaldi station, which is underground directly beneath the Centrale station and which is also used for subways. Express trains from Rome take a little over two hours for the journey.

Trains from Sorrento are operated by the private Circumvesuviana Railway, which does not accept railpasses. These stop at Pompeii and Ercolano *(Herculaneum)* en route, and take about one hour to reach Naples. They arrive at their own station underneath the Centrale station, two minutes before terminating at the Circumvesuviana station on Corso Garibaldi.

By car, Naples is 136 miles southeast of Rome via the A-2 Autostrada. Driving in Naples is an unnerving experience likely to result in disaster.

By air, Naples is served with flights from other major Italian cities as well as London, Paris, Frankfurt, and Zurich. Capodichino Airport is three miles northeast of the city.

WHEN TO GO:

The museums and the Royal Palace are closed on some major holidays. Avoid taking this walking tour on a Sunday morning, when the lavishly decorated churches are busy with services. Naples can be uncomfortably hot during July and August.

FOOD AND DRINK:

Neapolitan cooking comes the closest to being what foreigners usually think of as "Italian" food. *Pizza* is probably the most typical dish, along with the related *Calzoni*. Pasta specialties include *Macaroni* and *Spaghetti*, often served *al Sugo* (with meat sauce), *alle Vongole* (with clam sauce), or *al Pomodoro* (with tomato sauce). The local cheeses are *Mozzarella* and *Provolone*. Neapolitans do not eat very much meat, although *Bistecca alla Pizzaiola* (beef or veal steak with tomato, garlic, olive oil, and spices) and *Polpette* (meat balls) are fairly common. With the entire Mediterranean at their disposal, the restau-

rants of Naples are primarily noted for their superb seafood, especially fish soups. For dessert there is a wide variety of excellent pas-
tries and ice cream *(Gelato),* the most noted of which is *Spumone.*

The Campania region has always been famous for its tasty wines.
Of these, the most beloved is *Gragnano,* a dark and fruity red from
near Sorrento. Somewhat more refined is the popular *Lacrima Christi,*
a golden white grown on the slopes of Mount Vesuvius and named
for the tears the Christ supposedly shed after discovering that this
earthly paradise of Naples was inhabited by such wicked people. *Fal-
erno* has been around since antiquity, and is available as both a red
and a white. With luck, you might get to taste a genuine *Capri,* a dry
white of which far more is bottled than can possibly be grown on the
tiny island. The most appropriate liqueur is the sweet, yellow *Strega.*

Some good restaurants, roughly in the sequence that you will pass
or come close to them along the walking tour, are:

Avellinese da Peppino (Via Silvio Spaventa 31, 3 blocks west of
Centrale station) An inexpensive, simple and very popular
place. X: Sat. $

San Carlo (Via Cesario Console 18, just south of the Royal Palace) Crowded with local businessmen and politicians. X: Sun.,
Aug. $$$

La Cantinella (Via N. Sauro 23, between the Royal Palace and
Castel dell' Ovo) Famous for its seafood. X: Sun., Aug. $$

La Bersagliera (Borgo Marinaro 10, just north of Castel dell'
Ovo) A colorful seafood place in the Santa Lucia district. X:
Tues. $$

Amici Miei (Via Monte di Dio 78, 4 blocks west of the Royal
Palace) A local favorite with traditional dishes. X: Mon. Aug.
$$

Ciro a Santa Brigida (Via Santa Brigida 71, on the north side of
Galleria Umberto I) An old-fashioned trattoria and pizzeria in
the heart of town. X: Sun., Aug. $$

Dante e Beatrice (Piazza Dante 44, in Spacca-Napoli) Every-
one's favorite typical Neapolitan trattoria. X: Wed. $$

Pizzeria Bellini (Via Santa Maria di Costantinopoli 80, 2 blocks
northeast of Pza. Dante in Spacca-Napoli) A very old pizzeria
and restaurant, popular with locals. X: Sun. $

Trianon da Ciro (Via Pietro Colletta 44, 5 blocks southeast of
the cathedral) Possibly the best pizza in Naples. X: Sun. lunch.
$

TOURIST INFORMATION:

The provincial tourist office, phone (081) 40-53-11, is at Piazza dei
Martiri 58, north of Castel dell' Ovo. They have a convenient branch

within the Centrale train station, phone (081) 26-87-79. The local tourist office, phone (081) 41-87-44, is in the Royal Palace, with branches at Piazza del Gesù Nuova in Spacca-Napoli, by the docks, and elsewhere. Be sure to get a free copy of *Qui Napoli,* a "what's on" guide in English and Italian.

SUGGESTED TOUR:

Begin your tour at the modern **Centrale train station** (1), built by the noted architect Pier Luigi Nervi in 1954 and easily reached by bus, subway, or on foot from your hotel. *If you are staying closer to the Santa Lucia district or the Piazza del Municipo you should start the walk at the Castel Nuovo (2) instead.* Just in front of the train station is the Piazza Garibaldi, a vast square surrounded by hotels, cheap restaurants, and street peddlers. Get through it as quickly as you can and head down **Corso Umberto I**. This broad boulevard was cut through a notorious slum district in the late 19th century after a terrible cholera epidemic had decimated the population. Lined with shops, it is today virtually the main street of Naples. At Piazza Giovanni Bovio stands the lovely early-17th-century **Neptune Fountain**, embellished with sea monsters by Bernini.

Continue straight ahead on Via Agostino Depretis to **Piazza del Municipo**, a large open area bordered on the west by the city hall. Its south side is dominated by the massive 13th-century **Castel Nuovo** (2), sometimes called the *Maschio Angioino* after its Angevin ancestry. It was built by Charles I of Anjou and altered in the mid-15th century by Alfonso I of Aragon, two of Naples' many foreign rulers. The main entrance to the castle is through the famous **Triumphal Arch** of 1467, commemorating the entry of Alfonso I into Naples. This masterpiece of the Renaissance leads into a courtyard, which is as far as you can go as the castle now houses government offices.

Now stroll over to the nearby **San Carlo Opera House** *(Teatro San Carlo)* (3), the largest in Italy and the most famous after Milan's La Scala. Erected in 1737 and rebuilt within six months after a disastrous fire in 1816, its sumptuous interior seats an audience of 1,700. Guided tours are held in the mornings. You can ask at the box office or at the tourist office in the adjacent Royal Palace about this.

The **Royal Palace** *(Palazzo Reale)* (4) was begun in 1600 as a home for the Spanish viceroys and later enlarged into a palace for the Bourbon kings of Naples. Sometimes used by the kings of Italy, it has now been restored and is open to the public. Eight niches in its façade hold statues of the most famous kings of Naples, all foreigners. High drama took place here in 1799 when Ferdinand IV and his wife, Maria Carolina, the sister of Marie Antoinette, along with the royal family, escaped the advancing French—and probably the guillotine—through a

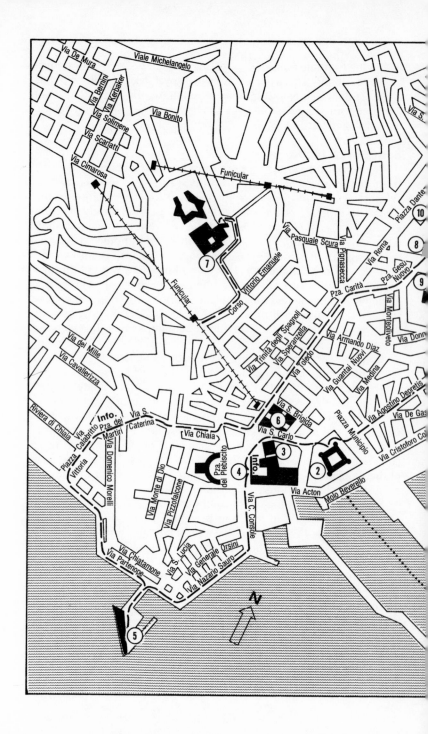

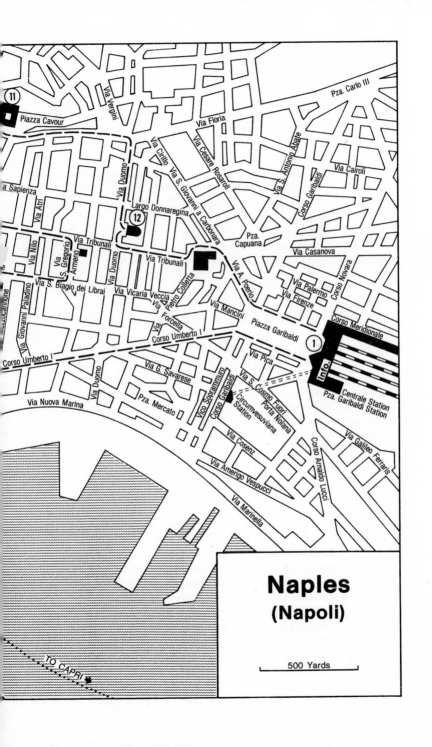

Naples
(Napoli)

500 Yards

Street and place labels (as shown on map):

- Pza. Carlo III
- Via Floria
- Via Vergini
- 11 Piazza Cavour
- Via Cairoli
- Via S. Antonio Abate
- Corso Garibaldi
- Via Cirillo
- Via S. Giovanni a Carbonara
- Via Cesare Rosaroll
- Via Duomo
- a Sapienza
- Via Atri
- Largo Donnaregina
- 12
- Pza. Capuana
- Via Casanova
- Via Tribunali
- Via Nilo
- Via S. Gregorio Armeno
- Via Tribunali
- Via Duomo
- Via Palermo
- Via Firenze
- Corso Novara
- Via A. Poerio
- Via S. Biagio dei Librai
- Via Vicaria Veccia
- Via Giovanni Paladino
- Via Pietro Colletta
- Via Forcella
- Via Mancini
- Piazza Garibaldi
- Corso Umberto I
- Corso Meridionale
- Corso Umberto I
- 1
- Via Pica
- Info.
- Via G. Savarese
- Via Duomo
- Vico Sopramuro
- Corso Garibaldi
- Via S. Cosmo Fuori Porta Nolana
- Centrale Station
- Pza. Garibaldi Station
- Via Nuova Marina
- Pza. Mercato
- Circumvesuviana Station
- Via Cosenz
- Corso Arnaldo Lucci
- Via Galileo Ferraris
- Via Amerigo Vespucci
- Via Marinella
- TO CAPRI

secret passageway to the port. In this escapade they were assisted by Britain's Lord Nelson and his mistress, Lady Hamilton, together with the unsuspecting Sir William Hamilton. The sumptuously appointed interior of the palace is filled with the original furnishings, and is well worth a visit. It is open on Mondays through Saturdays, from 9 a.m. to 2 p.m., and on Sundays and holidays from 9 a.m. to 1 p.m.

Directly across the enormous Piazza del Plebiscito from the palace is the early-19th-century **Church of San Francesco di Paola**, erected by Ferdinand IV (also known as the First) in thanks for his final deliverance from the Napoleonic menace. It is modeled on the Pantheon in Rome and is made far grander than it actually is by the sweeping colonnade on either side.

Stroll downhill past the little park on your left and continue on Via Nazario Sauro into the Santa Lucia district, from which there are magnificent views of the harbor and Mount Vesuvius. Made famous by that typically Neapolitan song, the small port of **Santa Lucia,** once home to fisherman, is now primarily devoted to seafood restaurants. At the end of its jetty stands the 12th-century **Castel dell' Ovo** (5), a highly picturesque medieval fortification. It was constructed by the Normans on the site of the villa of Lucullus, a Roman general during the 1st century B.C. who was famous for his lavish banquets. The villa later served as a place of exile for the last Roman emperor, Romulus Augustulus, who disappeared from history in A.D. 475. The castle's name—meaning egg— is rather curious, referring either to its shape or to the ancient legend that it was built upon an egg balanced on the seabed. Long notorious as a prison, it is now used for exhibitions and can usually be freely explored.

Now follow the map through Piazza Vittoria and Piazza dei Martiri back to the opera house (3). Via Toledo, also called *Via Roma,* is one of the busiest streets in Naples. Turn north on it and step into the **Galleria Umberto I** (6), a huge steel-and-glass shopping arcade from the late 19th century, similar to the earlier one in Milan. This is an excellent place to sit down at an "outdoor" café for some refreshments.

Just across the street is the lower station of the Centrale funicular, on which you can make a little side trip to the **Certosa di San Martino** (7) and its splendid museum. Get off the funicular at Corso Vittorio Emanuele and climb through the gardens to the entrance of the former monastery, founded in the 14th century but heavily altered in the 17th. It now houses the **National Museum of San Martino**, and enormous collection of art and objects relating to the life and history of Naples from the 16th century on. Of particular interest are the exhibits of nativity scenes, costumes, and 19th-century Neapolitan paintings. Don't miss the marvelously baroque church. The views from here sum

The Castel dell' Ovo

up what is meant by the phrase "See Naples and die." Visits may be made on Mondays through Saturdays, from 9 a.m. to 2 p.m.; and on Sundays and holidays from 9 a.m. to 1 p.m. You may want to save this for another day when there is more time.

Return on the funicular or on foot and turn north on Via Toledo to Piazza Carità. You are now entering the famed **Spacca-Napoli** district, the very heart of Old Naples. The crowded, chaotic narrow streets of this poor neighborhood are lined, perhaps surprisingly, with some of the most lavishly decorated churches you'll ever see. There are many of these, but since time is limited, head straight for the late-16th-century **Church of Gesù Nuovo** (8) and step inside to witness the lengths to which the baroque style could be carried in Naples. In total contrast to this is the **Church of Santa Chiara** (9), directly across the square. Built in 1328, its 19th-century rococo interior was demolished by incendiary bombs in 1943 and the church reconstructed in its original Gothic austerity. Take a look at the surviving remnants of the 14th-century Tomb of Robert I of Anjou, behind the high altar, then visit the enchanting **Cloisters** *(Chiostro delle Clarisse)* behind the church— a very unusual sight in this city. They are reached by way of a side alley to the east of the church.

Some other interesting churches along this colorful route are those of **San Domenico Maggiore** on the piazza of the same name, and **San Lorenzo Maggiore** on Via San Gregorio Armeno. Continue west on Via Tribunali to the Alba gate, opening onto **Piazza Dante** (10), a picturesque area rich in restaurants and cafés.

From here it is only a short stroll up Via Enrico Pessina to the **National Archaeological Museum** *(Museo Archeologico Nazionale)* (11), one of the major sights of Naples. Typically, it is only open until 1 or 2 p.m., so you may want to return on another day. Among the world's most important museums of Greco-Roman antiquities, it is especially rich in artifacts uncovered at Pompeii and Herculaneum. There are mosaics, bronzes, household utensils, furniture, and even preserved foods, as well as the expected classical sculptures. You would do well to see these before visiting the excavations themselves, which are described in later chapters. The museum is open on Mondays through Saturdays, 9 a.m. to 2 p.m.; and on Sundays and holidays from 9 a.m. to 1 p.m.

Now follow the map through Piazza Cavour and south on Via Duomo to the **Cathedral** *(Duomo)* (12), dedicated to San Gennaro, the patron saint of Naples. Construction of the present church began in 1294 in the French Gothic style on the site of earlier churches and a Roman temple. It has been altered many times since, and has a late-19th-century façade. The spacious interior opens, to the left, into the 4th-century Basilica of Santa Restituta which, though altered in the 14th-century, still retains much of its original atmosphere. Along the south aisle is the venerated **Chapel of San Gennaro**, preserving in a silver reliquary the head of the saint as well as two vials of his congealed blood. This is supposed to liquefy three times a year, on the first Saturday in May at Santa Chiara, and in the cathedral on September 19th and December 16th. Failure of this miracle to occur on schedule portends bad omens for Naples, so huge crowds gather to watch in anticipation.

From here you can follow the map back to the train station or go directly to your hotel. There are several other attractions in Naples that could not be included in this walk and which should be saved for another day. Foremost among these are the **Capodimonte Museum and Picture Gallery**, located in another former royal palace well to the north of the Archaeological Museum; the **Villa Floridiana**, a small museum beyond the Certosa di San Martino; the entire district of **Mergellina**; and the **Catacombs of San Gennaro**.

Capri

Spending only one day on the beguiling Isle of Capri may sound like an exercise in frustration, but it's done all the time and is, moreover, both worthwhile and highly enjoyable. It also gives you an excellent opportunity to sample this sparkling little bit of paradise and decide whether you'd like to return later for a real vacation.

People have been taking their holidays on this rugged, mountainous island ever since the ancient Romans, who called it *Capreae*. Even then it had already been inhabited as far back as prehistoric times, and was well known to the Greeks. Today it is international tourists who come by the millions each year to bask in the glorious sunshine and admire the incomparable scenery. Yet, despite the hordes, the island has lost none of its charm and still remains an intoxicating place. Unlike most resorts, Capri does have some real attractions in the true sense of the word. The Blue Grotto is world famous, and there are excellent Roman ruins to probe along with a lovely villa and an historic monastery.

Located some 17 miles south of Naples and eight miles southwest of Sorrento, the Isle of Capri is accessible only by boat or, if you are very rich, by helicopter. Cars are useless since there are few roads wide enough to accommodate them, and in any case tourists are not allowed to bring motor vehicles over between March and the end of October.

It is difficult to see all of the sights described on the suggested walking tour in one day and still have time for a leisurely lunch. Be selective and choose only those that really interest you, remembering that seductive Capri is no place to rush.

GETTING THERE:

Boats from Naples depart from the Molo Beverello, just below Piazza del Municipio and Castel Nuovo. You have a choice between a large, comfortable ferry *(Traghetto)*, which takes about 80 minutes and is operated by CAREMAR; or one of the much faster, more expensive hydrofoils *(Aliscafi)* operated by both CAREMAR and SNAV. Tickets are sold at the dock, where you should be sure to check the return schedule. Leave as early in the morning as possible to avoid the guided tours that come down from Rome, and be certain to get on the right boat as some go to other islands. Service operates all year round, but less frequently during the off-season.

Boats from Sorrento, both ferries and hydrofoils, are operated by CAREMAR. They depart from the Porto Marina Piccola just downhill from Piazza Tasso. The large ferry takes about 50 minutes to reach Capri.

WHEN TO GO:

The best time to see Capri is during the late spring or early fall, when the weather is warm and there are fewer tourists. It can get rather crowded in the summer. Depending entirely on the weather, a winter visit might be highly enjoyable. The monastery is closed on Mondays, and the chairlift to Monte Solaro does not run on Tuesdays in winter.

FOOD AND DRINK:

Many of the dishes served on Capri tend to be of the international or conventional Italian variety, influenced particularly by Neapolitan cooking. The few local specialties are usually identified by the word *Caprese*. Seafood, of course, is quite good on the island. The dry white wine of Capri is among the best from Southern Italy, although it is produced in very small quantity. Some choice restaurants in the town of Capri are listed below. Expect prices to be somewhat higher than on the mainland.

> **La Capannina** (Via le Botteghe 14, 2 blocks east of Pza. Umberto I) A simple but attractive place noted for tasty food. X: Wed. except in Aug., mid-Nov. to mid-Mar. $$$

> **La Pigna** (Via Lo Palazzo 30, just west of the bus station) A romantic old-time favorite with a garden. X: Tues. except July through Sept. $$$

> **Grottino** (Via Longano 27, 1 block northwest of Pza. Umberto I) A popular small trattoria with regional dishes. X: Tues. off season. $$

> **Da Gemma** (Via Madre Serafina 6, in an alleyway 1 block southwest of Pza. Umberto I) A cozy place noted for seafood. X: Mon., Nov. $$

> **Settanni** (Via Longano 5, just northeast of Pza. Umberto I) Good, inexpensive food in a friendly environment. X: Thurs. $

TOURIST INFORMATION:

There is a local tourist office, phone (081) 83-70-634, at the Marina Grande dock, with another on Piazza Umberto I, phone (081) 83-70-686. In Anacapri contact the office at Via Orlandi 19/A, phone (081) 83-71-524.

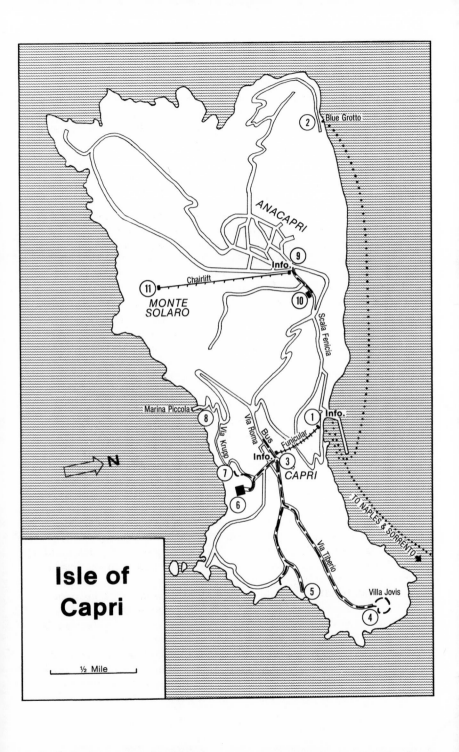

Isle of Capri

½ Mile

SUGGESTED TOUR:

Boats to Capri dock at the **Marina Grande** (1), located on the island's north shore. All but one of the major attractions are high up in the hills, so while you're still at sea level you should head directly to the famous **Blue Grotto** *(Grotta Azzurra)* (2) before the tour groups arrive. People come from all over the world to marvel at this fantastic cavern, and in the process of doing so have made it one of those inescapable tourist traps. Fortunately, it actually is an incredible, not-to-be-missed sight, one well worth the expense and bother of reaching. An entire local industry has sprung up around the transport of visitors to this highly inaccessible place on the water's edge at the bottom of a steep cliff. Motorboats takes groups of tourists from Marina Grande to the cave's tiny entrance, where you will be put into a small rowboat and taken inside.

The Blue Grotto was known to the ancient Romans, who used it as a temple of sorts. Several interesting underwater archaeological finds have been made there in recent years, but it appears to have been largely forgotten until being "rediscovered" by tourist promoters in 1826. The magical effect of its unearthly luminescence is, of course, caused by refraction of the sun's rays. The grotto is open daily from 9 a.m. until one hour before sunset, but not when the sea is rough.

Back at Marina Grande, you can take either the funicular (summers only) or a bus to the delightful little town of Capri, 465 feet above the port. Its main square, **Piazza Umberto I** (3), is a charming place lined with busy outdoor cafés. You will be returning to it several times during the day as nearly all of the paths and roads on the island radiate from there.

Next to the Blue Grotto, the most important sight on Capri is probably the **Villa Jovis** (4), once the palace of the emperor Tiberius. The only way of reaching it, short of hiring a donkey, is on foot—an uphill walk of about two miles. The paved trail, starting out as Via Le Botteghe and followed by Via Fuorlovado, Via Croce, and Via Tiberio, is very well marked and rewards you with stupendous panoramic views all along the way.

The entire Roman Empire was presumably ruled from this villa between A.D. 27 and 37, the last ten years of the reign of Tiberius. An ancient legend has it that the emperor took pleasure in having people who displeased him thrown off the thousand-foot-high cliff, but there is no factual evidence of this. Now in a state of ruin, the immense villa is, nevertheless, a fascinating place to explore. At its highest peak there is a chapel with a hugh bronze Madonna, installed in 1979. The villa is open daily from 9 a.m. until one hour before sunset.

On the way back, you will come to a fork in the road just before the town of Capri. This is marked for the **Arco Naturale** (5) and makes

View from the Trail to Villa Jovis

an interesting little side trip to a peculiar natural stone arch by the water's edge. It is not necessary to go all the way down to admire the view. Nearby, another trail leads to the **Matromania Grotto**, possibly used in prehistoric times for human sacrifices, and later decorated by the Romans.

Return to Piazza Umberto I, where you can sit down at an outdoor café for a welcome rest. From here you may want to continue on Via Vittorio Emanuele, Via Serena, and Via Certosa to the former **Carthusian Monastery** *(Certosa di San Giacomo)* (6), dating from the 14th century. Its restored Gothic church and cloisters are quite interesting, and there are a few Roman artifacts removed from the Blue Grotto on display.

A short distance beyond this are the **Augustus Gardens** *(Giardini di Augusto)* (7), a lovely public park overlooking some fabulous scenery. In its northwest corner there is a small statue of Lenin, who spent a very un-communistic exile in luxurious Capri after the abortive first revolution. From the gardens it is possible to descend the steep and narrow Via Krupp, also called Via Augusto, to the **Marina Piccola**, a small harbor and beach from which you can get a bus back to Capri town. Otherwise, return the way you came.

Back in the town, board a bus or taxi to the island's other settle-

View from the Augustus Gardens

ment, **Anacapri** (9). Perched nearly a thousand feet above the sea, this attractive village could only be reached via the *Scala Fenicia,* a staircase of over 800 steps probably built by the ancient Greeks, until a hair-raising road was constructed in the late 19th century. Once there, walk uphill from Piazza della Vittoria on Via Munthe to the **Villa San Michele** (10). Built about a century ago by the noted Swedish doctor and author Axel Munthe over the ruins of another of Tiberius's villas, it contains ancient sculptures as well as furnishings from the 17th and 18th centuries. The gardens are especially enchanting. Visits may usually be made on any day, from 9 a.m. to 6 p.m.

The highest vantage point on Capri is **Monte Solaro** (11), whose peak rises some 1,932 feet above the sea. You can get to the top in 12 minutes by riding the chairlift from Anacapri. On a clear day it is possible to see completely across the Bay of Naples to the Apennine mountains running down the spine of Italy, a breathtaking panorama indeed. The lift runs every day in summer, from 9 a.m. to 5 p.m. with shorter hours and no service on Tuesdays in winter.

Herculaneum and Vesuvius

(Ercolano e Vesuvio)

When Mount Vesuvius blew its top in A.D. 79 it destroyed more than just Pompeii. The residential and resort town of Herculaneum was also buried under as much as 80 feet of a muddy effluent that hardened into a form of tufa stone, preserving its buildings to a truly remarkable degree. Although it is much smaller and less famous than Pompeii, Herculaneum is in some ways more interesting—and a lot less crowded. The surrounding modern town of Ercolano is also the departure point for trips to the top of the volcano, so it is easily possible to combine visits to both the victim and the perpetrator in the same day.

Herculaneum began as the Greek settlement of *Herakleion*, founded, according to legend, by Hercules. Later occupied by Oscans and Samnites, it fell into Roman hands in 89 B.C. Possibly used as a retirement colony for veterans, the town became a resort for wealthy Romans, who built splendid villas there. At the time of its destruction it had a population of about 5,000.

There is a certain thrill about going to the top of Mount Vesuvius—after all, it is an active volcano, the only one on the European mainland. Since the last major eruption in 1944 it has lost the distinctive plume of smoke that often colored the Neapolitan skies, and today emits only scattered vapors. This can be deceptive, however, as the beast is only sleeping and certainly not dead.

GETTING THERE:
Commuter trains operated by the private Circumvesuviana Railway in the direction of Sorrento depart frequently from their own station underneath the Centrale station in Naples. These same trains leave a few minutes earlier from the Circumvesuviana station on Corso Garibaldi. Take one of these as far as the **Ercolano** stop, about 15 minutes from Naples. Return service operates until mid-evening. Railpasses are not accepted on this line, but fares are very low. Those coming from Sorrento should take the same line in the direction of Naples.

By car, take the A-3 Autostrada southeast to the Ercolano exit, about seven miles from Naples. From here follow signs a short distance to

Scavi di Ercolano for Herculaneum, and signs for Vesuvio to visit Mount Vesuvius.

WHEN TO GO:

The excavations at Herculaneum are open daily except on some holidays. Clear weather is absolutely essential for an enjoyable ascent of Mount Vesuvius, for which a light jacket or sweater may be welcome.

FOOD AND DRINK:

The local wine of Mount Vesuvius is the golden white *Lacrima Christi*, grown right on the slopes of the volcano. There are a few ordinary pizzerias and bars between the train station and the excavations in Ercolano. A good restaurant choice is:

La Piadina (Via Cozzolino 10) An old favorite with traditional cooking. X: Tues. $$

TOURIST INFORMATION:

Your best source is the provincial tourist office in Naples' Centrale train station, phone (081) 26-87-79. In Ercolano there is a small local tourist office, by the southwest corner of the square between the station and the excavations, which has up-to-date schedules of buses to Vesuvius.

SUGGESTED TOUR:

Begin your tour at the **Ercolano train station** (1). Normally, you should see the excavations at Herculaneum first, but in winter it is best to start with Vesuvius as the bus does not operate in the late afternoon then. The bus to Vesuvius leaves from directly opposite the train station. If you have any questions about this, stop at the local tourist office by the southwest corner of the square one block from the station, on the way to the digs.

Continue straight ahead along the main street for about three blocks to the entrance of the **Herculaneum Excavations** *(Scavi di Ercolano)* (2). Once inside, you will see several authorized guides who will offer to take you around, expecting a tip in reward. This is by far the best way to see Herculaneum since the guides are knowledgeable and have the keys to those houses that are locked. Attempting to identify the ruined structures by yourself is very difficult, even using the best guide books available. After the guided tour is finished you can retrace your steps—the site is quite small—and spend more time at those spots of greatest interest. The short descriptions given below are only a rough guide to the most important highlights.

Herculaneum was discovered in 1709 when a local prince came

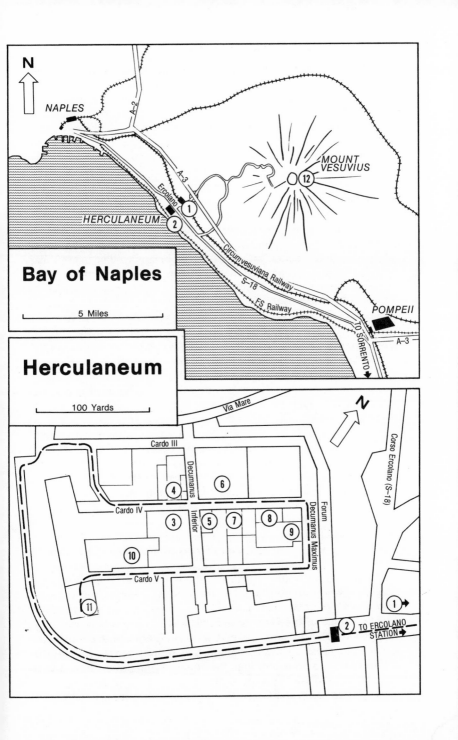

N

NAPLES

MOUNT
VESUVIUS

⑫

Ercolano

①

HERCULANEUM

②

A-2

A-3

Circumvesuviana Railway

S-18

FS Railway

Bay of Naples

5 Miles

POMPEII

TO SORRENTO

A-3

Herculaneum

100 Yards

N

Via Mare

Cardo III

Decumanus Interior

Cardo IV

Decumanus Maximus

Cardo V

Forum

Corso Ercolano (S-18)

④ ⑥

③ ⑤ ⑦ ⑧ ⑨

⑩

⑪

① →

② TO ERCOLANO STATION →

across ruins while digging a well. Further excavations were made with the support of the king of Naples after 1738 but, as was common in those days, the only interest was in recovering valuable artifacts. Real systematic archaeological work began in 1927 and is still under way. Digging is especially painstaking as everything is literally encased in stone. To date, only a portion of Herculaneum has been uncovered since most of it lies under the modern town of Ercolano, once known as Resina.

From the bottom of the long entrance ramp turn right to the **House of the Mosaic Atrium** (Atrio a Mosaico) (3), which has some very fine mosaic floors and a lovely garden. Some of its wooden window frames are preserved, a feature of Herculaneum that is missing in Pompeii, where the hot ashes ignited the wood. Just up the street is the **House of the Wooden Trellis** (Graticcio) (4), a plebeian dwelling using cheap wood-and-plaster construction and incorporating a shop. Not all of the wood here is original, of course. Next to this is the **House of the Wooden Partition** (Tramezzo di Legno), a multi-storied private house where parts of a wooden wall are still well preserved. Bits of furniture and even some ancient food are displayed in glass cases. The shop on the corner has a wooden clothes press in excellent condition.

On the opposite corner stands the **Samnite House** (Sannitica) (5) which, although modified, has interesting pre-Roman origins. Its interior atrium is especially noteworthy. The large **Baths** (Thermae) (6) have survived much as they were when first built during the reign of Augustus. Not as luxurious as those at Pompeii, they are nonetheless quite well planned and have separate entrances for men and women.

Cross the street to the **House of the Charred Furniture** (Mobilio Carbonizzato) (7), a charming middle-class home with some original furniture. Standing next to it is the **House of the Neptune Mosaic** (Nettuno e di Anfitrite) with a superbly well-preserved shop on the street, complete with merchandise that was for sale at the moment of destruction. Step into the courtyard to view the beautiful mosaics of Neptune and Anfitrite.

Continue up the street to the **House of the Beautiful Courtyard** (Bel Cortile) (8), an unusual structure in which objects of everyday life are displayed. Now turn right onto the main street, the Decumanus Maximus, where there is a public fountain. The Forum, not yet excavated, lies buried beyond this.

The **House of the Bicentenario** (9) was so named because it was unearthed 200 years after the first serious digs began. Curiously, the outline of a cross on a wall of an upstairs room seems to suggest that a Christian lived here, although the crucifix symbol was not known to have been used as early as A.D. 79.

Turn right onto the Cardo V street and follow it past many inter-

Inside the House of the Wooden Partition

esting sights, including the partially excavated **Palestra**, to the **House of the Deer** *(Cervi)* (10). This is the most luxurious villa yet unearthed at Herculaneum, and is filled with remarkable art and sculpture. A ramp from here leads down to the former port, now far away from the sea. The **Suburban Baths** *(Thermae)* (11) were constructed shortly before the disaster and are in exceptionally fine condition.

You have now seen the major attractions of Herculaneum, which is open daily except on some holidays, from 9 a.m. until two hours before sunset. Return to the entrance and walk up the street to the train station (1).

Buses to **Mount Vesuvius** *(Vesuvio)* depart from the corner diagonally opposite the station, or you can drive there following the signs. The road takes you most of the way up and ends at a parking lot. From there it's an easy climb of about 30 minutes over loose gravel. At the **summit** (12) you are required to use the services of a guide, who will take you around the crater. The view from the top, 4,189 feet above the sea, is simply fantastic.

Pompeii
(Pompei)

Just about everyone who visits southern Italy eventually goes to Pompeii, and sometimes they all seem to be there at the same time. Fortunately, the place is so huge that once beyond the Forum you'll have much of the site to yourself. Don't expect to see a reconstructed Roman town, however. Most of Pompeii is in a state of ruin, with only a few of the structures restored. Unlike partially excavated Herculaneum or the scattered remains in Rome, what you have here are the bits and pieces of a complete town where—with enough imagination—you can immerse yourself into the daily life of 1,900 years ago. Pompeii's isolated location, far from modern cities, helps enhance the illusion.

From its humble beginnings as an Oscan settlement in the 8th century B.C., Pompeii grew into a flourishing market town and eventually allied itself with the nearby Greek towns of Cumae and Neapolis. Occupied by the Etruscans in the 6th century B.C. and the Samnites in the 5th, it continued to maintain a Hellenistic identity until the Romans made it a colony in 80 B.C. After that, it became a favorite resort for wealthy Romans as well as a commercial center with a mixed population of some 20,000 souls.

A terrible earthquake in A.D. 63 caused extensive damage, which was still not completely repaired when the ultimate disaster struck on August 24th, A.D. 79. By the time Mount Vesuvius was done dropping its load of stones and burning ashes—lava never touched the town—Pompeii was buried at least one story deep in rubble. Scavengers grabbed what they could above the surface, but in time what remained underneath was forgotten. It was not until the late 16th century that workers building an aqueduct stumbled across some ruins. Excavations began in 1748 and were systematically organized in 1860. The digs are still under way and will continue to be so for a long time.

GETTING THERE:

Commuter trains operated by the private Circumvesuviana Railway in the direction of Sorrento depart frequently from their own station beneath the Centrale station in Naples. These same trains leave a few minutes earlier from the Circumvesuviana station on Corso Garibaldi. Take one of these as far as the **Pompei Scavi-Villa dei Misteri**

stop, about 30 minutes from Naples. This station is close to the main excavation entrance. First class is no more comfortable than second, but less crowded. Those coming from Sorrento should take the same line in the direction of Naples.

Trains operated by the State Railways *(FS)*, bound for Salerno or beyond, leave Centrale station *(main level)* in Naples at infrequent intervals for the modern town of Pompei. This is about a one-mile walk from the excavations. Only a few trains on this line stop at Pompeii, so check the schedule carefully.

By car, take the A-3 Autostrada to the Pompei exit, about 14 miles southeast of Naples.

WHEN TO GO:

The excavation site at Pompeii is open daily except certain holidays, from 9 a.m. until about an hour before sunset. Get there as early as you possibly can to beat both the tour groups and the afternoon heat in summer. Winter visits can be a real joy, leaving you alone among the ruins.

FOOD AND DRINK:

It's ironic that the best local wine—*Lacrima Christi*—should spring from the very ashes that buried the town. This golden white is made from grapes grown on the slopes of Mount Vesuvius. There are many tourist restaurants near the entrance to the site, but none that can be recommended. You're best off eating at:

> **Restaurant-Cafeteria Internazionale** (just north of the Forum in the excavation site) A large, modern, and inexpensive place to fill up right in the middle of the digs. $

> **Zi Caterina** (Via Roma 16-22, in the modern town near the basilica) Good food, nearly a mile from the excavations. X: Tues. $$

TOURIST INFORMATION:

Check with the provincial tourist office inside the Centrale station in Naples, phone (081) 26-87-79. There is also a local tourist office in the modern town of Pompei, at Via Sacra 1, phone (081) 85-07-255, and another near the train station.

SUGGESTED TOUR:

From the **Pompei Scavi-Villa dei Misteri station** (1) of the Circumvesuviana Railway it is only a short stroll to the main entrance of the excavations at **Porta Marina** (2). Just follow the crowds. Before entering, you might want to purchase an illustrated guide book in English to help identify the sights. Once inside you can, if you wish, engage the services of an authorized guide who will take you and probably several other English-speaking people around on a tour lasting about one hour. These usually cover only the highlights nearest the entrance, but are useful as an introduction before seeing the rest of the digs on your own. They also have the advantage of pointing out some little-known features, such as the racy frescoes hidden behind cloth drapes.

The do-it-yourself tour outlined below leads you to all of the favorite attractions, as well as some that are not so well known. Pass through the arches of the Porta Marina gate and walk uphill. To your right are the ruins of the **Basilica**, the largest building in Pompeii, which once held law courts and business offices and may date from about 120 B.C.

The front of the Basilica opens onto the **Forum** *(Foro)* (3), the civic center around which were grouped important public buildings. On its western side is the **Temple of Apollo,** built in the 3rd century B.C., and just north of that the **Horreum**, a shop probably selling grain, which is now used as a deposit for archaeological finds. The **Temple of Jupiter** *(Tempio di Giove)*, from the 2nd century B.C., closes off the northern side of the huge square. It was dedicated to Juno, Minerva, and Jupiter.

On the eastern side of the Forum is the **Building of Eumachia**, a wool market with a beautifully decorated doorway. Next to this is the **Temple of Vespasian**, dedicated to the worship of the emperor, which has an interesting altar depicting the scene of a sacrifice. Finally, there is the **Macellum**, a large covered market.

Leave the Forum by its northern end and pass the modern restaurant-cafeteria, which also has souvenir shops and rest rooms. On the right is the **Temple of Fortuna Augusta**, erected in A.D. 3 as a place to worship the emperor Augustus. Adjoining the restaurant are the **Forum Baths**, parts of which are in good condition. Step inside to see the rather elegant marble wash basin whose bronze letters proclaim the names of those who paid for it—along with the price.

A left on Via delle Terme brings you to the **House of the Tragic Poet** *(Poeta Tragico)* (4), a nice middle-class dwelling named after a mosaic found in it but now in the Naples Museum, where many of Pompeii's movable treasures are on display. The entrance floor has a mosaic of a dog with the words *Cave Canem* (Beware of the Dog). You will find stray dogs all over Pompeii, and could reasonably conclude that they are reincarnations of ancient Romans, paying for the sins of their past. The enormous house next to this, the **Casa di Pansa**, dates from the Samnite age and was divided into small rental apartments.

Now turn around and follow Via della Fortuna to the noted **House of the Faun** *(Casa del Fauno)* (5), a luxurious home—one of the best

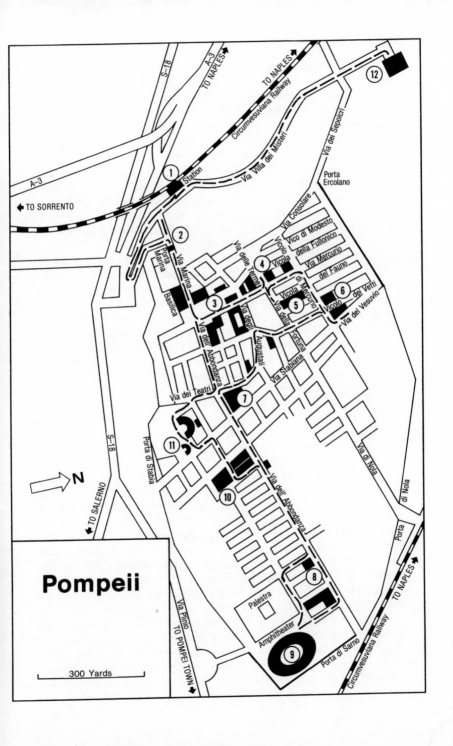

Pompeii

N

TO NAPLES
TO SORRENTO
TO SALERNO
TO POMPEI TOWN

Circumvesuviana Railway

S-18
A-3
S-18

Station

Via Villa dei Misteri
Via Consolare
Porta Ercolano
Via dei Sepolcri
Vico di Modesto
della Fullonico
Via Mercurio
del Fauno
Vicolo di Mercurio
Vicola
Vicolo dei Vetti
Via dei Vesuvio
Via delle Terme
Via degli Augustali
Via della Fortuna
Via Stabiana
Via Marina
Porta Marina
Basilica
Via dell' Abbondanza
Via dei Teatri
Porta di Stabia
Via dell' Abbondanza
Via di Nola
Porta di Nola
Porta di Sarno
Palestra
Amphitheater
Via Plinio

300 Yards

in the Roman world—which is reputed to have belonged to the nephew of the 2nd-century-B.C. dictator Sulla. Its magnificent bronze statute of a faun is a copy—the original is in Naples. Return to Via di Mercurio and turn right to the **House of the Large Fountain** *(Fontana Grande)*, whose main feature is—you guessed it—a large fountain. This has some wonderful Egyptian-style mosaics in colored glass.

Possibly the most famous dwelling in town is the **House of the Vettii** (6), which might also be called the House of the Dirty Pictures. The fabulous wall decorations reflect the sophisticated taste of its wealthy owners and were the height of fashion in the last ten years of Pompeii's existence. The notorious obscene statue near the entrance and the pornographic frescoes in one of the rooms may be covered, but you can ask the guard for a peek.

Nearby, on Via del Vesuvio, is the **House of the Golden Cupids** *(Amorini Dorati)*, possibly owned by a relative of Nero. Its splendid interior is in excellent condition. Continue on past the **Bakeries and Mills** *(Pistrinum)* on Vico Storto and follow the map to the ten-bed **Brothel** *(Lupanare)* on Vicolo del Lupanare. The wall pictures here advertise the various services that used to be available.

Just a few steps away are the **Stabian Baths** *(Terme Stabiane)* (7), the oldest in Pompeii, probably begun in the 4th century B.C. The extremely well-preserved interior should not be missed. You are now on the **Via dell' Abbondanza**, a largely commercial street stretching from the Forum to the eastern end of town. Some of its buildings are decorated with fascinating graffiti. Note the groove marks left in the pavement by heavy wagon wheels, and the stepping stones for crossing the street, which also served as a storm sewer.

Continue on past the **Fullonica Stephani**, a well-preserved laundry, and the **snack bar** *(Thermopolium)* which, judging from the graffiti, also served girls along with wine and prepared food. Farther down the main road is the **House of Loreius Tibertinue**, also known as the Casa di Octavius Quartio (8), another rich house in a fine state of repair. A block beyond it is the **Villa of Julia Felix** *(Giulia Felice)*, which has been restored and certainly merits a visit.

Every Roman town of any importance had an arena, but the **Amphitheater** *(Anfiteatro)* (9) of Pompeii, built in 80 B.C., is the oldest one known to exist. It is still in splendid condition. Next to it is the **Palestra**, a training ground for athletes.

Return to Via dell' Abbondanza and retrace your steps as far as the **Casa del Criptoportico**, whose underground passages were used for wine storage. When Vesuvius erupted, several people took refuge there, but were buried alive as they tried to escape. Plaster casts of the void left by their bodies may be seen in the crypt. To the south of this is the great **House of Menander** (10), an elegant and richly deco-

In the Forum Baths

rated villa which is among the best-preserved in town.

The route now leads to the **Small Theater** *(Odeon)* (11), dating from the earliest Roman colonization. Next to it is the **Large Theater** *(Teatro Grande)*, accommodating 5,000 spectators. Originally from the 5th century B.C., it was rebuilt in the 1st century A.D. On its north side is the **Temple of Isis**, curiously dedicated to an Egyptian goddess, while to the south is the **Court of the Gladiators**, built as a refuge for tired audiences during the long theatrical performances. It was later used as a barracks for gladiators. To the west side of the theater complex is the **Triangular Forum**, whose tiny temple may date from the 6th century B.C.

One more major sight remains to be seen, and that is outside the excavation site proper—although the same entrance ticket is valid. If the Porta Ercolano gate, in the northwest corner, is open you can get there by going through it. Otherwise return to the Porta Marina gate (2) and follow around past the train station (1) to the fabulous but seldom visited **Villa of the Mysteries** *(dei Misteri)* (12). Once the sub-urban home of a wealthy couple, it is famous for its frescoes depicting the initiation of a bride into the mysteries of the secret cult of Diony-sus. These are in a room to the right of the entrance, and are well worth the walk.

The Amalfi Coast

(Costa Amalfitana)

There are few places on earth as spectacularly beautiful as the Amalfi Coast. Stretching from Sorrento to Salerno and taking in the stunning little villages of Positano, Amalfi, and Ravello, it presents one breathtaking sight after another. Rugged mountains crash directly into the sea, leaving fantastically shaped rock formations in their wake. Innumerable gorges are cut deeply into the wild coastline, making the only road an endless series of hair-raising bends and turns. The Amalfi Drive, as it's called, is a real challenge to the skills of any driver. Fortunately, you won't even need a car to experience its thrills, since the route is well served by buses—offering the distinct advantage of allowing you to concentrate on the sights and not your brakes.

This one-day adventure begins with a visit to the popular resort of Sorrento, which can also be used as a convenient base instead of Naples, to which it is connected by commuter trains. It then moves on by bus or car through Positano to the ancient port of Amalfi, allowing enough time for an enjoyable exploration. A side trip to the gorgeous hill town of Ravello is possible before continuing on to Salerno, from which there is both rail service and an autostrada back to Naples. Those staying in Sorrento will probably want to return from Amalfi.

GETTING THERE:

Commuter trains operated by the private Circumvesuviana Railway depart frequently for Sorrento from their own station beneath the Centrale station in Naples. These same trains leave a few minutes earlier from the Circumvesuviana station on Corso Garibaldi. Take one of these from the platform marked Sorrento and ride it to the end of the line, about one hour from Naples. First class is no more comfortable than second, although less crowded. Buy a one-way ticket only, since you'll be returning a different way.

Buses operated by SITA depart from the train station in Sorrento about every two hours for the spectacular 90-minute ride to Amalfi, where they connect with buses to Salerno. That ride takes another 80 minutes. Schedules are posted at the bus stops, or may be had from the tourist offices. Fares can be paid on board if the ticket offices are closed.

Trains of the State Railways *(FS)* will bring you back to Naples from Salerno, a ride of about one hour. These run until late evening, and railpasses are accepted.

By car, leave Naples on the A-3 Autostrada and follow it to Castellammare di Stabia, then switch to the S-145 coastal road to Sorrento. It is 30 miles from Naples to Sorrento.

From Sorrento you can continue on the S-145 to the Amalfi Coast, but it is easier to return in the direction of Naples to the village of Meta, then take the S-163 south to the Amalfi Coast *(Coasta Amalfitana)*. Once on the coast take the S-163 into Amalfi, a distance of 21 miles from Sorrento. The road along the Amalfi Coast is one of the most enchanting anywhere, but is also treacherous and requires skillful driving. From Amalfi continue on the S-163 in the direction of Salerno as far as Vietri sul Mare, then turn north on the A-3 Autostrada and return to Naples. The distance between Amalfi and Naples by this route is 39 miles.

WHEN TO GO:

Late spring and early fall are the best times to savor the Amalfi Coast. Summers are usually pleasant but very crowded, especially on weekends and holidays. A sunny day in winter will allow you to enjoy the views without the traffic.

FOOD AND DRINK:

Seafood dominates the regional cooking of the Sorrento Peninsula and the Amalfi Coast. The local wine is the fruity red *Gragnano,* while the white *Lacrima Christi* from Mount Vesuvius is also popular. Restaurants here are geared to the tourist trade. Some good choices are:

In Sorrento:

La Favorita O' Parrucchiano (Corso Italia 71, 4 blocks west of Pza. Tasso) An old tavern with a lovely garden in the rear. X: Wed. from Nov. through May $$

La Pentolaccia (Via Fuorimura 8, just south of Pza. Tasso) Local cuisine in the old part of town. X: Thurs. $$

In Amalfi:

La Caravella (Via Camera 12, near the beach) A very casual place with local cooking. X: Tues. from Oct. to May and Nov. $$

Il Tari (Via Capuano, near the main street) Simple and unpretentious. X: Tues. except in July to Sept, Nov. $$

Da Gemma (Via Cavalieri di Malta, near the cathedral) A trattoria famous for its seafood. Reservations are suggested, phone (089) 87-13-45. X: Jan., Feb. $$

TOURIST INFORMATION:

The local tourist office in Sorrento is hidden away in the Foreigner's Club at Via Luigi De Maio 35, just north of Piazza Antonino. Its phone number is (081) 878-11-15. They can help you with room reservations if you choose to make Sorrento your base instead of Naples. Other places in town marked "Tourist Office" are in fact travel agencies.

In Amalfi, the local tourist office, phone (089) 87-11-07, is at Corso Roma 19, on the main street just east of the bus stop.

SUGGESTED TOUR:

Begin at the **Sorrento train station** (1). While this tour is strictly for fun, those in need of a daily cultural "fix" can get one at the nearby **Correale Museum** (2). Housed in an 18th-century villa, it contains superb examples of regional decorative arts from the 15th through the 18th centuries, including furniture, porcelains, and paintings. There are also some local archaeological finds, as well as rare editions of the works of Torquato Tasso, a famous locally born poet of the 16th century. Be sure to visit the lovely garden behind the museum, which accesses to a belvedere overlooking the bay. The museum is usually open daily except Tuesdays, holidays, and Sunday afternoons; from 9:30 a.m. to 12:30 p.m. and 5–7 p.m., with shorter hours in winter.

Now head for the main square, **Piazza Tasso** (3), a busy place lined with outdoor cafés. Sorrento has been a popular resort ever since the time of the Romans, and has long been a favorite of foreign vacationers—especially the British. Its many hotels in all price ranges makes it an ideal base for exploring the coastal region south of Naples. From the north side of the square there is a ramp leading down to the Marine Piccola, a harbor with boat service to Capri, Ischia, and Naples.

A stroll down Via Luigi De Maio brings you to the attractive Piazza Sant' Antonino, near which is the tourist office. Turn left to the baroque **Church of San Francesco** (4), noted for its 14th-century cloisters now used by an art school. Take a peek in, then walk out into the adjacent **public gardens** for a wonderful view across the bay.

Return through the narrow old streets to the station (1) and board a SITA bus to Amalfi, being sure to sit on the right-hand side. In about 20 minutes you will reach the unforgettable Amalfi Drive at the village of Colli di San Pietro. From here on it's a wild drive, up and down, twisting and turning, gasping at the magnificent scenery. The dreamlike fishing village of **Positano** (5), now a world-famous resort where tiny white houses cling to the steep mountainside, descending in steps to the sea, is reached in another 20 minutes. Continuing along this incredible road for 50 more minutes, the bus will come to Amalfi, where you get off.

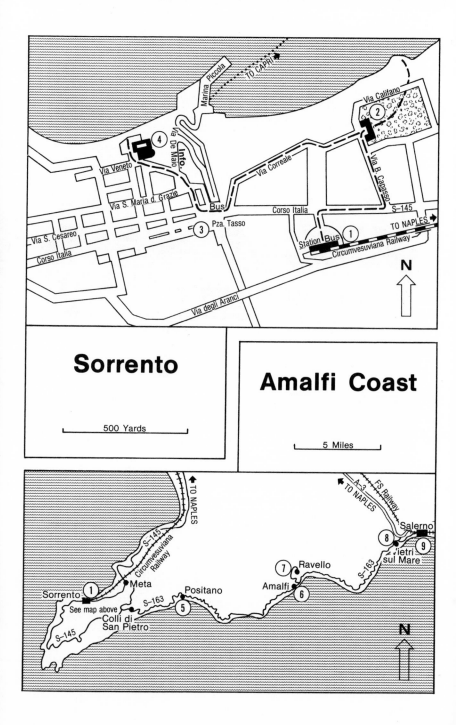

Sorrento

500 Yards

Amalfi Coast

5 Miles

N

View of Sorrento from the Public Gardens

It may not look it today, but **Amalfi** (6) was once a powerful maritime republic with a population of 70,000. That was in the 11th century; now it's down to 6,000 or so. As early as the 6th century it was already trading with the Middle East and later provided transportation to the Holy Land for the Crusaders. Conquered by the Normans and then the Pisans, most of the town was destroyed by the sea in 1343. It is now a popular resort, and a very lovely one at that. From the bus stop by the beach it is only a few steps into the Old Town, a warren of tiny passages squeezed between the sun-baked ancient buildings.

Be sure to visit the almost Byzantine **Cathedral of Sant' Andrea** *(Duomo)*, founded in the 9th century but rebuilt in the 13th. Reached by a broad flight of steps from the Piazza del Duomo, just one block inland, it is famous for its fabulous **cloisters** *(Chiostro del Paradiso)*, entered from the left side of the porch. Near this is the **Town Hall** *(Municipo)*, where you can see the original *Tavole Amalfitane*, a local 11th-century set of maritime laws that governed all Mediterranean shipping until 1570. Beyond this, you will find many other hidden corners to poke around in, or perhaps just sit down at a café.

From Amalfi it is possible to make a side trip to the astonishing little hill town of **Ravello** (7), long a hideout for celebrities. You won't have time to see its three major attractions—the **Villa Rufolo**, the **Villa**

The Harbor at Amalfi

Cimbrone, and the **Cathedral**, but perhaps even a short stop will entice you to return another time. It can be reached by bus in 30 minutes, or by a torturous four-mile road.

Now board the bus from Amalfi to Salerno, which continues along the Amalfi Drive. Those driving their own cars should turn off at **Vietri sul Mare** (8) and get on the A-3 Autostrada to Naples. If you are staying in Sorrento you would, of course, return there instead. The bus ends its journey at a terminal in **Salerno** (9), from which it is only a three-block walk east on Corso Garibaldi to the train station on Piazza Vittorio Veneto, where you can get a train to Naples.

Caserta

The Royal Palace at Caserta has often been called the Versailles of Italy, but in some ways it even surpasses the French original. Built by the Bourbon rulers of Naples in the mid-18th century as a monument to their megalomania, it remained a home for the kings of Naples until the unification of Italy in 1860, and was used by the kings of Italy until 1921. Perhaps its most famous resident was Joachim Murat, appointed to the position of king by Napoleon in 1808 and shot by rebellious forces in 1815. During World War II Caserta served as the headquarters of the Allied Mediterranean Command and was the scene of the unconditional surrender of the German forces in Italy on April 29th, 1945. Restored to its original splendor, it is now open to the public as a showcase of royal extravagance.

Truly stupendous in size, the palace was the last great building of the Italian baroque. It contains no fewer than 1,200 rooms, 1,900 windows, and 34 staircases. As is also the case with Versailles, the real glory of Caserta is in its magnificent gardens, which stretch for two miles behind the palace.

GETTING THERE:

Trains depart Centrale station in Naples at frequent intervals for Caserta, taking between 30 and 45 minutes for the trip, depending on the route followed. Almost all of these leave from the main level, with a few departures from the subway (*Metropolitana Piazza Garibaldi*) level. Railpasses are accepted, and return service runs until late evening. Those staying in Sorrento should take the private Circumvesuviana Railway to Naples first.

By car, take the A-2 Autostrada north to the Caserta exit, a distance of 20 miles from Naples. You can use your car in the gardens to avoid the long walk to the waterfalls. When finished, it is possible to drive to the picturesque medieval town of Caserta Vecchia, about six miles to the northeast.

WHEN TO GO:

Avoid going to Caserta on a major holiday, when everything is closed. Fine weather will make the gardens more enjoyable. Be sure to see the Royal Palace first as it closes for the day at 12:30 or 1:30 p.m.

The Majestic Staircase of the Royal Palace

FOOD AND DRINK:

Aside from the snack bar in the gardens and the mobile vendors in front of the palace, there are not many places to eat at Caserta. Perhaps you might want to bring along a picnic lunch to eat in the gardens. The town itself does have a few pizzerias and restaurants, of which the following can be recommended:

Antica Locanda-Massa 1848 (Via Mazzini 55, 2 blocks east of the palace and a bit north of Pza. Dante) Regarded as the best in town. X: Mon., Sun. eve., and mid-Aug. $$

TOURIST INFORMATION:

The provincial tourist office, phone (0823) 32-11-37, is at Corso Trieste 39 on the corner of Piazza Dante.

SUGGESTED TOUR:

Leave the **Caserta train station** (1) and stroll across the open square to the **Royal Palace** *(Palazzo Reale* or *La Reggia)* (2). Enter the courtyard and buy a ticket for both the palace and the gardens. The palace is open on Mondays through Saturdays, from 9 a.m. to 1:30 p.m., and on Sundays from 9 a.m. to 12:30 p.m., but closed on some holidays— while the gardens remain open until about one hour before sunset.

The majestic **staircase** leading to the **Royal Apartments** looks like something out of a set designer's wildest dreams, especially when you make the turn halfway up. It was created by the noted architect Luigi Vanvitelli, as was the rest of the palace. Sadly, or perhaps happily for the taxpayers, Vanvitelli's full plans for a grandiose royal complex were never realized. The apartments are about as sumptuously decorated as they could possibly be, although it is hard to understand how any person could feel at ease amid such lavish splendor. Perhaps the king had some simpler quarters tucked away elsewhere in the palace as a place to relax. The 25 or so rooms open to the public are, of course, only a small part of the entire structure—the servants had to live somewhere—but they will take at least an hour to explore.

The **park** with its splendid gardens was conceived of as an integral part of the palace complex, and is largely the work of the same architect. There is a regular bus service from the palace to the waterfalls at the far end, a distance of two miles, and horse-drawn carriages are also available. Those with cars are usually allowed to drive there. The best way to enjoy the beauty, however, is to walk one way and then return by bus.

Leaving the palace, the path to the left leads through the *Bosco Vecchio* woods to the delightful **Little Castle** *(Castelluccia)* (3), built in 1769 as a play house for the royal princes. Continue along the path to the **Great Fish Pond** *(Peschiera Grande)* (4), where mock sea battles were staged to amuse the king. Now follow around to the central alley and turn left past the **Dolphin Fountain** *(Cascata dei Delfini)* (5), where water gushes through the mouths of three stone dolphins. Next in line is the **Aeolus Fountain** *(Fontana di Eolo)* (6), a large ornamental group named for the Greek god of the winds. Behind its façade is a cool grotto where you can escape the heat.

The **Ceres Fountain** *(Fontana di Cerere)* (7) merrily splashes water from unexpected places. Continue on past several other waterworks to the marvelous sculptural groups of **Diana and Actaeon** (8) at the foot of the waterfalls. One of the huge statues depicts Actaeon transformed into a stag and attacked by his hunting dogs. From here the ambitious can climb up through woods past the waterfalls to the artificial **Grotto** (9), which offers a wonderful view of the entire park and palace. Returning to the sculptural group (8), you can reward yourself with a cool drink at the nearby snack bar.

To the east of the central alley is the picturesque **English Garden** (10), laid out in 1782 for Queen Maria Carolina of Austria. Its tiny lake, rare plants, and fake ruins make it an enchanting spot to end your visit before returning by bus or on foot to the palace and train station.

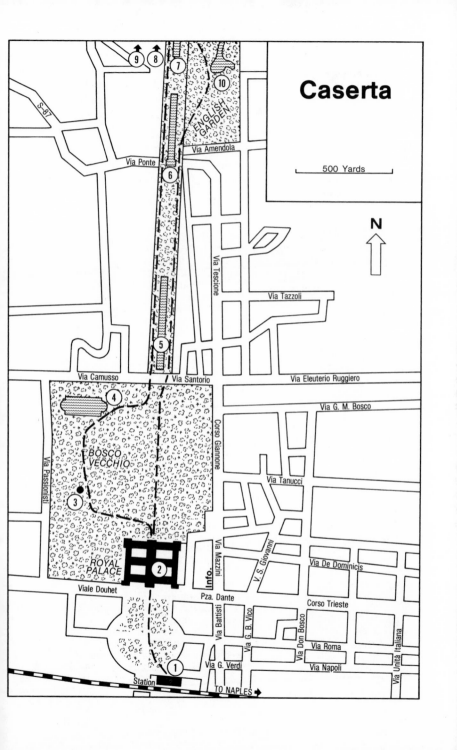

Index

The major selection of Cathedrals, Gardens, Museums, Palaces, and Roman Relics are listed individually under those category headings. *Names of persons are in italics.*

PAM HALL

The Coil
a history
in four parts
1988-1993

curated by Patricia Grattan

catalogue essays by Patrick O'Flaherty
and Nancy Shaw

Art Gallery, Memorial University of Newfoundland
St. John's, Newfoundland, Canada
1994

Contents

The Coil *on site... (clockwise from top left)*

Middle Cove Beach, Newfoundland, 1988

Futamigaura, Kyushu, Japan, 1993

near Milk River, Alberta, 1991

Harling Point, Victoria, B.C., 1990

The Coil that Binds, the Line that Bends...
an introduction

The Coil That Binds, the Line That Bends is a process of site-responsive environmental installation and subsequent studio work that has engaged Pam Hall for the past five years. Memorial University's Art Gallery gave the early Newfoundland Coil works their first public exposure in our 1989 exhibition, MASKUNOW A Trail A Path. We now are presenting selected works representing the entire project in **The Coil - a History in Four Parts**, an exhibition that we are pleased to be sharing with a Japanese audience and with other Canadian galleries.

Those who know Pam Hall know she has a way with words as well as with images. And it seems to me that Hall as author is very much in evidence in the Coil works — not only in the poetic incantatory phrases and the Biographical Notes, which are like pages from a journal, but in the basic structure of the project.

The Coil is the protagonist in a narrative the artist is "writing". It (or she as Hall refers to the Coil) comes into the story with a pre-history made of its physical origin, as a cod trap, and its symbolic associations for Hall. These, which have been reflected in most of the artist's earlier bodies of work, include cycles of birth and death, fecundity, ritual, the relationship of humans and nature. The narrative proceeds as the artist works with the Coil at various outdoor locations across Canada and in Japan: the Coil acquires its own history, with each site providing both the setting and the source for a direct encounter with the physical world and, at the same time, forming "chapters" in an unfolding biography. It is a history of incidents, accidents, relationships and accretions from the sites and cultures in which it temporarily rests: Shinto religious practices, ancient rock formations in the Alberta badlands, tools of the fishing trade, clear cut evidence of exploitation of nature...

Working with images gathered on site and with her own intuitive response to remembered experience of the physical and human contexts of each encounter, Hall makes that history manifest in the Biographical Notes. Their shifting format and overlayered maps, drawing, images and texts reflect the nature of history — fragments of experience, tentative observations, enticing paths of inquiry. Helping us to trace our way through Hall's dense web of information and allusion are guest essayists Patrick O'Flaherty, St. John's and Nancy Shaw, Vancouver, whom we thank for their perceptions. We also want to acknowledge, for their essential assistance with the exhibition and catalogue, the cultural staff at The Canadian Embassy, Tokyo; The Canada Council, which remains a vital source of support for the arts in Canada; and Pam Hall, who has been an energetic and enthusiastic collaborator.

Patricia Grattan

The first circle... Middle Cove Beach, Newfoundland, 1988

Pam Hall and the Coil

Patrick O'Flarerty

Pam Hall has internalized the Newfoundland experience in a new way. To me, she resembles Rockwell Kent or even the writer Norman Duncan, both outsiders for whom Newfoundland became a spiritual home, both forced to experiment with artistic forms, to wrench them out of their traditional shapes, in order to express a shocked awareness of ocean and landscape.

Pam Hall too has had to look beyond the resources of conventional artistry to express what is stirred up in her,as woman and as a creator, by the elemental forces on this hard edge of the North American continent. Do not picture her as sitting on a headland with palette and brushes. Think of her rather as akin to T.S. Eliot: a poet of shards and scissors. Not for her the straight lines and numinousness of the magic realists. (There are neat lines on the edges of her works: but the twisting, turning, breaking forms within the boundaries seem a flight from what is shapely and fixed.)

No boats sit peacefully at anchor in her work. Throw words like idyll and rustic out of the skiff. She is in the business of inventing rather than inheriting forms; that's the only way she can tell what she has witnessed and felt. Her work does not just provide an image of life; it seems to participate in it in some way. Though purposeful underneath, it has in it the jaggedness of seascape, a littoral clutter, suggesting the untamed and shapeless forces of nature.

It is typical of her that her art springs from muscular contact with earth and ocean. The pleasures of the gazebo, sitting back and watching butterflies in the flowery meadow, are not her pleasures. She has gone out to confront and explore her world in a brazen fashion. She fishes, works, hauls, lifts rocks. Then creates out of the lifting and hauling. The hand that draws and takes photos has sores on it from the rub of real rope and the bones of real fish.

The Coil, on the deck of the Whispering Sea ready to come ashore at Quidi Vidi, Newfoundland, 1988

The first spiral... heavy with water on Elis wharf, Quidi Vidi, Newfoundland, 1988

She goes about her job of creation in a number of ways. She will make a scene with, say, driftwood, photograph it, photograph it again slightly altered, create a sequence of photographs, find a topographic map to place it over or under, alter the map with various devices of art - - then write about it, this mixture, as if meaning were too precious a commodity to be left entirely to the visible objects.

Or she will do it differently.

Throughout, as a dominant motif, there is the Coil.

A cod trap is an unwieldy, heavy object which demands the greatest care and skill of the fisherman or - woman if it is to catch fish. Knitting a trap is hard enough. Placing it in a skiff so it can be put out properly with a lop on is taxing too. But setting it in the salt water is the thing. Tides, depth of water, the shape of the bottom — all this and more must be understood; the leader, anchors, kegs, trap-mouth, all have to positioned just so. Get something a foot or so wrong, no fish. A successful trap-setter (as Hall well knows) is thus a kind of artist.

Hall's Coil — made by sewing part of a real, though discarded cod trap into a 110-foot length with red fishing twine — is not just the metaphor through which she replicates what she sees in the world of work and anxiety she has entered. It is her way of sharing the daily grind of the fishing life: the trap-man or -woman pulls the twine out of the water; Hall pulls the Coil (a "she", of course) into varying shapes. This ropy object is at different times, depending on how her hand shapes it — and what you, the viewer, are open to seeing in it — a nest, a string of kelp, a worm or snake or dragon, a long tail, a set of layers, the tentacles of some sea creature, a circle, a ring of circles, a puzzle, a contour line on a map, a whip, an umbilical cord, something dead, something living.

Every knot, as she says, a thought.

Sea-water wet and too heavy to lift by hand, **The Coil** *being lowered by the winch onto Eli's wharf, Quidi Vidi, Newfoundland, 1988*

A trap is hard to handle, massive, heavy. So is the Coil, for it must be lugged around the world in a great bag to find a place to yield its significance. A beach, maybe. A hillside. A grassy field. The Alberta Badlands. Japan, even. The floor of a gallery. But always it summons up the sea and the things that lurk in it and the life of the men and women who toil on it and near it.

Coil means spiral, vortex, gyre, spring. It is something wound up, a force contained, one that can be unleashed. There is energy pent up in Hall's work. An impression of energy and motion is the first thing we get from her work. There is a daring in it too, a willingness to toy with broken images, to make art out of flotsam. And there is a woman's wish — no, not wish merely, a fierce determination — to see this strange, grim world in a woman's way, truly, not being restricted to the traditional linear modes defined by men and showing how men think.

Hall is off on a sea-voyage of her own. We can follow in her wake. If she seems, at first, to lead us into unfamiliar waters, be advised she is steering by her own compass and stars. Following, we soon become more at ease, for she is an artist. The ship is in good hands.

What does art do? To answer this question, Wallace Stevens used the metaphor of a jar:

> *I placed a jar in Tennessee,*
> *And round it was, upon a hill.*
> *It made the slovenly wilderness*
> *Surround that hill.*
>
> *The wilderness rose up to it,*
> *And sprawled around, no longer wild.*
> *The jar was round upon the ground*
> *And tall and of a port in air.*

*Three lines on the land... **The Coil** (from top to bottom) at Harling Point, Vancouver Island, 1990, in the Drumheller Badlands, and near East Coulee, Alberta 1991*

Though both are "round upon the ground", I prefer Pam Hall's Newfoundland Coil to Stevens' Tennessee jar. The jar, Stevens insists, has "dominion" over the wilderness; it organizes and subdues it. But Hall's Coil, unlike the jar, is a part of the world of flux and motion. It lies next to the wilderness too but, though it seeks and makes connections, leaves it slovenly and primitive. It is art that coexists with what is wild and true.

A Time Between Times

Nancy Shaw

> Ritual takes place in the temporal framework of myth,
> in that Celtic "time between times" of twilights, mist,
> and hybrids which John Sharkey has compared to the
> "entrelacs" of Celtic visual arts, the visual knots
> and puns and curves– repetitive images arising from
> tasks set the contemplative mind.
>
> –Lucy R. Lippard

Resistance to Western modes of domination– especially our alienated and divisive relationship to nature is charted by Pam Hall's five year expedition, **The Coil That Binds, the Line that Bends**. Suspended in the liminal space of ritual, she addresses the sense of loss perpetuated by patriarchal capitalism in site-specific landscape installations with **The Coil**– the floor of a cod trap reclaimed and intricately bound. Her journey of discovery draws connections between human labour and the land to form an intricate web of meaning akin to the life cycle of birth, growth, sacrifice and rebirth. This is all documented in the **Biographical Notes**, collages full of poetic and photographic elements. Layers of correspondence rife with symbolic resonance between past, present and future remind us of marginalized narratives, particular myths of ancient matriarchal societies celebrating the earth's association with the feminine. This is not an epic of heroic conquest. Hall's is a tale of regeneration and reflection arrived at through drawing, knotting, spiralling and binding.

Drawing - the long line

As with all stories of discovery, **The Coil's** begins with introductions, drawing interrelations between the tale's various elements – setting a scene against which the action can take place. Initiated by its birth, **The Coil** emerges as an artist's tool from a hunter's implement; **The Coil**; Hall says "falls artlessly onto the land" and its making has quite a history. While a set director on a film shoot, Hall become engrossed in one location, Quidi Vidi Gut– a harbour in St. John's where she later learned to fish with Eli Tucker and sons. Fascinated by the process and history of this local inshore industry, she launched her Coil, mimicking fishing gestures and imbuing her artistic practice with a ritual social function.

Through an arduous and labour-intensive process, with red twine she hand-bound the floor of Eli's old cod trap into a 32m rope. After thirty-three days of preparation, **The Coil**, as she christened it, was ritually retrieved from the ocean's depths onto the long liner **Whispering Sea**. To celebrate its rebirth and acknowledge its history, Hall wrapped **The Coil** around the **Whispering Sea's** hold and placed it on the wharf in the shape of a nest.

The nest, like the net, is a space where one form of life sustains another to establish The Coil as both womb and tomb and create a dynamic tension upon which Hall's work thrives. Her appropriation of fishing gestures forges archetypal connection between the art of retrieving hidden meaning from unconscious depths and the laboured gathering of sustenance from the deep sea. Other rites she practised included the cleaning of salt water from The Coil and laying it on the land to dry. During certain times of the season it is not unusual in Newfoundland to see the land decorated with nets being cleaned and repaired.

In the face of drastic economic fluctuations, the inshore fishery still embodies vestiges of its pre-industrial form that coexisted symbolically with nature. Hall's artistic statement is instructive on the issue. She writes;

> **The Coil** emerged both physically and conceptually from one of the last remaining **primitive** interactions between humans and Nature ...the fishery of inshore Newfoundland. Primitive in that it is direct, unmediated, and full of both terror and comfort... primitive in that it is a vestige of the hunt...one of the first and formative ways the species interacted in the natural world...and primitive in that the distance between hunter and the hunted is minimal, the technology used is ancient and simple, and the relationship with the natural world is still bound by respect and dependency, rather than by mastery and control.

***The Coil**, wrapping the hold of the Whispering Sea, North Atlantic, 1988*

Binding - the line that begins again

...ral, the Canadian Embassy, Tokyo, 1993

After situating Western conceptions of nature within a larger geological frame, Hall returns to the present to a multitude of personal, artistic, cultural and symbolic correspondences. An intricate web of meaning emerges, fleshing out her hopes of developing a harmonious existence with nature. To do this, she travelled to Japan, where unexpected connections emerged, allowing Hall to feel at home in unfamiliar surroundings. Remembering Newfoundland, she set up **The Coil** on beaches, fishing wharfs, as well as in gardens and at sacred shrines. She noted many similarities: Newfoundland and Japan are islands with thriving coastal cultures reliant on fishing to a certain extent, and are roughly the same geographical size. Both are identified as Eastern (although not in relationship to each other) and have been subject to colonial exploits. Nevertheless, records state that Japanese settlement is much older and more densely populated than Newfoundland (the population of Japan is 111,057,485 compared to Newfoundland's population of 567,681).

Japanese notions of nature were most striking to Hall, especially those that emerged through Shinto. Unlike Western Christianity, Shinto's spirits exist in the material world rather than outside and above it. In Shinto, there is no word for nature that situates humans as separate and dominant. Howard Fox states that in Shinto:

> ...man is equivalent to and involved with nature and the spirits and life force embodied therein, that the art object is the locus of the individual's spiritual encounter with nature, that the artist works "with" the materials to discover their "inner being," rather than against them to impose his technical virtuosity... [2]

Moreover, in both art and nature, arrangement and order are important as each component is integral to universal harmony. Even though nature in both Western Christianity and Shinto contexts is replete with human manipulations, the Japanese approach is based on order and harmony rather than domination, accumulation and consumption.

Near the Canadian Embassy in Tokyo, Hall circled **The Coil** around a pristine and highly arranged garden, most unlike the wind-worn and sea-sculpted terrain traced in Victoria's cityscape. Recalling the sittings on Eli's wharf, she set up **The Coil** at wharfs on the Japanese island of Kyushu, comparing fishing methods and tools to Newfoundland's. More transcultural comparisons emerge in the **Biographical Notes** where compositions resembled holy crosses, kimonos, and fishing oil-skins hung to dry.

Shimenawa, at a shrine in Hita, Kyushu, Japan, 1993

Hall visited spiritual places like Hita where she wrapped a Shinto shrine and traced a Sumo Ring. Significantly, rope is used for many sacred purposes in Japan, especially within Shinto, where each gateway to each shrine in draped with a shimenawa (sacred rope). Consequently, **The Coil** sitings were enriched by new contextual and symbolic meaning. Her trip to Futamigaura was perhaps the most revealing for Hall. She discovered Meoto-iwa – two rocks protruding from the sea bound by rope signifying their marriage. In this uncanny place she laid one significant rope leading to another. On a nearby beach she drew a circle marking the end of her journey... an echo of the first circle drawn on a Newfoundland beach five years earlier. She describes this as a signing off, a returning home in the process of running into her origins across the world. Perhaps the following poetic fragment best summarizes **The Coil's** acquired function in this work of discovery:

one rope tied
by Shinto hands
one laid down
from distant land
one for binding
one for finding
both bound by
the sea – the sand
one to lead
a caring eye...
one to wed
two rocks to tie...
one to map
unveil a site...
one to manifest
a rite.

Although in retrospect it is easy to recount the polyphony of symbolic resonance accumulating through out the five year project, it is crucial to note that the artist did not consciously plan the course of her journey. Her overriding concern resides in **The Coil's** physical encounter with and engagement in the landscape. The work and the process it emerges from , is ephemeral, non-intrusive, material-dependent and site-responsive. Moreover, **The Coil's** sitings are domestic in scale and greatly determined by such details as the weather and the crew she works with. As an engaged explorer, Hall is fully awake in the land, attentive and respectful, searching out methods of coexistence with nature.

1. Lucy R. Lippard, **Overlay** (New York: Pantheon, 1983) 160
2. Howard N. Fox, "A Primal Spirit", A Primal Spirit: Ten Contemporary Japanese Sculptors (Los Angeles County Museum of Art, 1991) 26

newfoundland
1988-1989

a line drawn
a drawn line
a bound trap
trap- bound
a berth on the water
a birth on the water
from a long-liner
comes a long line

one long line
from sea...to me

The Coil on site in Newfoundland, 1988
(from top to bottom)

Eli Tucker's wharf, Quidi Vidi

Hawke Hill barrens

Middle Cove Beach

Middle Cove Beach